NEW DIRECTIONS IN INFORMATION ORGANIZATION

LIBRARY AND INFORMATION SCIENCE

Series Editor: **Amanda Spink**

Recent and Forthcoming Volumes

Gunilla Wuff and Kim Holmberg
Social Information Research

Dirk Lewandowski
Web Search Engine Research

Donald Case
Looking for Information, Third Edition

Amanda Spink and Diljit Singh
Trends and Research: Asia-Oceania

Amanda Spink and Jannica Heinstrom
New Directions in Information Behaviour

Eileen G. Abels and Deborah P. Klein
Business Information: Needs and Strategies

Leo Egghe
Power Laws in the Information Production Process: Lotkaian Informetrics

Matthew Locke Saxton and John V. Richardson
Understanding Reference Transactions: Turning Art Into a Science

Robert M. Hayes
Models for Library Management, Decision-Making, and Planning

Charles T. Meadow, Bert R. Boyce, and Donald H. Kraft
Text Information Retrieval Systems, Second Edition

A. J. Meadows
Communicating Research

V. Frants, J. Shiparo, and V. Votskunskii
Automated Information Retrieval: Theory and Methods

Harold Sackman
Biomedical Information Technology: Global Social Responsibilities for the Democratic Age

LIBRARY AND INFORMATION SCIENCE

NEW DIRECTIONS IN INFORMATION ORGANIZATION

EDITED BY

JUNG-RAN PARK
The iSchool at Drexel, College of Information Science & Technology, Drexel University, Philadelphia, PA, USA

and

LYNNE C. HOWARTH
Faculty of Information, University of Toronto, Toronto, Canada

Series Editor: Amanda Spink

Emerald

United Kingdom • North America • Japan
India • Malaysia • China

Emerald Group Publishing Limited
Howard House, Wagon Lane, Bingley BD16 1WA, UK

First edition 2013

British Library Cataloguing in Publication Data
A catalogue record for this book is available from the British Library

ISBN: 978-1-78190-559-3
ISSN: 1876-0562 (Series)

Contents

List of Contributors

Yunseon Choi	Department of Information and Library Science, Southern Connecticut State University, New Haven, CT, USA
Elizabeth J. Cox	Morris Library, Southern Illinois University Carbondale, Carbondale, IL, USA
Stephanie Graves	Morris Library, Southern Illinois University Carbondale, Carbondale, IL, USA
Birong Ho	University of Richmond, Richmond, VA, USA
Laura Horne-Popp	University of Richmond, Richmond, VA, USA
Lynne C. Howarth	Faculty of Information, University of Toronto, Toronto, ONT, Canada
Andrea Imre	Morris Library, Southern Illinois University Carbondale, Carbondale, IL, USA
Heejung Kim	International Vaccine Institute, Seoul, South Korea
Yan Yi Lee	Horrmann Library, Wagner College, New York, NY, USA
Shawne Miksa	Department of Library and Information Sciences, University of North Texas, Denton, TX, USA
Xi Niu	Indiana University, Indianapolis, IN, USA
Jung-ran Park	The iSchool at Drexel, College of Information Science and Technology, Drexel University, Philadelphia, PA, USA
Ziyoung Park	Division of Knowledge and Information Science, Hansung University, Seoul, South Korea

Alan Poulter	University of Strathclyde, Glasgow, UK
Emma Stuart	University of Wolverhampton, Wolverhampton, UK
Sarah H. Theimer	Syracuse University Library, Syracuse, NY, USA
Barbara B. Tillett	Library of Congress, Washington, DC, USA
Cassie Wagner	Morris Library, Southern Illinois University Carbondale, Carbondale, IL, USA
Sharon Q. Yang	Moore Library, Rider University, Lawrenceville, NJ, USA

Editorial Advisory Board

Introduction

New information standards and digital library technologies are being developed at a rapid pace as diverse communities of practice seek new ways to organize massive quantities of digital resources. Today's digital information explosion creates an increased demand for new perspectives, methods, and tools for research and practice in information organization. This new direction in information organization is even more critical owing to changing user needs and expectations in conjunction with the collaborative decentralized nature of bibliographic control.

The evolving digital information and technology environment will likely require the more active collaboration of the library and information communities as data are increasingly mined and shared from multiple information providers.

This environmental change affords researchers and practitioners unprecedented opportunities as well as challenges. This book aims to provide readers with the current state of the digital information revolution with the associated opportunities and challenges to information organization. Through interdisciplinary perspectives, it presents broad, holist, and more integrated perspectives on the nature of information organization and examines new directions in information organization research and thinking. The book highlights the need to understand information organization and Web 2.0 in the context of the rapidly changing information world and provides an overview of key trends and further research.

Topics covered include areas such as the Semantic Web, linked data, new generation library catalogs, *Resource Description and Access* (RDA), which is the new cataloging code, social cataloging and tagging, Web 2.0 technologies, organizing and sharing digital images, faceted browsing and searching, and metadata quality standards.

Semantic Web and Linked Data

Tim Berners-Lee, Director of the World Wide Web Consortium (W3C) and inventor of the Internet, defines the Semantic Web as "a web of data that can be processed directly and indirectly by machines" (http://en.wikipedia.org/wiki/Semantic_Web). As indicated in this definition, one of the salient characteristics of the Semantic Web concerns understanding of word meanings by machine. The meanings of natural language are complex and can be expressed indirectly with multiple related and associated senses. In order for a machine to process the meaning, the meaning of the data needs to be represented in a rudimentary and formal manner. Toward this end, the Resource Description Framework (RDF), which centers on Semantic Web technologies, models the data into three parts called RDF triples: a subject, a predicate, and an object. Breaking the data into triples facilitates the ability of the machine to process meanings and establish relationships among data elements in the Semantic Web.

The Semantic Web is also described as a web of linked data, Web 3.0 versus current Web 2.0, and the Giant Global Graph (Baker et al., 2011; Berners-Lee, Hendler, & Lassila, 2001; Gruber, 2007, 2008). Linked Data is structured metadata that allows links to be created between data elements and value vocabularies. In contrast to library data, which is based on the bibliographic record, linked data is based on a graph data model that centers on statements (Baker et al., 2011). In principle, linked data employs the Uniform Resource Identifier (URI) as names for things (Berners-Lee, 2009). A unique identifier is assigned to a resource, data element, or value vocabularies. These identifiers allow a resource to be accessed and used unambiguously in Semantic Web environments.

The Semantic Web has great potential for improving traditional library metadata functions expressed in library catalogs. Structured metadata in the linked data model represents the meanings of the information object and document in relation to its association to other related contents or documents. The creation of such robust library metadata is critical for today's library users who desire seamless one-stop searching for their information needs.

RDA and the Future of the Bibliographic Control

Library data created by cataloging and metadata professionals has the potential for interconnecting with related data distributed across the web and improving resource discovery beyond the traditional silos of library catalogs. However, the cataloging community is bracing for another significant time of major change and uncertainty, as *Anglo-American Cataloguing Rules*, 2nd edition (AACR2) is set to be replaced by a new cataloging code — *RDA: Resource Description & Access* — for the first time in more than 30 years (see Tosaka & Park, 2013 for details).

In the same way as the Semantic Web, RDA is based on entity relationships. Based on the new Functional Requirements for Bibliographic Records (FRBR)/Functional Requirements for Authority Data (FRAD) conceptual models, which delineate entities, attributes, and relationships in bibliographic and authority records, RDA is designed to provide a robust metadata infrastructure that will position the library community to better operate in the web environment, while also maintaining compatibility with AACR2 and the earlier descriptive cataloging traditions. RDA provides a set of guidelines and instructions for formulating data representing the attributes and relationships associated with FRBR entities in ways that support user tasks related to resource discovery and access. AACR2 had been developed in the days of the card catalog, designed for the predominantly print-based environment. AACR2 centers on manifestations by classes of materials. On the other hand, RDA is intended to provide a flexible and extensible framework that is easily adaptable to accommodate all types of content and media within rapidly evolving technology environments. In the RDA framework, the content of the information object can be distinguished from its carrier.

RDA is also intended to produce well-formed data that can be shared with other metadata communities in an emerging linked data environment. How well RDA data will be compatible and shareable with other metadata standards will be a main test of RDA's stated goal to open up bibliographic records out of library silos, make them more accessible on the web, and support metadata exchange, reuse, and interoperation. Since the traditional Machine Readable Cataloging (MARC) formats are not well-equipped to take advantage of RDA's new entity-relationship model for RDA implementation, its full capabilities cannot be fully evaluated until the U.S. Library of Congress completes its work on the Bibliographic Framework Transition Initiative to redesign library systems and better accommodate future metadata needs within the library community. The impact of the emerging data standard on the future of bibliographic control should inspire and inform a wide array of new research agenda in the cataloging and metadata communities.

More in-depth, systematic research in relation to practitioners' views on the new cataloging code, ease of application, and benefits and costs of implementation is essential. Research also requires further in-depth studies for evaluating how the additional information provided by RDA — such as bibliographic relationships, and content, media, and carrier types — will improve resource retrieval and bibliographic control for users and catalogers. RDA brings with it guidelines for identifying bibliographic relationships associated with entities that underlie information resources. Future library catalogs can become a set of linked data the meaning of which can potentially be processed by machine. This may open library catalogs to the world in an unprecedented way. However, the question of how the cataloging community can best move forward to the RDA environment must be systematically examined for future bibliographic control.

Library Catalogs: Toward an Interactive Network of Communication

One of the salient characteristics of Web 2.0 can be found in its principle of communication and user participation. Sharing personal data (e.g., photos), opinions (e.g., news article reviews and comments), and experiences on products and services (e.g., books, medical treatments) online is becoming a part of our daily lives. This trend may be further accelerated owing to the rapid advancement of communication and information technologies. The spread and prevalent usage of social media and networking indicates the changing information landscape centering on user interaction and data sharing. This trend has led information practitioners as well as researchers to fundamentally reexamine information organization and library catalog functions. The implementation of Web 2.0 technologies including social tagging in libraries and the emergence of next generation catalog brings into relief this phenomenon.

As a typical application of Web 2.0, the social tagging system allows users to annotate resources with free-form tags. In contrast to the traditional web, today's web invites active user participation. This participation and communication brings forth an unprecedented amount of data and content. Generation of such collective intelligence is another prominent aspect of Web 2.0 (O'Reilly, 2005). User-generated content can be strategically harnessed for furthering information organization and library catalog function.

The advantage of social tagging lies in its ability to allow users to index and catalog resources with their own vocabulary and needs in mind. In short, users become indexers, catalogers, or metadata creators. In this sense, indexer-searcher consistency would be more easily accomplished; heretofore this has been the indicator of retrieval effectiveness (Furner, 2007). That is, when individuals are from the same population, the degree to which they agree on the subjects and concepts of a given resource and on the combinations of terms that are used to express given subjects and concepts can be assumed to be high.

Another advantage of social tagging comes from its capacity for adaptation; that is the ability to very quickly change in response to flux in user needs and vocabulary. As social culture and technology evolve, new words and phrases continue to emerge in every domain. Controlled vocabularies tend to react slowly to new terms and phrases because of high maintenance cost. However, the addition of new terms and phrases to a social tagging system can be highly efficient with low cost.

An important advantageous aspect of social tagging also derives from its social property. It creates a sense of community among users through shared tags and resources. Many social tagging systems have the recommendation function. When a user tags a new resource, the system can show the tags that have been assigned by other users to the same resource. Further, when users assign a tag to an item, they can see the resources that carry the same tag.

Successful implementation and use of social tagging in the library setting depends on a better understanding of various issues surrounding user behavior on tagging information resources, linguistic structures of vocabulary that users employ, and relations between user and professional's vocabulary. This understanding needs to underlie the assessment related to integration of social tagging into library catalogs.

The attention to the emergence of next generation catalogs is vital. The first generation of Online Public Access Catalog (OPAC) appeared in late 1970 and mostly reflected card catalogs; second-generation catalogs present more advanced features including keyword searching and browsing. Web-based catalogs emerging in late 1990 present a more sophisticated interface featuring book jackets/covers, hyperlinks, and electronic resources. However, the lack of user interaction and participation is evident even in web-based OPACs.

The static and inflexible nature of catalogs does not reflect changing user needs and expectations; today's users are familiar with web search engines, and tend to expect the same features such as relevance feedback and ranking, recommendations, and user interactions in library OPACs. Making catalogs an interactive network of communication requires versatile OPAC interface design in the context of web. Development of interactive library catalogs in Semantic Web environments should also engender an even wider array of issues for future research.

Organization of the Book

This volume consists of three main sections consisting of a total of 11 chapters: (1) RDA, Semantic Web, and linked data; (2) Web 2.0. technologies and information organization; (3) library catalogs: toward an interactive network of communication.

Below is a brief introduction to the contributed studies.

Section I: RDA, Semantic Web, and Linked Data

The U.S. Library of Congress will implement RDA beginning in 2013, yet many librarians do not fully understand the benefits of RDA and its relevance to linked data and the Semantic Web. The study by Sharon Q. Yang and Yan Yi Lee, "Organizing Bibliographical Data with RDA: How Far Have We Striven toward the Semantic Web," aims to help librarians get to know the underlying rationale for RDA and to see the great potential of the Semantic Web for libraries. It explains the linked data model and Semantic Web technologies in basic, but informative terms, and describes how the Semantic Web is constructed. Semantic Web standards and technologies are discussed in detail including URI, RDF, and ontologies. The study also traces the development of RDA and some of the major library Semantic Web projects. The authors explore how RDA shapes bibliographic data and prepares it for linked data in the Semantic Web. In addition, this study examines what libraries in the United States and the rest of the world have achieved toward implementing RDA since its release. Included is a discussion of the obstacles and difficulties that may occur in the work ahead. It ends with a vision for the future when libraries join the Semantic Web and become part of the Giant Global Graph.

In her chapter, "Keeping Libraries Relevant in the Semantic Web with *RDA: Resource Description and Access*," Barbara B. Tillett underscores the importance of the new international cataloging code, *RDA* in addressing fundamental user tasks through the creation of well-formed, interconnected metadata. The metadata constructed throughout the life cycle of a resource is especially valuable to, and available for repurposing by, many types of users — from creators of resources, to publishers, subscription agents, book vendors, resource aggregators, system vendors, libraries and other cultural institutions, and end users of these resources. Such structured, rich metadata is well-aligned with linked data initiatives associated with the Semantic Web ensuring the continuing importance and relevance of RDA as an international standard.

Unlike AACR2, *RDA* is intended to provide subject access. Alan Poulter's chapter, "Filling in the Blanks in RDA or Remaining Blank? The Strange Case of FRSAD," outlines possible strategies for RDA to move forward in providing subject access, based on the model given in the recent Functional Requirements for Subject Authority Data (FRSAD) (IFLA Working Group, 2010). The study covers significant developments in subject access in the FR (Functional Requirements) family of models, which underpin RDA. It presents in detail the development of FRSAD and explains the differences between it and the earlier FR models. The author suggests that the linguistic theory underlying the Preserved Context Index System might provide an alternative model for developing entities in FRSAD.

Linked data, which is based in the Semantic Web, enables specific identification and linkage of information through open HTTP protocols. Linked data has great potential for expanding bibliographic and authority data in libraries in the web environment. The chapter, entitled, "Organizing and Sharing Information Using Linked Data," by Ziyoung Park and Heejung Kim, introduces the fundamental concepts and principles of linked data. Introduced are such major linked data projects as the W3C Library Linked Data Incubator Group, the British National Bibliography, Faceted Application of Subject Terminology, and Virtual International Authority File. The study discusses benefits that linked data can provide in and to libraries, and presents a short history of the development of library linked data.

Section II: Web 2.0. Technologies and Information Organization

In her chapter, "Social Cataloging: Social Cataloger," Shawne Miksa observes that, over the past several years, we have seen in catalog records in local systems an increase in the amount of user-contributed content in the form of social tags and user commentary. Miksa defines this activity of "social cataloging" as, "…the joint effort by users and catalogers to interweave individually- or socially- preferred access points in a library information system as a mode of discovery and access to the information resources held in the library's collection." The popularity of social tagging, Web 2.0, and folksonomies challenges long-held professional practices and values wherein the cataloger creates — using standardized codes and procedures — a record which the user may use to locate and retrieve library materials. Following a review of relevant literature pertaining to social tagging and library catalogs from 2006 to 2012, Miksa suggests a rethinking of the role of the cataloger based on emerging trends, subsequently defining the "social cataloger" as "… an information professional/librarian who is skilled in both expert-based and user-created vocabularies, who understands the motivations of users who tag information resources and how to incorporate this knowledge into an information system for subject representation and access." This, she argues, is not an abrogation of a cataloger's professional responsibility, or of well-articulated, codified practice across time, but rather a role consistent with Jesse Shera's vision of social epistemology.

"Social Indexing: A Solution to the Challenges of Current Information Organization," by Yunseon Choi, continues the exploration of the concept of social tagging by investigating the quality and efficacy of user-generated tags in subject indexing. She notes that subject gateways, and web directories as tools for internet resource discovery, are problematic in two key respects. First, they were developed using traditional library schemes for subject access based on controlled vocabularies — vocabularies not always well-suited to the range of digital objects, or demonstrating either a lack of, or excessive specificity in, certain subject areas. Second, web documents were organized and indexed by professional indexers. Consequently, subject terminology may not reflect the natural language of users searching subject gateways and professionally indexed web directories. Choi's comparison of indexing consistency (1) between professional indexers (BUBL and Intute), and (2) taggers and professional indexers (Delicious and Intute), provides an empirical backdrop to understanding the extent to which social indexing might or could be used to replace (and in some cases to improve upon) professional indexing. The chapter concludes with suggestions for future research, including an evocative call for research on subjective or emotional tags which, though usually discounted, could be metadata crucial to describing important factors represented in the document.

Image production and photography have gone through many changes since photography was first introduced to society in 1839, in terms of photographic equipment and technology, the kinds of things people photograph, and how people organize and share their photographs and images. While it is technological advancements in cameras (from analog to digital), which have fundamentally transformed the physical way in which images are both taken and subsequently organized, it is thanks to technological advancements in both the Internet and mobile phones that have truly revolutionized the ways in which we think about taking, organizing, and sharing images, and even the kinds of things we photograph.

The chapter by Emma Stuart, entitled, "Organizing Photographs: Past and Present," discusses the switch from analog to digital and how this switch has altered the ways in which people capture and organize photographs. The emergence of Web 2.0 technologies, and online photo management sites, such as Flickr™, is also discussed in terms of how they aid with organization and sharing, and the role that tagging has on these two functions. Camera phones and the proliferation of photography applications is discussed in terms of impact on how images are shared, and specific emphasis is placed on how they have fundamentally changed the kinds of things that people photograph.

Section III: Library Catalogs: Toward an Interactive Network of Communication

In the introduction to their study, "VuFind — an OPAC 2.0?," Birong Ho and Laura Horne-Popp lament that library online public access catalogs

(OPACs) have been relatively the same for years. They then challenge readers to consider the following: "If Web 2.0 OPACs can provide the sophistication and ease of use needed by the average searcher, then it may be possible to bring users back to the library catalog as a starting point." Following a discussion of the characteristic features and functionalities of Web 2.0 OPACs, and a comparison of products supporting the Universal Graphics Module (UGM), the authors focus on VuFind, an open-source, library discovery tool. They suggest that VuFind has been a viable option for libraries needing to implement a Web 2.0 OPAC due to its lack of fees, and its low hardware costs and server maintenance. Ho and Horne-Popp illustrate their conclusion that VuFind represents "an inexpensive solution to an improved library catalog" by describing usability studies conducted at a number of academic libraries, including the author's institution, the University of Richmond.

Information technologies today are experiencing greater use than at any other time in their history, and, more importantly, by regular laypeople other than scientists. Massive amounts of information are available online and web search engines provide a popular means to access this information. We live in an information age that requires us, more than ever, to seek new ways to represent and access information. Faceted search plays a key role in this program. The study, entitled, "Faceted Search in Library Catalogs" by Xi Niu, explores the theory, history, implementation, and practice of faceted search used in library catalogs. The author offers a comprehensive perspective of the topic and provides sufficient depth and breadth to offer a useful resource to researchers, librarians, and practitioners about faceted search used in library.

In the current economic climate, libraries struggle to do more with less as collection budgets shrink. Southern Illinois University Carbondale's (SIU) Morris Library changed its default catalog from the local catalog (SIUCat) to the consortial catalog (I-Share) in 2011. VUFind has been employed with Voyager as the catalog interface for I-Share libraries since 2008. Morris Library is one of 152 members of the Consortium of Academic and Research Libraries in Illinois (CARLI), 76 of which contribute records to I-Share. Users from any of these 76 libraries can request materials from other libraries through the consortial catalog. In essence, the library users have access to over 32 million items located at 76 member libraries instead of being limited to the local library collection. The chapter, "Doing More With Less: Increasing the Value of the Consortial Catalog," by Elizabeth J. Cox, Stephanie Graves, Andrea Imre, and Cassie Wagner relates the steps taken to implement this change, the pros and cons of the change, evaluation and assessment, as well as potential future enhancements.

General data studies, web quality studies, and metadata quality studies contain common dimensions of data quality, namely, accuracy, consistency, completeness, timeliness, trust, and relevance. Sarah H. Theimer's contribution, entitled, "All Metadata Politics Is Local: Developing Meaningful Quality Standards," discusses the importance of recognizing and utilizing local needs in the metadata quality process. Her chapter reviews the importance, and multiple definitions of data quality, exploring how egregious metadata errors can thwart discovery systems and make resources virtually irretrievable. Quality data should meet customer expectations. Businesses determined that customers want relevant, clear, easy to understand, low-cost data. The chapter describes how quality dimensions are applied in practice to local quality procedures. It is necessary to identify high priority populations, and resources in core subject areas or formats, as quality does not have to be uniform throughout all metadata. The author emphasizes the importance of examining the information environment, documentation practice, and development of standards for measuring quality dimensions. The author points out that in order to provide optimum service we must vigilantly ensure that quality procedures rapidly evolve to reflect local user expectations, the local information environment, technology capabilities, and national standards.

Summary

The information revolution in the digital environment affords researchers and practitioners unprecedented opportunities as well as challenges. Through systematic research findings using various perspectives and research methods, this volume addresses key issues centering on information organization in the context of the information revolution, and future research directions. The reader is provided with the breadth of emerging information standards and technologies for organizing networked and digital resources. Readers may also benefit from practical perspectives and applications of digital library technologies for information organization. We hope that this volume stimulates new avenues of research and practice and contributes to the development of a new paradigm in information organization.

Jung-ran Park
Lynne C. Howarth

Reference

Baker, T., Bermès, E., Coyle, K., Dunsire, G., Isaac, A., Murray, P., … Zeng, M. (2011). *Library linked data incubator group final report*. http://www.w3.org/2005/Incubator/lld/XGR-lld-20111025/

Berners-Lee, T. (2009). *Linked data – In design issues*. World Wide Web Consortium. Retrieved from. http://www.w3.org/DesignIssues/LinkedData.html

Berners-Lee, T., Hendler, J., & Lassila, O. (2001). The semantic web: A new form of Web content that is meaningful to computers will unleash a revolution of new possibilities. *The Scientific American*, *284*(5), 34–43.

Furner, J. (2007). User tagging of library resources: Toward a framework for system evaluation. In *World Library and Information Congress: 73RD IFLA general conference and council*, Durban, South Africa (pp. 1–10).

Gruber, T. (2007). Ontology of folksonomy: A mash-up of apples and oranges. *International Journal on Semantic Web & Information Systems*, *3*(1), 1–11.

Gruber, T. (2008). Collective knowledge systems: Where the social web meets the semantic web. *Journal of Web Semantics: Science, Services and Agents on the World Wide Web*, *6*(1), 4–13.

IFLA Working Group on the Functional Requirements for Subject Authority Records (FRSAR) (2010). *Functional requirements for subject authority data (FRSAD): A conceptual model*. Retrieved from http://www.ifla.org/files/classification-and-indexing/functional-requirements-for-subject-authority-data/frsad-final-report.pdf

O'Reilly, T. (2005). *What is web 2.0: Design patterns and business models for the next generation of software*. Retrieved from http://oreilly.com/web2/archive/what-is-web-20.html

Tosaka, Y., & Park, J. R. (2013). RDA: Resource Description & Access – A survey of the current state of the art. *Journal of the American Society for Information Science and Technology*, *64*(4), 651–662.

SECTION I: SEMANTIC WEB, LINKED DATA, AND RDA

Chapter 1

Organizing Bibliographical Data with RDA: How Far Have We Stridden Toward the Semantic Web?

Sharon Q. Yang and Yan Yi Lee

Abstract

Purpose — This chapter aims to help librarians understand the underlying rationale for Resource Description and Access (RDA) and recognize the great potential of the Semantic Web for libraries.

Design/methodology/approach — It explains the linked data model and Semantic Web technologies in basic, informative terms, and describes how the Semantic Web is constructed. Semantic Web standards and technologies are discussed in detail, including URI, RDF, and ontologies. The study also traces the development of RDA and some of the major library Semantic Web projects. The authors explore how RDA shapes bibliographical data and prepares it for linked data in the Semantic Web. In addition, this study examines what libraries in the United States and the rest of the world have achieved in implementing RDA since its release.

Findings — RDA is the correct approach libraries should take.

Originality/value — This is the first and only chapter that covers the development of RDA in other countries as well as in the United States. It is highly informative for anyone who wishes to understand

New Directions in Information Organization
Library and Information Science, Volume 7, 3–27

ISSN: 1876-0562/doi:10.1108/S1876-0562(2013)0000007005

the RDA and Semantic Web and their relevance to libraries in a short period of time.

1.1. Introduction

Resource Description and Access (RDA) is a new cataloging standard that can organize bibliographical metadata more effectively and make it possible to be shared and reused in the digital world. Since its release in 2010, RDA has been tested in libraries, museums, and information centers. Recognizing its potential advantages, many librarians have started to familiarize themselves with RDA, and are planning to implement it in their libraries. On the other hand, some still have doubts about RDA which led to questions such as "Do we have to implement RDA?", "Why RDA, not AACR3?", and "What are the real benefits of RDA to library users?" These questions have subjected the new cataloging standard to resistance and criticism worldwide. Understanding the Semantic Web and related technologies will help clarify some of those questions.

This chapter will explain Semantic Web technologies and their relevance to RDA. It will trace the development of RDA and some of the major library Semantic Web projects. The authors will explore how RDA shapes bibliographical data and prepares it for linked data in the Semantic Web. In addition, this chapter will examine what libraries in the United States and the rest of the world have achieved toward implementing RDA since its release. Included is a discussion on the obstacles and difficulties that may occur in the work ahead. It will end with a vision for the future when libraries join the Semantic Web and become part of the Giant Global Graph.

1.2. IFLA Standards and RDA Development

The Anglo-American Cataloging Rules, Second Edition (AACR2) was created prior to the digital age in 1978, and is obviously outdated. When the time came to write a new cataloging code, namely AACR3, the Joint Steering Committee for Revision of AACR was formed with representatives from national libraries of four English-speaking countries — the United States, Canada, the United Kingdom, and Australia. Halfway through the discussion, the committee realized that AACR3 was not the direction they would take. Instead, RDA should be the modern cataloging standard. Thus, the Joint Steering Committee for Revision of AACR became the Joint Steering Committee for Development of RDA (JSC).

RDA is the new cataloging standard designed for the digital age and metadata. It is built on the foundations of the previous cataloging standard, AACR2. However, RDA is very different from AACR2 in concept, structure, and scope. Based on International Federation of Library Associations (IFLA)'s conceptual models FRBR (Functional Requirements for Bibliographical Records) and FRAD (Functional Requirements for Authority Data), RDA is designed for describing resources in both digital environment and traditional library collections. Both FRBR and FRAD are conceptual models for organizing bibliographical data. Developed and revised by IFLA between 1998 (IFLA Study Group on FRBR, 2011) and 2009 (IFLA Working Group on Functional Requirements and Numbering of Authority Records, 2012), FRBR defines an item as entity and its bibliographical relationships by work, expression, manifestation, and item. The Semantic Web is an excellent technology to represent such bibliographical relationships defined by BRFR.

1.3. Semantic Web Technologies

The significance of RDA lies in its alignment with the Semantic Web requirements. The RDA will help to prepare bibliographical data for their future use in the Semantic Web. Implementing RDA is the first step for libraries to adopt Semantic Web technologies and exchange data with the rest of the metadata communities. Linking data will be the next logical move.

The Semantic Web is a vision expressed by Tim Berners-Lee, Director of the World Wide Web Consortium (W3C) and inventor of the Internet, in 1999. According to him, the Semantic Web is "A web of data that can be processed directly and indirectly by machines." Other descriptions of the Semantic Web include a Web of Linked Data, the Giant Global Graph, and Web 3.0 vs. current Web 2.0. The Semantic Web is not meant to replace the current Web as the mission impossible. Instead it will be an extension of current Web as an enhancement.

The Semantic Web remained a vision, a standard, and a movement more than a reality until recent times. Even now it is still under development. As time goes by, more and more applications begin to embed Semantic Web elements. As those implementations are on a small scale, most people are not aware of the benefits of the Semantic Web. The latest deployment is by Google.com that acquired Metalib, a leading company in the Semantic Web movement and the creator of Freebase, a Semantic Web knowledgebase with structured data. In May 2012, Google.com linked its search to Freebase and began to provide "smart search results" (Cameron, 2010). One CNN report states that "Google revamps search, tries to think more like a person" (Gross, 2012). The new Google search provides a glimpse of how the Semantic Web works.

There are three characteristics of the Semantic Web that differentiate it from the current Web. First of all, machines understand the meanings of data and process them accordingly. They know how to make logical inferences and establish relationships among data elements. In other words data is actionable by machines. In the current Web, only humans can read and infer meanings from data. Second, the Semantic Web is based on entity relationships or structured data. The Semantic Web is about people, things, their properties, and entity relationships. For instance, if we establish that Tom is a cat and all cats are mammals in the Semantic Web, machines can establish a new relationship such as that Tom is a mammal by the power of inference. Library data is rich in bibliographical relationships. For instance, William Shakespeare is the author of "A Midsummer Night's Dream." Theseus is a character in this play. Hippolyta is another character in the same play. The Semantic Web is supposed to understand the above said relationships and make inferences between Shakespeare, Theseus, Hippolyta, and the work "A Midsummer Night's Dream." In the Semantic Web, searching one of them will retrieve the others through linked data even though they are not related directly by word patterns. The current Web is not capable of doing that.

Finally, the Semantic Web is a Web of linked data, while the current Web is a Web of linked documents. In the current Web, searching keywords will bring up HTML documents and we follow links to other HTML documents. Searching in the Semantic Web will retrieve all the relevant information on a subject through relationships even though the searched keywords are not contained in the content. For instance, a search of Bill Clinton may bring up his wife, daughter, schools and colleges he attended, his friends and White House associates, his speeches and works, and more. The information about Bill Clinton is not a pre-composed HTML page. Rather it is data assembled from different sources based on entity relationships and the display is created on the fly. Such information retrieval is based on structured and linked data in the Semantic Web. A click on the link to Hillary Clinton will bring up similar information about her. Data about her contains relationships that lead to other relationships. This is done through linked data.

The Semantic Web is made possible through a series of W3C (World Wide Web Consortium) standards and technologies. Those standards and technologies are still being defined and developed at this moment. In the center of Semantic Web standards and technologies are URI (Uniform Resource Identifier), RDF (Resource Description Framework), subject ontologies, and vocabularies. Those are the most basic building blocks in constructing the Semantic Web and linked data. Web Ontology Language

(OWL), SPARSQL, and Simple Knowledge Organization System (SKOS), and many more are also important standards and technologies for the Semantic Web.

1.3.1. URI: Uniform Resource Identifier

A word may have different meanings. For instance, the word "Boston" may mean any of the 26 geographical locations around the world (MetaLib Inc, 2012). In most Internet search engines and databases, search is not case sensitive. Therefore, Apple (Mac computer) and apple (fruit) are literally the same word in the eyes of a machine. How can computers tell the Mac Apple from the fruit apple? How does the Semantic Web manage to distinguish between the different meanings of a word with the same spelling? On a different note, there may be multiple ways to describe a place. For instance, there are 50 different ways that people address UC Berkeley on the Internet (MetaLib Inc, 2012). How can the Semantic Web tell that all those different spellings mean the same thing? The secret lies in the fact that the Semantic Web uses entities, not words, to represent meanings. In the Semantic Web, people, things, and locations are defined as entities and entities can be anything including concepts or events. An entity may have its own unique properties or attributes. One such entity can be "person" whose properties or attributes may include height, weight, gender, race, birth date and place, and more. Another entity can be garment with properties or attributes such as size, color, texture, and price. Using entities to represent meanings in the Semantic Web are less ambiguous than words.

Each entity is also called a resource on the Internet. In fact, an Internet resource is most likely to be a description of the entity. In the Semantic Web each resource is found by a URI that comprises a unique string of characters to identify a resource on the Web. The URI can be a Uniform Resource Locator (URL) or a Uniform Resource Name (URN) or both. While the former is an Internet address, the latter is the name of a persistent object. Examples of the URI may be http://www.rider.edu/library (URL) or urn:isbn:9781844573080 (URN). A URI may be used to identify a unique resource such as a document, an image, an abstract object, or the name of a person. Another example of URI looks like "http://id.loc.gov/authorities/subjects/sh2001000147.html" which is the URI of the Library of Congress (LC) Subject Heading for the September 11, 2011 terrorist attack.

If each of the 26 Bostons has a unique URI with a detailed description of their geography, country, climate, population, and cultures, then it would be easy for a researcher to quickly retrieve and choose the right location that is linked to other URIs with related information. Likewise, all the various forms addressing UC Berkeley can be mapped to one URI. The Semantic

Web search engines use SPARSQL as their query language. They will query URIs and assume that the data containing the same URI should be about the same entity. The Semantic Web search engines will retrieve and assemble the data containing the same URIs and present them to humans in a meaningful way. The URI is used for linking data and is a fundamental building block of the Semantic Web. The more URIs are created, the more linking can be accomplished.

1.3.2. RDF: Resource Description Framework

The URI is a standalone location identifier, but does not define relationships between entities. They must be connected by syntax into meaningful units and RDF serves this purpose. RDF stands for Resource Description Framework. Simply put, RDF is a structure of three parts called RDF triples. A triple includes a subject, a predicate, and an object. See Figure 1 for a graphic representation of an RDF triple. The subject is generally the entity or thing to be described. The predicate is often defined as the properties or attributes of the subject and the object as the value. Using our previous example, in the RDF triples, Shakespeare is the subject. The predicate or the property comprises "is the author of" and the object or the value could be "A Midsummer Night's Dream" or any of his plays. The RDF data model isolates data into separate elements for machines to process, establish relationships, and make inferences leading to more relationships. Likewise, MARC format is also created for machines to read, but it is not made for the Semantic Web and linked data. It is not an easy job to translate MARC into RDF triples. Another drawback of MARC is that it is a standard only known and used by the library community, while RDF is being used by the Semantic Web and other metadata communities.

The subject in the RDF triples must contain URIs. The predicate must also hold URIs. The object of the triple is more flexible. It can have URIs or text. The URIs are capable of linking with other data, while text will be the dead end. When constructing the RDF triples, URIs are used wherever it is possible (Coyle, 2012). The Semantic Web is built upon billions of RDA triples.

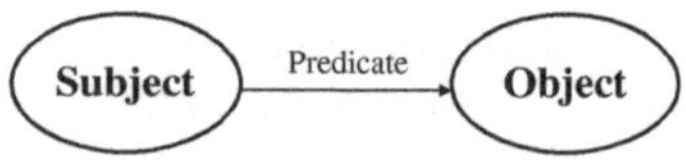

Figure 1: RDF.

The current Web is not capable of defining relationships between entities as RDF does. In the Semantic Web, machines are programmed to interpret and understand RDF triples and entity relationships. SPARSQL is the query language for the Semantic Web. The SPARSQL query will search for RDF triples with the same URIs and follow the relationships in RDF triples for linked data. HTML is very limited in defining entity relationships. Therefore, RDF and the Semantic Web are not written in HTML, but in one of the several other languages such as RDF/XML, N3, Turtle, and N-Triples. RDF/XML is a far more commonly used language than the others in the Semantic Web.

1.3.3. Ontologies and Vocabularies

RDF only includes basic vocabulary defining relationships and it is not sufficient. Ontologies, vocabularies, and controlled values are developed to supply more properties and relationship definitions for a specific subject. Simply put, an ontology is a Web-based database that contains definitions of classes, subclasses, properties or elements, and URIs. Ontology defines the relationships in a specific subject or discipline which in Semantic Web jargon is called a "subject domain." Each subject domain has its own unique properties and relationships. For instance, bibliographical relationships are specific for publishers or libraries which may include classes and subclass of relationships between publishers and items, authors and works, editions, and manifestations of a work. Likewise, an ontology for higher education may define the relationships and hierarchies between professors and students, classes, universities, colleges, schools, and departments. Biology has its ontology and so do music, math, and many other fields. RDF refers to ontologies and related languages for definitions of relationships and values.

Ontologies are created according to a W3C standard in languages called RDF Schema or Web Ontology Language (OWL). Simple Knowledge Organization System (SKOS) is a W3C OWL ontology for taxonomies and thesauruses. Friend of A Friend (FOAF) is another ontology for defining people and their relationships. A list of existing and completed ontologies can be found at http://semanticweb.org/wiki/Ontology. Once created, an ontology of a subject domain can be shared and used subsequently by others in the Semantic Web. Sharing the same ontologies makes it easier for linking and exchanging data cross-domains. Like RDF triples and URIs, the more ontologies there are, the more data that can be linked.

The library community is developing its own ontologies and vocabularies. Open Metadata Registry is one of the Web sites for depositing controlled vocabularies (metadaregistry.org). IFLA has been active in standardizing cataloging principles and promoting the Semantic Web. One initiative related to FRBR and FRBRoo is a formal ontology "interpreting conceptualizations expressed in FRBR and of concepts necessary to explain the intended meaning of all FRBRer attributes and relationships" (CIDOC and the CIDOC Documentation Standards Working Group, 2011). It is jointly developed by two international working groups CIDOC Conceptual Reference Model and Functional Requirements for Bibliographic Records. A vote by IFLA FRBR Review Group is eminent for its final approval. FRBRoo will play an important role in bridging RDA with the Semantic Web. Open Metadata Registry is another effort in building library vocabularies and controlled values.

Shared ontologies and vocabularies provide a common set of elements between disparate databases. Linking of data can take place through shared data elements. Furthermore, a URI as subject in one RDF triple may be the URI of an object in another triple. Thus, triples are being linked through common URIs and shared ontologies or vocabularies. RDF and inference are powerful for presenting relationships in the Semantic Web. "Broadly speaking, inference on the Semantic Web can be characterized by discovering new relationships. On the Semantic Web, data is modeled as a set of (named) relationships between resources. 'Inference' means that automatic procedures can generate new relationships based on the data and based on some additional information in the form of a vocabulary, e.g., a set of rules" (W3C, 2012). Ontologies, vocabularies, URIs, RDF, and power of inference in combination will link data into a huge network called the Giant Global Graph.

1.3.4. Storage of RDF Data

RDF triples can be stored in a graph database or triple store. A graph database is one of several data storage structures. "In a data graph, there is no concept of roots (or a hierarchy). A graph consists of resources related to other resources, with no single resource having any particular intrinsic importance over another" (LinkedDataTools.com, 2009). Figure 2 is an illustration of relational, hierarchical, and graph databases. To search and retrieve relationships in the Semantic Web, the Semantic Web search engines are used and the query language is SPARSQL.

To summarize, the architecture of the Semantic Web is continuously being revised. The basis of the Semantic Web is URI, a unique way to identify Web resources. RDF is the bone structure and RDF/XML is one of the languages to build the Semantic Web. Ontologies and vocabularies serve as the flesh and extend RDF to identify meanings for a specific subject domain. SPARSQL is the language to retrieve data in the Semantic Web

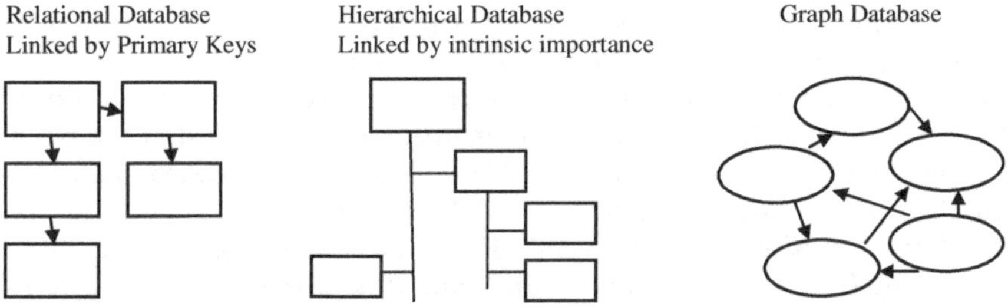

Figure 2: Databases.

environment. Work on Semantic Web standards and technologies will be an ongoing project. RDA breaks bibliographical data into data elements for relationships and the Semantic Web can link those relationships in a meaningful way.

1.4. RDA and the Semantic Web

Currently, Semantic Web technologies have been widely deployed in industry and business. In library and information communities, Semantic Web applications have also been developed and used in recent years.

In 2009, the LV started to deliver LC Subject Authority File as linked-data in a Web-based service named LC Linked Data Service — Authorities and Vocabularies. Later on, more LC's authority data has been added to this Web service. In addition to LC Subject Headings, the Web service includes Name Authority File (NAF), Genre/Form Terms, Thesaurus of Graphic Materials, as well as MARC Relators, MARC Countries, etc. Written in SKOS, this Web service provides authority data which can be accessed not only by humans but also by machines (Library of Congress, 2012a).

Another successful application is xISBN. Developed by Online Compute Library Center, Inc. (OCLC), this Web service provides FRBRized information in WorldCat. Users can retrieve a core record and all manifestations by one search. For example, when we search for a book and get one record in WorldCat Local, we can easily find all different editions and formats of this title from "Editions and formats" in this record, such as translations in different languages, or non-print formats like computer file, audio disc, etc. (OCLC, 2012)

Library professionals and experts have made great efforts to exchange information with the outside world, and have achieved a lot to share data in the digital environment. However, the primary and largest database, bibliographical catalog, is still "closed" in libraries.

The current cataloging rule AACR2 is focused on describing manifestations by classes of materials. Bibliographical data, created by AACR2 or previous cataloging rules, is now stored in MARC format in library databases. Entries (or elements) such as title, subject, and ISBN are bound together in a bibliographical record. These elements are indexed and can be searched in the Web-based library catalogs, but they still reside in silos called the "invisible or dark Web." Thus, the bibliographical data is not indexed by Internet search engines and cannot be searched or shared across the Internet with other metadata sources. All the data elements reside in a record only. Without the record, the data elements will be decomposed and there is no way to find or retrieve those scattered data elements in the vast digital ocean. The Web-based online catalogs are simply an electronic version of card catalogs. Library users cannot get more information from a library online catalog than in a card catalog. Even if there are some hyperlinks in a bibliographical record, the links only point to a few external Web pages and therefore are not linked data.

What is the possibility to make bibliographical data usable outside the library catalogs? Obviously, there needs to be bibliographical data in an entirely different manner. The newly released cataloging rule RDA provides us with an effective method to turn a "solid" record into flexible, well-labeled metadata, which can serve as the foundation of the Semantic Web.

As a content standard, RDA guides the recording of data. The key features of RDA (RDA Toolkit, 2012) are:

1. flexible and extensible framework for description of resources;
2. efficiencies and flexibility in data capture, storage, retrieval, and display made possible with new database technologies; and
3. clear line of separation between the guidelines and instructions on recording data and those on the presentation of data.

The basic goal of RDA is to help users to identify and link the resources they need from our collections. "RDA provides relationship designators to explicitly state the role a person, family, or corporate body plays with respect to the source being described" (Tillett, 2011). Based on the "entity-relationship" model, which is similar to the structure of RDF, RDA provides a way to build bibliographical entities as RDF triples, the primary building block of linked data in the Semantic Web.

Figure 3 illustrates an example of the "triple" derived from a traditional catalog record. The work "Through the looking glass" was written by Lewis Carroll and illustrated by John Tenniel. The entities and relationships can be represented by URIs (see Figure 4).

The advantage of URI is that it points to exactly the correct place to obtain the appropriate bibliographical resource, agent, or relationship.

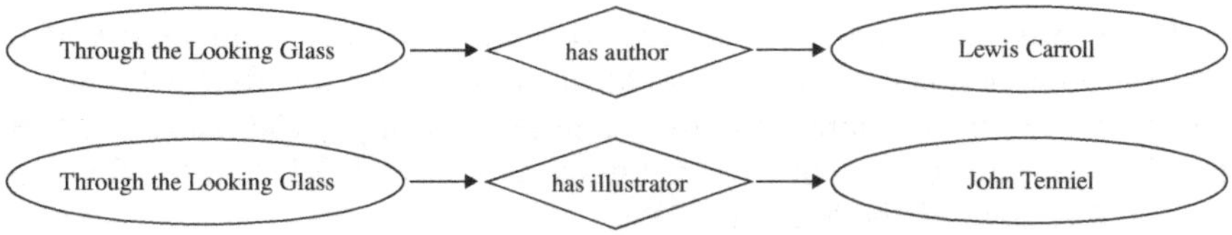

Figure 3: An Author and a Contributor, in Triple Form (Coyle, 2010).

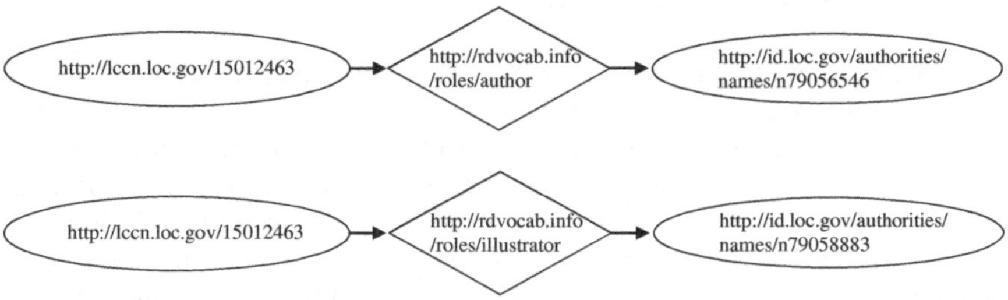

Figure 4: An Author and a Contributor Represented by URIs (Coyle, 2010).

The subject in this case is represented by the URI of a LC control number, which points to the record in the LC online catalog. The URI of the predicate points to the namespace http://revocab.info, where RDA element set "roles" have been stored. The objects, author and illustrator in this case, are personal names. Their pointers are URIs in the domain http://id.loc.gov, which was mentioned above. All authority data files LC are stored there, including the NAF.

Speaking about library data and the Semantic Web, Karen Coyle stated, "I do think that the move towards open declaration of vocabularies and the freeing of data from databases and even from records is the key to expending the discovery and navigation services that we can provide information seekers" (Coyle, 2010). "Freeing" data from the library databases is the ultimate goal. First of all, a traditional catalog record needs "to be decomposed into a set of instance triples, all using the same URI for the subject" (Dunsire & Willer, 2011). The URI of the predicate identifies the property, such as "is the author of" or "has publisher" or "illustrated by." The object, which contains the value of the property, can be a character string, or a URI. The future catalog "record" will be an aggregated set of "triples." These triples have "meaning," and can be read and accessed by machines. This makes it possible to deliver library catalog as linked data. Assisted by Semantic Web technologies, bibliographical database will be connected to databases created by other information communities.

RDA provides us the guidelines to identify entities and clarify their relationships explicitly. Bibliographical and authority data should be constructed with well-labeled entities and relationships, and made available for the future development toward linked data model. RDA is the first step on the way toward the Semantic Web.

1.5. RDA in the United States

LC participated in RDA development from its early inception, but the journey to RDA is not smooth in the United States. During the development stage, LC Working Group on the Future of Bibliographic Control recommended to "suspend work on RDA" in its final report in January 2008 (The Working Group, 2008). In response to the recommendation in its *Response to On the Record: Report of the Library of Congress Working Group on the Future of Bibliographic Control*," LC rejected the recommendation and decided to "Continue to support RDA development and subsequent testing; estimate resources needed to assign Web-based identifiers retroactively to data elements in existing LC online records" (Marchum, 2008). The release of RDA in 2010 was met with strong opposition initially. The arguments in favor of RDA include "Greater potential for machine-assisted cataloging," "Fewer inconsistencies in cataloging process because of automated RDF (URI) linking and use of controlled vocabularies," "Less redundancy in cataloging process," "More cooperation between different bibliographical communities (publishers, aggregators)," "Leeway in many areas for local cataloging interpretations," "Adaptable to new formats," and "Visibility of library collections on the web" (Yang & Quinn, 2011). Arguments against RDA include the difficulty in using RDA Toolbox, cataloging becoming too complex caused by fields and statement being broken into smaller pieces, too much flexibility to be a standard, and too much training involved just to name a few. Some questioned if the vendors of Integrated Library Systems (ILS) were ready to incorporate RDA into the cataloging module, while others had suspicion if records cataloged under MARC 21 could ever be converted into RDA records. There was also voiced concern about discarding years of training and teaching in AACR2 and accepting a mysterious new standard. Most librarians were not aware of the Semantic Web and did not understand some of the new practices. Some of those are legitimate concerns.

In spite of the controversies, both LC and OCLC have taken the lead in the work toward the Semantic Web. In 2008, LC Network Development and MARC Standards Office started to make MARC Format changes to accommodate RDA. "MARC 21 Updates 9, 10, 11, and 13 include all changes to MARC for use with RDA approved through 2011" (Library of Congress, 2011). Immediately upon the release of RDA in June 2010, LC formed U.S. RDA Test Coordinating Committee to organize testing of RDA in cataloging. The testers included three National libraries (LC), National Agricultural Library (NAL), and National Library of Medicine (NLM) and 23 other entities representing research, academic, and public libraries and vendors. The RDA testing project continued for 9 months from July 1, 2010 to March 31, 2011. In the first 90-day period, testing participants familiarized themselves with the content of RDA and Toolkit; in the second 90-day period, RDA testers produced RDA records; in the third 90-day period, the Coordinating Committee evaluated the test results and submitted its final report on May 9, 2011. The report entitled "Report and Recommendations of the U.S. RDA Test Coordinating Committee" was revised for public release on June 20, 2011 (U.S. RDA Test Coordinating Committee, 2011).

In its final report, the LC Coordinating Committee pointed out that out of the 10 goals of RDA, only 3 had been met or mostly met, and 3 were partially met. Therefore, the committee recommended to LC/NAL/NLM that a series tasks should be well underway before RDA implementation. Among the recommendations to the JSC is the major task to "Rewrite RDA in clear, unambiguous, plain English." Some core tasks recommended by the committee, such as "Define process for updating RDA in the online environment," "Improve RDA Toolkit," and "Develop RDA record examples in MARC and other schemas" have been completed, while others are still on track.

After the completion of RDA testing, some participants continued RDA cataloging, such as Chicago University, Stanford University, and State Library of Pennsylvania. In March 2012, LC announced that they would move forward with full implementation of RDA on March 31, 2013. LC's partner national libraries, NAL and NLM, will also target Day One of their implementation of RDA in the first quarter of 2013 (Library of Congress, 2012c).

Fully aware of the limitation of MARC for data management in digital age, LC formed the Working Group on the Future of Bibliographic Control to find how bibliographical control can effectively support management of and access to library materials in the digital environment. Based on the recommendations made by both the Working Group and the final report on the RDA Test, LC made its decision to investigate a solution to replace MARC 21. LC announced its initial plan for Bibliographic Framework Transition Initiative on October 21, 2011 (Library of Congress, 2011a). In the plan the LC made a commitment to obtaining funding for the development of a Semantic Web compatible bibliographical display standard. In spite of the lack of concrete details, the initial plan lists requirements for the new standard. The new framework should accommodate bibliographical data regardless of cataloging rules so that it can be used internationally in different languages under diverse cataloging codes. More importantly, it should be able to accommodate linked data with URIs. W3C Semantic Web standards are mentioned as a possible approach, specifically RDF, XML, library domain ontologies, and triple stores. The LC pledged its determination to work with vendors, libraries of all types, and the Internet community in seeking a new bibliographical framework. On May 22, 2012 the LC announced its contract with Zepheira, a company headed by Eric Miller, a well-known Semantic Web proponent and library researcher, to accelerate the launch of the Bibliographic Framework Transition Initiative (Library of Congress, 2012b). The project is developing a solution to translate MARC into linked data model.

Program for Cooperative Cataloging (PCC) is another LC organization. In preparation for future implementation of RDA, PCC formed three working groups at the end of June 2011: PCC RDA-Decisions-Needed Task Group, PCC Task Group on AACR & RDA Acceptable Heading Categories, and PCC Task Group on Hybrid Bibliographic Records. In the late summer of 2011, the three task groups came up with separate and combined reports. PCC Task Group on AACR & RDA reviewed (discerned) the LC NAF. The result revealed that "Less than 5% of the 7.6 million name authority records need to undergo a heading change as part of RDA implementation. Of the 397,000 NARs needing a change to the 1XX field in order to be used in RDA, 172,000 can be changed by automated means. Over 95% of the existing authority record 1XX fields can be used in RDA without modification." AACR2 and RDA bibliographical records will co-exist for a long time in a hybrid environment. The PCC Task Group on Hybrid Bibliographic Records investigated the use of hybrid records and made recommendations for the best practices. Working with PCC Task Group on AACR & RDA Acceptable Heading Categories, it recommended non-energy-intensive means of implementing a new set of rules, while gaining a maximum of the benefits from RDA (PCC Task Group on Hybrid Bibliographic Records, 2011). No one knows how long the interim of the hybrid situation will be before a solution can be reached.

OCLC is another national leader in the transition to RDA and one of the 26 formal test partners of the U.S. National Libraries RDA Test. In June 2011, OCLC issued its RDA policy and encouraged member libraries to contribute RDA records. OCLC members are allowed to:

1. contribute original cataloging using RDA;
2. change a record from AACR2 (or earlier rules) to RDA if the record describes continuing resources; and
3. change a record from AACR2 (or earlier rules) to RDA if the record is minimal-level or less than minimal-level.

Once the RDA records exist in WorldCat, no one will be allowed to change them back to AACR2. In addition, OCLC has implemented most of the MARC 21 format changes for initial support of RDA (OCLC, 2010). It has also embedded links to the RDA Toolkit for toolkit subscribers in the Connexion Browser and in Connexion Client.

Many institutions, including LC, are experimenting with and contributing RDA records to OCLC WorldCat. The daily growth rate of RDA records in OCLC database is estimated to be 200 on average. At the time this chapter was written, the total number of RDA records was over 70,000 in WorldCat. "OCLC urges that cataloging staff members take time to become familiar with the content and use of RDA before beginning the creation of RDA records" (OCLC, 2011).

Vendors of most major ILS are preparing for RDA implementation in the near future, including Ex Libris, SirsiDynix, Innovative Inc., and Polaris. They have made or are making changes to MARC in ILS to accommodate RDA by following MARC 21 Updates 9, 10, 11, and 12. The newly added RDA fields can be displayed in most ILS. Some vendors have also indexed newly added RDA fields making them searchable (American Library Association, Canadian Library Association, and CILIP: Chartered Institute of Library and Information Professionals, 2010).

1.6. RDA in Other Countries

RDA is intended as an international cataloging standard. The interest in RDA is strong in the rest of the world. Upon its release in 2010, LC has been the leading force in testing and implementation. At the beginning, many countries were watching and waiting. As time goes by, RDA is gathering momentum along the way. Now more countries are actively engaged in RDA preparation and training. Originally there were four countries in the JSC. In November 2011, German National Library joined the JSC. Following the LC's decision to implement RDA starting March 31, 2013, Canada, the United Kingdom, Australia, and Germany also set up their RDA implementation schedule to be about the same time or no later than the middle of 2013. RDA is being translated into French as a joint effort by France, Canada and volunteers from Belgium, German by Germany and Austria, and Spanish by Spain and Latin American countries. Translation of RDA into Chinese started in May 2012.

Most of the non-English-speaking countries are busy conducting research on applicability of RDA to local cataloging. RDA is considered a drastic or even revolutionary departure from AARC2 tradition by English-speaking countries, but criticized as too AACR or Anglo-American for a true international cataloging code by some non-English-speaking countries. Some countries had gone ahead and developed their own FRBR-based cataloging code. For instance, Italian National Library released their home-grown FRBR-based cataloging code REICA in 2009.

The Semantic Web is not a new concept for European libraries. Prior to the release of RDA in 2010, the European libraries had started experimenting with the Semantic Web because they had anticipated its potential for libraries. Many library Semantic Web projects were in Europe such as Talia, Cacao Project, and JeromeDL, just to mention a few. One of the more visible Semantic Web library applications is LIBRIS, the Swedish union catalog of 170 libraries, which is the first library catalog that has been built with Semantic Web components in its blueprint. The interest in the Semantic Web is much more intense in Europe and the concept of the Semantic Web and digital libraries are not foreign to European librarians. Thus, RDA is a natural extension of such enthusiasm. In the United States, most Semantic Web projects have been initiated by LC and OCLC with little involvement from other libraries.

Cataloging follows various standards in Europe. Some countries use AACR2 and MARC 21, while others created their local standards. Most countries face the daunting task of translating RDA into their national languages. In September 2011, European libraries formed a European RDA Interest Group known as EURIG. The goal of EURIG is to promote cooperation in RDA among European libraries. Many national libraries are EURIG members such as the British Library, National Library of Norway, Bibliothèque nationale de France (BnF), and Swiss National Library, just to name a few. The membership grew fast and now they have 30 members (SLIC/EURIG, 2012). They hold meetings regularly, share research, and discuss RDA-related issues.

Bibliothèque nationale de France (BnF) is working with Library and Archives Canada (LAC) to translate RDA into French. BnF also formed working groups to investigate RDA and possible French implementation. The legitimacy of FRBR and FRAD models are fully recognized in the final recommendations of the working groups, but RDA is not considered too favorably as it is deemed too AARC and therefore lacks flexibility for non-English-speaking cataloging. "Adoption of RDA in the state would not meet the needs of French libraries, or even imply a decline from the current cataloging practice in France" (BnF, 2012). The working groups even hinted in their report that some part of RDA may even slow down the library's progress toward the Semantic Web. Subsequently, BnF decided not to implement RDA, but expressed interest in joining RDA users in the future. There is a possibility that BnF may draft its own cataloging code based on FRBR and FRAD or adopt Italian cataloging code REICAT

(National Library of France, 2011). The BnF's view on RDA is very thought-provoking.

Prior to the release of RDA in 2010, Office for Library Standards of German National Library had undertaken a project to study the possibility to convert German cataloging standard RAK and display format MAB to AACR2 and MARC 21. It seems that the release of RDA came at a good time and is very relevant to the decision that German National Library will make regarding its future cataloging standard and display format. Therefore, the response to RDA was much more positive and welcoming by the German National Library which was quick in translating some key parts and major principles of RDA into German language. It also organized internal RDA testing. In addition to joining the JSC in November 2011, German National Library developed plans paving way for implementing RDA in the middle of 2013. "Those of us who have been buffeted by many years of RDA Wars in the U.S. were impressed by the clear, centralized path the German speakers have taken to RDA adoption, as well as their well-organized program for training" (Tarsala, 2012). Germany and Australia are working together translating RDA into German.

The national libraries of Britain, Canada, and Australia are all original participants in RDA development along with LC. As early as 2007 the representatives of the four countries agreed to coordinate RDA implementation. Therefore "not sooner than early 2013" is also the implementation plan for Australia, Britain, and Canada (Australian Committee on Cataloguing, National Library of Australia, 2011). The decisions and activities of LC in the United States are closely watched and followed by the other three national libraries. When LC announced its plan to implement RDA on March 31, 2013, Britain, Canada, and Australia followed and RDA was implemented in March of 2013.

Although not a tester itself, the National Library of Australia (NLA) monitored the LC testing closely and focused its attention instead on planning RDA implementation. Its preparations include testing the exchange of records between local catalogs and libraries and OCLC, a survey for training needs, compiling a list of trainers, and developing training materials. Its cataloging policy and decision group, Australian Committee on Cataloguing (ACOC), put up a Web site with all the information about RDA and links to the LC to inform its librarians of recent decisions and activities in the United States. Upon the release of RDA in June 2010, the NLA solicited public responses and compiled them for the JSC. A discussion list server was created to facilitate communication, questions, discussion, and feedback. The NLA shared its experience from those activities with other national libraries to avoid duplicate efforts (Australian Committee on Cataloguing, National Library of Australia, 2011).

In the United Kingdom, the Chartered Institute of Library and Information Professionals/British Library Committee on AACR (CILIP/BL) is the primary group working with RDA. The British Library follows the lead of LC in its RDA implementation timeline and focused on two priorities: "Responding to the hybrid environment which RDA has already created" and "Preparing for implementation in 2013" (Metadata Services, British Library, 2011). The detailed plan includes preparation for training, documentation of policy and workflows, modification of their existing library system for RDA, and redistribution of RDA records in 2012. The initial release of RDA was also met with ridicules in Britain. RDA was criticized as more theoretical than practical and "After years of development RDA is still terribly flawed and virtually unusable in its current form" (Batley, 2011). The cost of RDA Toolkit also caused problems of "have" and "have-not." After "The general attitude of 'wait and see' towards RDA in the UK" (Carty & Williams, 2011), the British Library finally made its decision to implement RDA in March of 2013.

The Canadian Committee on Cataloging (CCC) is the primary contact group for RDA in Canada. LAC has a slightly different implementation plan for RDA due to the need for French language cataloging. The more urgent need for LAC is to have a French translation of RDA before it can decide on a date for implementation. Therefore, LAC is working with several partners on the French translation of RDA. In the meantime LAC has incorporated changes in MARC 21 in its system AMICUS. "Decisions on which RDA options and alternatives LAC will follow will be made in conjunction with the other Anglo-American national libraries to minimize differences in practice. Similarly, LAC will work with the national libraries on decisions regarding retrospective changes in legacy headings, with the aim of keeping differences to a minimum" (Library and Archives Canada, 2011). The full implementation of RDA will take place in the first quarter of 2013 in sync with the United Kingdom, Germany, and Australia.

After initial silence, the National Library of New Zealand took action and announced its plan to implement RDA in April of 2013. After April of 2013, it will still use AARC2 for older or non new-zealand materials. The preparation for RDA includes training and working through a list of RDA core elements for evaluation (Stanton, 2012).

The significance of RDA is recognized by Asian librarians. At this stage most Asian countries are collecting information about and conducting research on RDA. For instance, National Library of Vietnam hosted a seminar "Resource Description and Access and its Applicability in Vietnam" in 2011 and invited the JSC to speak on RDA. In Japan, a conference was held in 2012 entitled "RDA, Trends and Challenges in Organizing Bibliographic Data" where Japanese librarians exchanged opinions about FRBR, RDA, and possible revision of their local cataloging rule, a non-AACR-based cataloging rule called Nihon/Japan Cataloging Rules (NCR). The conference attendees identified the challenges from adopting RDA in several areas such as cataloging, authority control, and library systems. Even though the Japanese library researchers have been monitoring the RDA development with great interest, the Japanese leading organizations such as National Diet Library (Japanese National Library), the National Institute of Informatics (Bibliographic Utilities of University in Japan), and Japan Library Association have remained undecided about RDA so far (Katrura, 2012). Fully adopting RDA in Japan is difficult.

China, the biggest country in Asia, has been monitoring the development of RDA with strong interest. Their cataloging involves multiple standards. Foreign language and Chinese materials are cataloged separately under different rules. Implementing RDA and standardizing cataloging practice will be a challenge. However, there has been published research on RDA in Chinese language journals such as the *Journal of the National Library of China and Digital Library Forum* as well as government sponsored projects related to RDA and internationalization of cataloging rules. Most of the research focused on adoption of RDA by Chinese libraries and comparing Chinese cataloging standard to RDA. Two major views exist regarding the implementation of RDA. One argues for adoption of RDA directly to Chinese cataloging, while the other view recommends a modified RDA to suit the local needs. In May 2012, the project of translating RDA into Chinese started. There will be a long wait before Asian countries will adopt RDA (Gu, 2011; Lin, 2012).

1.7. Future Prospects

The road to Semantic Web will not be an easy one. The release of RDA is the first step toward the Semantic Web and it is the start of a paradigm shift in the cataloging world. The amount of work yet to be done is tremendous before libraries can truly join the Semantic Web.

The immediate work ahead includes the timely completion of translation of RDA into various languages, staff training, and preparation for RDA implementation, and continued work on ontologies, controlled vocabularies, and values. Another urgent task is the replacement of MARC 21 with a new display and data linking model based on Semantic Web standards. On May 22 the LC announced its project headed by Eric Miller which will develop means to translate MARC into linked data model (Library of Congress, 2012b). This will give the libraries a starting point for further discussion. Yet LC Bibliographic Framework Transition Initiative still has to find a new display standard to replace MARC.

Bibliographical relationships involve different forms of an author's name and different titles of the same work, different formats and editions of the same work, and more. The Semantic Web is well suited to make use of the above-mentioned relationships in the linked data environment. Even though MARC 21 has newly added fields to accommodate RDA, it only displays those relationships behind closed doors. It cannot utilize the potential of those relationships in presenting and linking data in a meaningful way on the Web. Therefore, one approach to a new bibliographical framework is a display format independent of cataloging rules so that it can truly be an international display standard. Its design should center on FRBR entity relationships and promote linked data model. LC listed three possible RDA implementation scenarios: "flat file" database structure, linked bibliographical and authority records, and relational/object-oriented database structure (Library of Congress, 2011c). To truly merge with the Semantic Web and linked data community, libraries must adopt the last scenario at the least.

Library data has been hidden in catalogs and databases for so long that it is time to promote data exchange and merge with the outside world. Toward this goal, libraries should embrace the existing ontologies and vocabularies developed by other metadata communities. Otherwise libraries will create another silo (the library Semantic Web) and isolate themselves from the Semantic Web. It is important for libraries to follow W3C standards and technologies and share ontologies and vocabularies with people in other subject domains.

This chapter will visualize the future of cataloging in the Semantic Web environment. What is called "authority records" will be a formal ontology with URIs to definitions of established and variant names and relationships. In parallel, a formal ontology for titles exists containing URIs and definitions of established and variant titles and associated relationships. FRBRoo ontology will define FRBR-based relationships. Library of Congress Subject Headings are online already and in RDF, what we know today as SKOS. RDA vocabularies and controlled value lists are complete and registered in a coordinated manner. Catalogers will code bibliographical data into an RDF-based interface that can fully represent entity relationships. The data would be ready for direct use in the Semantic Web. All the bibliographical data will automatically be saved in RDF structures in a stripe store or as flat XML pages. When searching for a title, the Semantic Web search engines will retrieve and display library bibliographical data together with other linked data about the title. The display may include other works by the same author, author biography, edition and publishing history, and different formats of the same work. The linked data may also include presentations about the work, critiques, comments, and the author's family members and friends, schools he attended, etc. Through semantic linking, information retrieval is not limited to library resources only. Everything about the title will show up from all other Web resources.

1.8. Conclusion

In spite of the controversies, RDA is a revolutionary move toward a better future. It started a paradigm shift in cataloging and library and information science. The JSC has done an incredible job breaking the boundary of cataloging traditions and embracing changes against all odds. Without doubt, FRBR principles and the Semantic Web are the right direction libraries should take. Releasing bibliographical data and better information retrieval are our ultimate goals. The Semantic Web and linked data are instrumental in helping libraries reach those goals. IFLA, LC, and non-library metadata communities should make coordinated, not duplicated, efforts in developing ontologies, vocabularies, controlled values, and cataloging code and display standards.

Research-based evidence is needed to guide the library community on the road toward the Semantic Web. Some non-English cataloging communities questioned the acclaimed internationalization of RDA. According to a French study, "Though RDA was developed with the goal of being used in an international context, it *reflects* an Anglo-American conception of information handling and leaves but little place for international reference documents" (National Library of France, 2011). This view has been echoed by others. FRBR is recognized widely to be the basic principle for cataloging by all, "Yet it seems that librarians still do not recognize the full potential of a networked library environment and want to hold on to some tools and practices that have lost their purpose with library automation. In this sense, initiatives that allow continuation of current practices will not help" (Žumer et al., 2011). Is RDA the only and best way to lead libraries to linked data model? Does AACR tradition in RDA hinder its applicability to cataloging practice of those countries that do not have AARC tradition? Is there a truly intuitive cataloging code that provides a shortcut to our goals? This is the time that librarians should think outside the box. Research should be done in this area to clarify existing doubts and focus resources on urgent issues.

The authors are optimistic about the future. It has been two full years since the release of RDA. The complaints are becoming less aggressive. The initial confusion is over. LC has made progress in testing and improving RDA. In parallel development, library communities are continuing to build RDA vocabularies and values in Open Metadata Registry in preparation for RDA implementation. As any new innovation will go through the circle of confusion, doubts, revision, and acceptance, RDA is no exception.

References

American Library Association, Canadian Library Association, and CILIP: Chartered Institute of Library and Information Professionals. (2010). *Vendor interviews*. RDA Toolkit. Last modified 2010. Retrieved from http://www.rdatoolkit.org/blog/category/29. Accessed on January 2, 2012.

Australian Committee on Cataloguing, National Library of Australia. (2011). *Implementation of RDA*. Resource Description and Access (RDA) in Australia. Last modified 2011. Retrieved from http://www.nla.gov.au/lis/stndrds/grps/acoc/rda.html#rdaaust. Accessed on December 19, 2011.

Batley, S. (2011). Is RDA ReDundAnt? *Catalogue & Index*, *164*(Fall), 20–23.

BnF. (2012). *Resource description and access: RDA in France*. BnF: National Library of France. Last modified March 15, 2012. Retrieved from http://www.bnf.fr/fr/professionnels/rda/s.rda_en_france.html?first_Art = non. Accessed on July 28, 2012.

Carty, C., & Williams, H. (2011). (RDA in the UK: Reflections after the CIG E-forum on RDA. *Catalogue & Index*, *163*(June):2–4. Retrieved from http://search.ebscohost.com/login.aspx?direct=true&db=ofm&AN=503016719&site=ehost-live

CIDOC and the CIDOC Documentation Standards Working Group. (2011). *FRBRoo introduction*. The CIDOC Conceptual Reference Model. Last modified December 1, 2011. Retrieved from http://www.cidoc-crm.org/frbr_inro.html. Accessed on December 29, 2011.

Cameron, C. (2010). *Google makes major semantic web play, acquires freebase operators metaweb*. ReadWriteWeb: Featured Sections-Mobile & Start. Last modified July 16, 2010. Retrieved from http://athena.rider.edu:2069/noodlebib/defineEntryCHI.php. Accessed on July 4, 2012.

Coyle, K. (2010). RDA vocabularies for a twenty-first-century data environment. *Library Technology Reports*, *46*(2), 5–11, 26–36.

Coyle, K. (2012). Libraries and linkded data: Looking to the future. *ALATechSource Webinar*. Podcast video. July 19, 2012. Retrieved from https://alapublishing.webex.com/alapublishing/lsr.php?AT=pb&SP=EC&rID=5519872&rKey=747359f5ad28e543. Accessed on July 23, 2012.

Dunsire, G., & Willer, M. (2011). Standard library metadata models and structures for the Semantic Web. *Library Hi Tech News*, *28*(3), 1–12.

Gross, D. (2012). Google search: Google revamps search, tries to think more like a person. *CNN Tech*. Last modified May 16, 2012. http://articles.cnn.com/2012-05-16/tech/tech_web_google-search-knowledge-graph_1_search-results-google-search-search-engine?_s=PM:TECH. Accessed on July 4, 2012.

Gu, B. (2011). Recent cataloging-related activities in Chinese library community. *IFLA ScantNews: Newsletter of the Standing Committee of the IFLA Cataloguing Section*, *36* (December). Retrieved from http://www.ifla.org/files/cataloguing/scatn/scat-news-36.pdf. Accessed on December 20, 2011.

IFLA Study Group on FRBR. (2011). *Final report*. Functional Requirement for Bibliographic Records. Last modified August 11, 2011. Retrieved from http://www.ifla.org/publications/functional-requirements-for-bibliographic-records/. Accessed on July 29, 2012.

IFLA Working Group on Functional Requirements and Numbering of Authority Records. (2012). *Final report*. Functional Requirement for Authority Data. Last modified July 24, 2012. Retrieved from http://www.ifla.org/publications/functional-requirements-for-authority-data. Accessed on July 29, 2012.

Katrura, K. (2012, July 27). Japanese libraries and RDA. E-mail message to the author.

Library and Archives Canada. (2011). *Cataloguing and metadata*. RDA: Resource Description and Access Frequently Asked Questions. Last modified June 21, 2011. Retrieved from http://www.collectionscanada.gc.ca/cataloguing-standards/040006-1107-e.html. Accessed on December 21, 2011.

Library of Congress. (2011a). *Library of Congress bibliographic framework initiative general plan*. News and Announcements. Last modified October 31, 2011. Retrieved from http://www.loc.gov/marc/transition/news/framework-103111.html. Accessed on July 30, 2012.

Library of Congress. (2011b). *"RDA in MARC" MARC Standards*. Last modified September 12, 2011. Retrieved from http://www.loc.gov/marc/RDAinMARC29-9-12-11.html. Accessed on July 20, 2012.

Library of Congress. (2011c). *RDA referesher training at LC (October 2011)*. RDA Supplement Documents, R-7: Some Possible RDA Implementation Scenarios. Last modified December 23, 2011. Retrieved from http://www.loc.gov/aba/rda/Refresher_training_oct_2011.html. Accessed on December 28, 2011.

Library of Congress. (2012a). *LC linked data service authorities and vocabularies*. Library of Congress Linked Data Service. Retrieved from http://id.loc.gov/. Accessed on July 28, 2012.

Library of Congress. (2012b). *The Library of Congress announces modeling initiative (May 22, 2012)*. News and Announcements. Last modified May 22, 2012. Retrieved from http://www.loc.gov/marc/transition/news/modeling-052212.html. Accessed on July 28, 2012.

Library of Congress. (2012c). *U.S. RDA implementation updates from the U.S. RDA Test Coordinating Committee*. Implementation Updates from the U.S. RDA Test Coordinating Committee. Last modifies June 20, 2012. Retrieved from http://www.loc.gov/aba/rda/pdf/RDA_updates_20jun12.pdf. Accessed on July 30, 2012.

Lin, M. (2012). RDA in China from Lin Ming. E-mail message to the author. Accessed on March 20, 2012.

LinkedDataTools.com. (2009). *Toturial 1: Introducing graph data*. Free Tools, Information, Resource for the Semantic Web. Last modified 2009. Retrieved from http://www.linkeddatatools.com/introducing-rdf. Accessed on December 29, 2011.

Marchum, D. B. (2008). *Response to On the record: Report of the Library of Congress Working Group on the future of bibliographic control*. http://www.loc.gov/bibliographic-future/news/LCWGResponse-Marcum-Final-061008.pdf. Accessed on July 28, 2012.

Metadata Services, British Library. (2011). *Cataloging standards*. Standards. Retrieved from http://www.bl.uk/bibliographic/catstandards.html. Accessed on December 20, 2011.

Metalib Inc. (2012). *Linked data tutorial*. Metalib Freebase. Last modified July 10, 2011. Retrieved from http://wiki.freebase.com/wiki/Main_Page. Accessed on March 18, 2012.

National Library of France. (2011). *RDA in Europe: Report of the work in progress in France; proposal for an EURIG technical meeting in Paris*. European RDA Interest Group. Last modified August 2011. Retrieved from http://www.slainte.org.uk/eurig/docs/BnF-ADM-2011-066286-01_%28p2%29.pdf. Accessed on December 23, 2011.
OCLC. (2010). *Technical bulletin 258 OCLC-MARC format update 2010 including RDA changes*. OCLC: The world's libraries connected. Last modified May, 2010. Retrieved from http://www.oclc.org/us/en/support/documentation/worldcat/tb/258/default.htm. Accessed on July 28, 2012.
OCLC. (2011). *OCLC policy statement on RDA Cataloging in WorldCat through March 30, 2013*. OCLC: The world's libraries connected. Last modified June, 2011. Retrieved from http://www.oclc.org/rda/old-policy.en.html. Accessed on January 17, 2013.
OCLC. (2012). *xISBN at a glance*. OCLC: The world's libraries connected. Last modified 2012. Retrieved from http://www.oclc.org/us/en/xisbn/about/default.htm. Accessed on July 28, 2012.
PCC Task Group on Hybrid Bibliographic Records. (2011). *PCC Task Group on Hybrid: Final report*. Program for Cooperative Cataloging. Last modified September 2011. Retrieved from http://www.loc.gov/catdir/pcc/Hybrid-Report-Sept-2011.pdf. Accessed on January 2, 2012.
RDA Toolkit. (2012). *RDA: Resource description & access*. RDA Toolkit. Last modified June 12, 2012. Retrieved from http://access.rdatoolkit.org/. Accessed on July 28, 2012.
SLIC/EURIG. (2012). *EURIG members and their representatives*. European RDA Interest Group. Last modified May 31, 2012. Retrieved from http://www.slainte.org.uk/eurig/members.htm. Accessed on July 28, 2012.
Stanton, C. (2012). *RDA updates from the National Library of New Zealand*. New Zealand Cataloguers' Wiki. Last modified June 18, 2012. Retrieved from http://nznuc-cataloguing.pbworks.com/w/page/25781504/RDA_updates_from_the_National_Library_of_New_Zealand. Accessed on July 28, 2012.
Tarsala, C. (2012). *The RDA Worldshow Plus one*. Retrieved from http://cbtarsala.wordpress.com/2012/07/01/the-rda-wordwide-show-plus-one/. Accessed on May 18, 2013.
The Library of Congress Working Group on the Future of Bibliographic Control (The Working Group). (2008). *On the record: Report of the Library of Congress Working Group on the future of bibliographic control*. Library of Congress — News and Press Releases. Last modified January 9, 2008. Retrieved from http://www.loc.gov/bibliographic-future/news/lcwg-ontherecord-jan08-final.pdf. Accessed on July 29, 2012.
Tillett, B. B. (2011). Keeping libraries relevant in the Semantic Web with Resource Description and Access (RDA). *Serials*, *24*(3), 266–272.
U.S. RDA Test Coordinating Committee. (2011). *Report and recommendations of the U.S. RDA Test Coordinating Committee*. Library of Congress — News and Press Releases. Last modified June 20, 2011. Retrieved from http://www.loc.gov/bibliographic-future/rda/source/rdatesting-finalreport-20june2011.pdf. Accessed on July 28, 2012.

W3C. (2012). *What is inference?* W3C Semantic Web. Last modified 2012. Retrieved from http://www.w3.org/standards/semanticweb/inference. Accessed on January 2, 2012.

Yang, S. Q., & Quinn, M. (2011). Why RDA? Its controversies and significance and is your library prepared for it? Managing the Future of Librarianship — Library Management Institute Summer Conference, Arcadia University, Glenside, PA, July 12, 2011.

Žumer, M., Pisanski, J., Vilar, P., Harej, V., Merèun, T., & Švab, K. (2011). "Breaking Barriers between Old Practices and New Demands: The Price of Hesitation." Paper presented at World Library and Information Congress: The 77th IFLA-general conference and assembly. Retrieved from http://conference.ifla.org/past/ifla77/80-zumer-en.pdf. Accessed on December 26, 2011.

Chapter 2

Keeping Libraries Relevant in the Semantic Web with RDA: Resource Description and Access[☆]

Barbara B. Tillett

Abstract

Purpose — To raise consciousness among librarians and library directors about the need to structure our descriptive data for library resources in a way that is machine-actionable in the Semantic Web, not just the library silos of MARC-based systems.

Design/methodology/approach — Narrative overview.

Social implications — By assuring library metadata is in a well-formed structure, libraries can place access to their collections on the Web where their users are.

Findings — The new cataloging code, Resource Description and Access (RDA), is one step in the direction toward more interoperability in the Semantic Web.

Originality/value — New perspective on this issue is to urge librarians to work with systems people and vendors for next generation systems that build on the relationships and identifying characteristics of well-formed metadata arising from use of the RDA.

[☆] First appeared in *Serials*, November 2011 issue, Volume 24, No. 3, doi: 10.1629/24266.

New Directions in Information Organization
Library and Information Science, Volume 7, 29–41

ISSN: 1876-0562/doi:10.1108/S1876-0562(2013)0000007006

2.1. Introduction

If we are to keep libraries alive, we must make them relevant to user needs. More and more services are on the Web, and many people expect it to have everything they would need in terms of information resources.

Libraries have made great strides to have a Web presence, but many also offer only an electronic version of their old card catalogs. The catalog approach of linear displays of citations to holdings may include a link to a digitized version of the described resource, but typically excludes machine-actionable connections to other related resources or beyond. The approach of building a citation-based catalog needs to expand to describing resources by their identifying characteristics in a way that computer systems can understand and by showing relationships to persons, families, corporate bodies, and other resources. This will enable users to navigate through linked surrogates of the resources to get information they need more quickly. It also will lead to better systems to make the job of cataloging easier.

Since mid-2010, Resource Description and Access (RDA) has offered us an alternative to past cataloging practices. This new code for identifying resources has emerged from many years of international collaborations, and it produces well-formed, interconnected metadata for the digital environment, offering a way to keep libraries relevant in the Semantic Web.

2.2. How Did We Get to this Point?

Resource Description and Access is built on the traditions of the Anglo-American Cataloging Rules (AACR). The Joint Steering Committee for Development of RDA (JSC), formerly the Joint Steering Committee for Revision of AACR, recognized during the 1990s that AACR2 (the second edition of AACR) had served us well during the 20th century, but there was growing concern that AACR2 was not a code that would help us in the 21st century. It was structured around the statements from card catalog days and linear displays of citations, before the Internet and before well-formed metadata that could be used by computer systems.

During the 1990s, the JSC received many complaints about AACR2 becoming increasingly complex, as updates continued to be added, particularly to address the new digital resources. People expressed concerns about AACR2 lacking a logical structure and instead focusing on individual rules for each type of material rather than seeing the commonalities and basic principles for a simplified, consistent approach. AACR2 was arranged by class of materials, which caused problems when cataloging e-resources with multiple characteristics. Other complaints were that AACR2 did not adequately address bibliographic relationships, whereas the Web is all about relationships, networks of interconnected information. AACR2's strong Anglo-American bias was cited as a problem even though it is being used around the world. It was also widely recognized that bibliographic data was segregated from the rest of the information community's data in a world of its own with MARC (MAchine-Readable Cataloging[1]) formatted records. Although MARC is widely used among libraries worldwide, it is not used by the larger information community.

There were complaints about AACR2's terminology for describing materials ("general material designations" or GMDs), which was a mix of types of content and carrier data. GMDs were irregularly applied if at all, with different practices by catalogers in North America from catalogers elsewhere.

In response to these complaints about AACR2, the JSC called an international conference on the "Principles and Future Development of AACR" for cataloging rule makers and experts from around the world to meet in Toronto in 1997. As a result of the Toronto meeting, specific problems were identified, and a strategic plan was put in place for future directions. Work began to develop AACR3, keeping the same structure as AACR2 and incorporating the recommended changes.

By April 2005, after an initial draft of AACR3 went out for worldwide comments, the JSC received a very negative response to the first draft. It was clear that people felt the JSC had not gone far enough to embrace the new conceptual models and vocabulary emerging from the international efforts within IFLA (International Federation of Library Associations). In particular, there were calls for more attention to the conceptual models FRBR and FRAD (Functional Requirements for Bibliographical Records and Functional Requirements for Authority Data)[2] from IFLA.

Those conceptual models brought a new perspective on describing resources to focus on the content and carriers and viewing the persons, families, and corporate bodies associated with those resources in terms of their identifying characteristics. The FRBR entities and relationships and

---

1. *The MARC formats are standards for the representation and communication of bibliographic and related information in machine-readable form.* MARC Standards at: http://www.loc.gov/marc/

2. *Functional requirements for bibliographic records.* Final report. IFLA Study Group on the Functional Requirements for Bibliographic Records. Approved by the Standing Committee of the IFLA Section on Cataloguing, September 1997, as amended and corrected through February 2009, p. 79. PDF available at: http://www.ifla.org/files/cataloguing/frbr/frbr_2008.pdf; *Functional requirements for authority data, a conceptual model.* Final report, December 2008. IFLA Working Group on Functional Requirements and Numbering of Authority Records (FRANAR), 2009, Saur, Munich.

the vocabulary used to describe them were important to the international community of responders. Probably one of the most important aspects coming from the conceptual models was a focus on using the identifying characteristics in describing resources to meet basic user tasks: find, identify, select, and obtain.[3] The user comes first. This is why we do cataloging.

There was also a call to move to an element-based approach to metadata, rather than building citations, to be more compatible with metadata services for Web use in the broader information community. This fitted nicely with the entity-relationship approach of IFLA's conceptual models.

This also was the time when IFLA's work toward *International Cataloguing Principles*[4] was well underway. Even within IFLA it was recognized that the basic "Paris principles" from 1961 were in need of review in light of the digital environment. Five regional conferences were held between 2003 and 2007 with rule makers and cataloging experts worldwide to develop the new *International Cataloguing Principles* of 2008. Those principles are part of the foundation for RDA.

RDA emerged in response to those worldwide comments from and beyond the Anglo-American community of libraries and other information agencies: publishers, book dealers, archives, museums, developers of Web services, and more. It is built on the idea of reusing identifying information coming from publishers and vendors, building on descriptions, and making relationships not just by libraries but all stakeholders in the information chain.

2.3. Collaborations

Following the Toronto conference, the concern about AACR2 dealing inadequately with seriality was addressed in a meeting of representatives. The result was the harmonization of ISBD, ISSN, and AACR2 standards, and those discussions will be resumed this year in light of RDA.

The JSC also initiated many collaborations with various special communities, such as with the publishing community, to work together to

3. International Federation of Library Associations and Institutions. *Functional requirements for bibliographic records*. Final report. IFLA Study Group on the Functional Requirements for Bibliographic Records. Approved by the Standing Committee of the IFLA Section on Cataloguing, September 1997, as amended and corrected through February 2009 as amended through February 2009, p. 79. PDF available at: http://www.ifla.org/files/cataloguing/frbr/frbr_2008.pdf

4. *IFLA Cataloguing Principles*. The statement of International Cataloguing Principles (ICP) and its glossary in 20 languages, edited by Barbara B. Tillett and Ana Lupe Cristán, 2009, Saur, Munich, p. 28.

develop a new vocabulary for types of content, media, and carriers. The result was the RDA/ONIX Framework and a plan for ongoing review and revision of that controlled vocabulary to share consistent data.

In 2003, representatives from the JSC met in London with representatives from the Dublin Core, IEEE/LOM, and Semantic Web communities, resulting in the DCMI/RDA Task Group to develop the RDA Registries and a library application profile for RDA. The controlled vocabularies and element set from RDA are now available as a registry on the Web as a first step to making library data accessible in the Semantic Web environment.

The JSC also met with various library and archive communities to initiate discussions about more principle-based approaches to describing their collections. An example of changes resulting from those discussions was the approach to identifying the Bible and books of the Bible, so they could be better understood by users and more accurately reflect the contained works. The JSC is resuming those discussions with the law, cartographic, religion, music, rare book, and publishing communities to propose further improvements to RDA.

2.4. Technical Developments

FRBR-based systems have existed for over a decade, and have been tested and used worldwide to enable collocation and navigation of bibliographic data. Some examples are systems developed by the National Library of Australia, the VTLS Virtua system (see their FRBR collocation of all the Atlantic monthly issues through all the title changes), the linked data services of the National Library of Sweden, and the music catalog of Indiana University's Variations 3 project. The Dublin Core Abstract Model is built on the FRBR foundation, and current work within the World Wide Web Consortium is looking at the potential for using libraries' linked data, such as the Library Linked Data Incubator Group. RDA positions us to enter that realm. Recent research articles like those from Kent State University[5] and the University of Ljubljana reaffirm the use of FRBR as a conceptual basis for cataloging in the future.[6]

5. Žumer, Maja, Marcia Lei Zeng, Athena Salaba. (2010). FRBR: A generalized approach to Dublin Core application profiles. *Proceedings of the international conference on Dublin Core and metadata applications.*

6. Pisanski, J., & Žumer, M. (2010). Mental models of the bibliographic universe. Part 1: Mental models of descriptions. *Journal of Documentation*, *66*(5), 643–667 and Pisanski, J., & Žumer, M. (2010). Mental models of the bibliographic universe. Part 2: Comparison task and conclusions. *Journal of Documentation*, *66*(5), 668–680.

It is important that libraries join the rest of the information community on the Web—share our expertise, our controlled vocabularies (multilingual), and organizational skills. The element-based approach of RDA facilitates identifying persons, families, corporate bodies, as well as works in a manner that machines can more easily use, better than we could with previous cataloging codes. We have already started posting our controlled vocabularies for RDA as "registries" on the Web along with other controlled vocabularies from our traditional authority files.

For example, we now have freely available authority data from hundreds of national libraries and other institutions through the Virtual International Authority File (VIAF, at http://viaf.org). VIAF now includes names and identifying data for the following types of entities: persons, corporate bodies/conferences, and uniform titles (for works and expressions in FRBR terminology). VIAF demonstrates how library metadata can be reused and packaged in ways beyond traditional catalogs. It provides a multi-lingual, multiscript base that has the potential to serve as a switching mechanism to display the language and script a user prefers, assigning a distinctive Uniform Resource Identifier (URI) to each entity. Although VIAF can manipulate authority data from various schema or communication formats like MARC, having the data clearly identified, as RDA does, will make it easier for services like VIAF and future linked data systems to use the specific identifying characteristics to describe persons, corporate bodies, works, etc. It will make it easier for machines to use that data to link related information and to display information users want.

The RDA registries include terms for description and access elements, such as title proper, date of publication, and extent, as well as values for specific elements, such as the terms to use when describing types of carriers, including computer disc, volume, microfiche, video disc, etc. Those terms are posted on the Open Metadata Registry,[7] giving URIs for all of the terms, which then can be used in the Semantic Web to enable greater use by Web services. This positions the library community to move access to our resources out of the silos of data used only by other libraries onward to the broader information community on the Web.

2.5. So What Is Different?

AACR2 said it was based on principles, basically IFLA's Paris Principles of 1961, but never really told a cataloger what those principles were. RDA not only is based on IFLA's *International Cataloguing Principles*, but also

7. Open Metadata Registry. RDA vocabularies at: http://metadataregistry.org/rdabrowse.htm

describes the principles for each section of elements. For example, RDA follows the ICP principle of representation, instructing to take what you see for transcribed data (e.g., title proper, statement of responsibility, publication statement). This translates into time savings and building on existing metadata that may come from the creators of resources or publishers or vendors.

There is the principle of common usage, which means no more Latin abbreviations, such as s.l. and s.n. Even some catalogers didn't know what they meant. There are also no more English abbreviations, such as col. and ill., which users do not understand.

RDA relies on cataloger's judgment to make some decisions about how much description or access is warranted. For example, the "rule of 3" to only provide up to three authors, composers, etc. is now an option, not the main instruction, so RDA encourages access to the names of persons and corporate bodies and families important to the users. RDA ties every descriptive and access element to the relevant FRBR user tasks: find, identify, select, and obtain in order to develop cataloger's judgment to know not only *what* identifying characteristic to provide, but *why* they are providing it — to meet a user need.

RDA requires that we name the contained work and expression as well as the creator of the work when that is appropriate. The concept of "main entry" disappears. However, while we remain in a MARC format environment, we will still use the MARC tags for the main entry to store the name of the first-named creator.

RDA provides instructions for authority data, which were not covered in AACR2. RDA states the "core" identifying characteristics that must be given to identify entities, including persons, families, corporate bodies, works, expressions, etc., such as their name. In addition other characteristics may be provided when readily available. For example, the headquarters location for corporate bodies may be included, or the content type for expressions, such as text, performed music, still image, and cartographic image.

These identifying characteristics, or elements in RDA, are separate from the authorized access points that may need to be created while we remain in the MARC-based environment. While RDA describes how to establish authorized access points, it does not require authorized access points. Instead, RDA looks toward a future where the identifying characteristics needed to find and identify an entity can be selected as needed for the context of a search query or display of results.

Also, very important for the Web, RDA provides relationships. The Web is all about relationships. RDA provides relationship designators to explicitly state the role a person, family, or corporate body plays with respect to the resource being described. It enables description of how various works are related, such as derivative works to link motion pictures or books based on other works, musical works, and their librettos, to link textual works and their adaptations, etc. It connects the pieces of serial works in successive relationships through title changes. The inherent relationships connect the contained intellectual and artistic content to the various physical manifestations, such as paper print, digital, and microform versions.

2.5.1. RDA Toolkit

The RDA instructions are packaged in a Web-based form as the "RDA Toolkit." It is also available in print, but was designed as a Web tool with hyperlinks among the various sections with advanced search capabilities to show related instructions. The RDA Toolkit also has mappings to and from the MARC format. There are tools for developers to embed links to RDA instructions from their products. There are tools for catalogers to include their own procedures with links to the RDA instructions and MARC formats. There are policy statements from the Library of Congress (LC) freely accessible through the RDA Toolkit, and other policy statements can be added for national or regional or local use. The RDA Toolkit site is at http://www.rdatoolkit.org/.

2.5.2. The U.S. RDA Test

Although the LC had publicly committed to implementation of RDA in 2007 in a joint statement with the British Library, the Library and Archives Canada, and the National Library of Australia,[8] that commitment had to be postponed. In response to the 2008 report to the LC from the Working Group on the Future of Bibliographic Control[9] recommending all work on RDA be stopped, the LC together with the National Library of Medicine and the National Agricultural Library instead launched a U.S. test of RDA to explore whether or not to implement the new code. This included gathering information about the technical, operational, and financial implications of implementation.

---

8. *Joint statement of Anglo–heritage national libraries on coordinated RDA implementation*, October 22, 2007. Available at: http://www.rda-jsc.org/rdaimpl.html

9. *On the record*. Report of the Library of Congress Working Group on the Future of Bibliographic Control, January 2008. PDF available at: http://www.loc.gov/bibliographic-future/news/lcwg-ontherecord-jan08-final.pdf

In preparation for the test, the LC provided "train-the-trainer" modules[10] and examples, which are freely available as Webcasts, PowerPoint presentations, and Word documents in the public domain.[11] The Policy and Standards Division also set up an e-mail address that remains available at LChelp4rda@loc.gov for anyone in the world to use to ask questions about the RDA instructions and LC policies for RDA. Initial policy decisions for the test were established and posted on the Web site as well as in the RDA Toolkit. Those LC policy decisions are now being adjusted, informed by the test results and feedback from participants in conjunction with discussions with the Program for Cooperative Cataloging and preliminary suggestions from the Library and Archives Canada, the British Library, the Deutsche Nationalbibliothek, and the National Library of Australia regarding their implementation decisions.

The 26 U.S. RDA Test participants included a wide range of sizes and types of libraries, as well as archives, museums, book dealers, library schools, system vendors, consortia, and funnel projects in the Program for Cooperative Cataloging. They created 10,570 bibliographic records and 12,800 authority records and documented their findings in more than 8000 surveys. The analysis of that data provided helpful feedback for needed improvements to the RDA Toolkit, to the language used to convey the instructions, as well as suggestions for moving beyond the current MARC format.

The report from that test recommended implementation no sooner than January 2013 provided certain conditions were met.[12] Those conditions

---

10. RDA Test "Train the Trainer" (training modules). Presented by Judy Kuhagen and Barbara Tillett, January 15, 2010, Northeastern University, Boston, MA, Modules 1–9 available at: http://www.loc.gov/bibliographic-future/rda/trainthetrainer.html. PowerPoint files of the modules (with speaker's notes) and accompanying material are freely available at: http://www.loc.gov/catdir/cpso/RDAtest/rdatraining.html

- Module 1: What RDA Is and Isn't
- Module 2: Structure
- Module 3: Description of Manifestations and Items
- Module 4: Identifying Works, Expressions, and Manifestations
- Module 5: Identifying Persons
- Module 6: Identifying Families *(filmed at the Library of Congress, March 1, 2010)*
- Module 7: Identifying Corporate Bodies
- Module 8: Relationships
- Module 9: Review of Main Concepts, Changes, Etc.

11. U.S. RDA Test Web site is known as "Testing Resource Description and Access (RDA)": http://www.loc.gov/bibliographic-future/rda/

12. *Report and recommendations of the U.S. RDA Test Coordinating Committee*, May 9, 2011, revised for public release June 20, 2011. PDF available at: http://www.loc.gov/bibliographic-future/rda/rdatesting-finalreport-20june2011.pdf

were stated as recommendations to the JSC, to the ALA Publishers who created the RDA Toolkit, to system vendors, to the Program for Cooperative Cataloging, and to the senior managers at the LC, the National Library of Medicine, and the National Agricultural Library. The conditions were met and implementation was effective March 31, 2013.

2.5.3. RDA Benefits

Participants in the U.S. test reported benefits to using RDA as follows.

Benefits

RDA testers in comments noted several benefits of moving to RDA paraphrased as follows:

- RDA brings a major change in how we look at the world as identifying characteristics of things and relationships with a focus on user tasks.
- It provides a new perspective on how we use and reuse bibliographic metadata.
  - It brings a transition from the card catalog days of building a paragraph style description for a linear card catalog to now focus more on identifying characteristics of the resources we offer our users, so that metadata can be packaged and reused for multiple purposes even beyond libraries.
  - It enables libraries to take advantage of pre-existing metadata from publishers and others rather than having to repeat that work.
- The existence of RDA encourages the development of new schema for this more granular element set, and the development of new and better systems for resource discovery.
- The users noticed RDA is more user-centric, building on the FRBR and FRAD user tasks (from IFLA).
- Some of the specific things they liked were:
  - using language of users rather than Latin abbreviations,
  - seeing more relationships,
  - having more information about responsible parties with the rule of 3 now just an option,
  - finding more identifying data in authority records, and
  - having the potential for increased international sharing — by following the IFLA International Cataloguing Principles and the IFLA models FRBR and FRAD.[13]

13. *Report and recommendations of the U.S. RDA Test Coordinating Committee,* public release June 20, 2011, p. 111. Available at: http://www.loc.gov/bibliographic-future/rda/rdatesting-finalreport-20june2011.pdf

2.5.4. RDA, MARC, and Beyond

The test had not specifically focused on the MARC format, but responses from the participants made it clear that the MARC format was seen as a barrier to achieving the potential benefits of RDA as an international code to move libraries into the wider information environment. As a result one of the recommendations was to show credible progress toward a replacement for MARC. Work is well underway toward that end through the new LC initiative, "Transforming the Bibliographic Framework."[14]

2.5.5. Implementation of RDA

About eight institutions that participated in the test decided to continue to use RDA, regardless of the test recommendations. Their bibliographic and authority records are being added to bibliographic utilities, such as SkyRiver and OCLC, and are available now for copy cataloging.

The LC had about 50 catalogers engaged in the U.S. test. Those catalogers resumed using RDA in November 2011 in order to assist with training and writing proposals to improve the code, as well as to inform related policy decisions.

Many Europeans also expressed interest in learning more about RDA. Several countries joined EURIG, the European RDA Interest Group, which held conferences before the IFLA meetings in 2010 (Copenhagen, Denmark) and 2011 (San Juan, Puerto Rico) to share news. These interested parties are also expected to submit proposals to improve RDA from their perspective, and the JSC has already received one such proposal for review in 2011.

Translations of RDA are also underway, so more people will be able to read RDA for themselves in their own language and determine whether they wish to implement the new code or not. Translations are expected for Spanish, French, and German among several other suggested languages. People interested in translating RDA into their own language should contact Troy Linker at ALA Publishing (tlinker@ala.org).

In recognition of the international intentions for RDA, the governance for the JSC will be expanded to include 1–3 new members from countries that intend to implement RDA. Those interested in participating should contact a member of the Committee of Principals, the group that oversees the JSC activities. The Committee of Principals includes representatives from the American Library Association, Canadian Library Association,

---

14. *Bibliographic framework transition initiative*. Available at: http://www.loc.gov/marc/transition/

CILIP (Chartered Institute of Library and Information Professionals), LC, Library and Archives Canada, British Library, and National Library of Australia.

2.6. Conclusion

Libraries are in danger of being marginalized by other information delivery services, unable to have a presence with other services in the information community on the Web. Our bibliographic control is based on the MARC format, which is not adequate for the Semantic Web environment. For example, MARC is not granular enough to distinguish among different types of dates, and it puts many types of identifying data into a general note which cannot easily be parsed for machine manipulation.

Our online catalogs are no more than electronic versions of card catalogs with similar linear displays of textual information. Yet, the metadata we provide could be repackaged into much more interesting visual information, such as timelines for publication histories and maps of the world to show places of publication (see the VIAF visual displays). We could also build links between works and expressions, like translations, novels that form the basis for screenplays, etc., to navigate these relationships rather than rely on textual notes that are not machine-actionable. Libraries need to make our data more accessible on the Web.

In order to help reduce the costs of cataloging, we need to reuse cataloging done by others and take advantage of metadata from publishers and other sources. Change is needed in our cataloging culture to exercise cataloger judgment and, equally important, to accept the judgment of other catalogers.

Libraries must share metadata more than we have in the past to reduce the costly, redundant creation and maintenance of bibliographic and authority data. RDA positions us for a linked data scenario of sharing descriptive and authority data through the Web to reuse for context sensitive displays that meet a user's needs for language/scripts they can read.

By providing well-formed metadata that can be packaged into various schema for use in the Web environment, RDA offers a data element set for all types of materials. It is based on internationally agreed principles. It incorporates the entities and relationships from IFLA's conceptual models. It focuses on the commonalities across all types of resources while providing special instructions when there are different needs for types of resources such as music, cartographic materials, legal materials, religious materials, rare materials, and archives, or refers to specialized manuals for more granular description of such materials.

Vendors and libraries around the world are being encouraged to develop better systems that build on RDA. Once RDA is adopted, systems can be redesigned for today's technical environment, moving us into linked data information discovery and navigation systems in the Internet environment and away from Online Public Access Catalogs (OPACs) with only linear displays of textual data.

We are in a transition period where libraries want and need to move bibliographic data to the Web for use and reuse. RDA isn't the complete solution to making that move, but its role as a new kind of content standard may be the component to smooth the path in that move. Two other components are needed to complete the move:

1. an encoding schema that maintains the integrity of RDA's well-labeled metadata — the aforementioned transition from MARC, and
2. systems that can accommodate RDA to harness its full potential to express relationships among resources.

We also need understanding by library administrators that the full benefits of investment in these components now will not be realized immediately, but the investment is critical to the future health and role of libraries.

RDA makes our bibliographic descriptions and access data more internationally acceptable. There is still more work to be done, but the direction is set.

Chapter 3

Filling in the Blanks in RDA or Remaining Blank? The Strange Case of FRSAD

Alan Poulter

Abstract

Purpose — This chapter covers the significant developments in subject access embodied in the Functional Requirements (FR) family of models, particularly the Functional Requirements for Subject Authority Data (FRSAD) model.

Design/methodology/approach — A structured literature review was used to track the genesis of FRSAD. It builds on work by Pino Buizza and Mauro Guerrini who outlined a potential subject access model for FRBR. Tom Delsey, the author of Resource Description and Access (RDA), also examined the problem of adding subject access.

Findings — FRSAD seemed to generate little comment when it appeared in 2009, despite its subject model which departed from that in previous FR standards. FRSAD proposed a subject model based on "thema" and "nomen," whereby the former, defined as "any entity used as the subject of a work," was represented by the latter, defined as "any sign or sequence of signs." It is suggested in this chapter that the linguistic classification theory underlying the PRECIS Indexing System might provide an alternative model for developing generic subject entities in FRSAD.

Originality/value — The FR family of models underpin RDA, the new cataloguing code intended to replace AACR2.Thus issues with

New Directions in Information Organization
Library and Information Science, Volume 7, 43–59

ISSN: 1876-0562/doi:10.1108/S1876-0562(2013)0000007007

FRSAD, which are still unresolved, continue to affect the new generation of cataloguing rules and their supporting models.

3.1. Introduction

Resource Description and Access (RDA) was released in July 2010, and made available for use, in an online form, the RDA Toolkit (http://beta.rdatoolkit.gvpi.net/) or in printed form, in a large loose-leaf binder. In July 2011, the Library of Congress, the National Library of Medicine, and the National Agricultural Library announced the decision to adopt RDA after conducting trials (US RDA Test Coordinating Committee, 2011). The decision to adopt RDA though carried riders on certain perceived issues to be resolved, related to rules readability, online delivery issues of the RDA Toolkit and a business case outlining costs and benefits of adoption. It appears though that, allowing for these issues to be dealt with, RDA will begin adoption in 2013 and will gradually replace the aged *Anglo-American Cataloguing Rules*, Second Edition (AACR2).

Unlike AACR2, RDA was intended to also provide subject access. As RDA currently stands, Chapters 12–16, 23, 33–37 are intended to establish guidelines for providing subject access, but only Chapter 16, "Identifying Places" is complete.

This chapter will outline possible strategies for moving forward in completing the remaining blank chapters, based on the model given in the recent Functional Requirements for Subject Authority Data (IFLA Working Group, 2010), hereafter referred to as FRSAD.

3.2. Chapter Overview

This chapter begins by outlining significant developments prior to the appearance of FRSAD, which was formerly known as FRSAR. This involves coverage of the two preceding reports, the Functional Requirements of Bibliographic Records (FRBR) (IFLA, 2008) and the Functional Requirements for Authority Data (FRAD) (IFLA, 2009), which was formerly known as FRANAR.

The final version of FRSAD, released in 2009, will be contrasted to earlier efforts to extend the FRBR/FRAD models to fully cover subject access.

Finally, a prospective proposal to take FRSAD forward to implementation using Preserved Context Indexing System (PRECIS) will be examined, as well as the general reception of FRSAD.

3.3. Before FRSAD

The roots of FRSAD go back to a critical juncture in the revision of AACR2. In April 2004 two bodies managing the development of a revision of AACR2, the funder, the Committee of Principals (CoP) and the developers, the Joint Steering Committee (JSC) decided that the level of change was no longer at the amendment level and was instead a comprehensive revision of AACR2. In April 2005 it was decided that AACR2's structure should be abandoned and that a new alignment with two abstract models of publication based on ER (entity-relationship) models, FRBR (IFLA Study Group on the Functional Requirements for Bibliographic Records 2009), and FRAD (IFLA Working Group on Functional Requirements and numbering of Authority Records 2009; Patton, 1985) was to be used as the basis for the new rules to replace AACR2: their name was changed to RDA to indicate this fundamental shift.

An "entity" is a thing which is capable of an independent existence and which can be uniquely identified. Every entity must have a minimal set of uniquely identifying attributes, which is called the entity's primary key. A "relationship" expresses how entities are related to one another. Entities and relationships can both have "attributes," named features. The intention in using ER modeling was to make explicit what was being described and how the elements of the model related.

The entities in FRBR were split into three groups. Group 1 was for "intellectual products" and there were four entities for these: "works," "expressions," "manifestations," and "items" (WEMI). The "work" entity was a distinct intellectual creation, for example, Daniel Defoe has the idea of a story about a man stranded on an island. The "expression" entity is the realization of a work in some form (a language, music, etc.). Defoe thinks of the story in English but it can be realized in other languages and media. The "manifestation" entity is the embodiment of an expression of a work, for example, the first edition in English, a later English version in the Penguin Classics, etc. The "item" entity represented a single physical copy of a manifestation, for example an owned copy of the Penguin Classic. Using ER relationships, a work can have many expressions, each expression can have many manifestations, and each item can only come from one manifestation. Generally, most works will have one expression and one manifestation of that expression. Manifestations of the same expression may have identical content but will vary in some other detail, for example, publication date. Manifestations of different expressions equate roughly to editions.

Group 2 entities were those responsible for intellectual/artistic content, that is "persons," "corporate bodies," and "families," while Group 3 entities were proposed to represent subjects: "concepts," "objects," "places," and "events" as well as all entities in Groups 1 and 2. Thus, a place can be the subject of a travel guide, a person can be the subject of a biography, and a poem can be the subject of a critical text. However, the Group 3 entities were only intended as place holders to indicate a future desire to represent subjects.

FRBR was explicitly designed to support user tasks. It does this by defining a set of user tasks:

Find: find entities that match a need
Identify: confirm that entities match a need and be able to distinguish them
Select: find the entity most appropriate
Obtain: get access to the required entity

and then explicitly highlighting particular attributes of WEMI entities as being required for one or more of the above tasks. Again, as far as subject access was concerned, these tasks were insufficient.

3.4. Precursors to FRSAD

Prior to the appearance of FRSAD there were two significant attempts to extend the FRBR/FRAD models to subject access. Pino Buizza and Mauro Guerrini had been involved in creating and testing an Italian version of PRECIS for Italian libraries and in their paper (Buizza & Guerrini, 2002) they outlined a potential subject access model for FRBR. Tom Delsey, the author of RDA, also examined the problem of adding subject access.

Buizza and Guerrini note that, uniquely, FRBR tried to bring cataloguing and subject access together, rather than consider them as distinct, as in the past. There was also an international aspect, which tried to make subject access a feature not restricted by language:

> While certain aspects of semantic indexing have necessarily national characteristics .... It is indispensable for the theoretic development to take place within international debate, and that the new working instrument be conceived as part the logic of international cataloguing co-operation and integration. (Buizza & Guerrini, 2002, p. 33)

Buizza and Guerrini note that subject is not an entity present in an item nor does it exist in its own right, it is a mediator between the topic of a work and the universe of inquiries which seek answer. Rather, subject persists independently and allows us to recognize common themes and distinguish competing claims of relevance.

They point out that because of the relationship between work and expression, manifestation and item, there was no need to investigate entities other than work as they would inherit their subject from the source work. In FRBR they recognize that the expression of Group 3 subjects is not meant to be exhaustive. For example, there is no category for living organism. The entities in the subject group, even when supplemented by the Groups 1 and 2 entities, correspond to a very simple categorization, which is there as a placeholder, and which is intended to be built upon and expanded. While FRBR does not perform an analysis of publication models but rather defines a practical generic structure, it makes no claim to be a semantic model. Unlike the other entities, subjects are presented as individual instances of atomic units, with no attributes.

They attempt to extend the ER model to indexing by proposing two new entities: "subject," the basic theme of a work, and "concept", each of the single elements which make up the subject. The entity types making up subject are suggested as "object," "abstraction," "living organism," "material," "property," "action," "process," "event," "place," and "time." "Person," "corporate body," and "work" are also included from FRBR. This is a much more extensive model and appears to cover the full range of potential classes of entities.

Having two distinct entities ('subject' and 'concept') allowed statements of the subjects of works, as well as allowed for recurring elements of subjects and the generic set of relationships (broader/narrow, related, use for, etc.) between them. The main attribute of "subject" is defined as "verbal description," the statement of the subject. Further attributes would include "identifier" and "language." Both these attributes would be required for managing multilingual systems. For "concept" the main attributes are given as "term for the concept" and "qualifier," for example, for a limited date range. An example "subject" might be "training dogs" in which there are two "concepts," "dogs" as an entity type of "living organism," and "training" as an "action" type entity.

They proposed three types of relationship to exist. There is the primary relationship of the "subject" to its constituent "concept" elements. The second relationship was between the potentially different constituent "concepts" in "subjects" which are identical. Finally, there would be relationships between the concepts themselves. These would be hierarchical, associative, and synonymous/antonymous. They also proposed to expand the set of user tasks given in FRBR to add some appropriate tasks for subject access, for example, "search for a known topic."

Finally, they emphasized the importance of maintaining the distinction between the "subject" and "concept" entities, as they had defined them, although they note a potential issue with the former. Their analysis did not give any attention to citation order within "subjects," which would be essential for the coherence and readability of the strings of "concepts" used in subjects. They conclude that their proposal:

> demonstrates a greater affinity with systems based on logical analysis and synthesis techniques, rather than those systems based on lists of pre-constituted headings. (Buizza & Guerrini, 2002, p. 44)

The second attempt at expounding a subject extension for FRBR/FRAD came from Tom Delsey, who, as the chief author of RDA, recognized it as the next hurdle. In Delsey (2005), he stated that neither FRBR nor FRAD were complete in their conceptual analysis of data relevant to subject access as performed by bibliographic and authority records. Refining and extending their models to reflect subject access fully would require a significant re-examination of the entities in those models and their attributes and relationships. The new entities when defined would have to completely cover the range of topics that would be required for subjects as understood by library users. Also needed would be all the attributes for the construction and use of subject access points and subject authority records. Finally, there would be the need for a model to provide a clear and robust representation of the range of subject access tools — thesauri, subject headings, classification schemes, and the syntactic structures — used in indexing strings, as these would all be needed. Major expansions of the FRBR and FRAD models would be required:

> In examining the entities in the existing models, we need to check whether they cover the whole "subject universe" and whether they can forge the range of tools used to implement the subject universe. (Delsey, 2005, p. 52)

For each Group 1 entity in FRBR, an identifier (one or more attributes) and other appropriate attributes are defined. In FRBR, the entities "work," "expression," "manifestation," and "item" get attributes "title" and "identifier" as well as additional attributes that may be needed for clarification in entries, for example, "form," "date," and "language." Again, for the FRBR entities "person" and "corporate body," the identifying attribute is "name," which can be supplemented by, for example, "date," "number," and "place." This is not the case for each of the "concept," "object," "event," and "place" entities for which only one attribute was currently defined — "term" for use as an entry element in a subject access point and for all other roles needed in subject access. Delsey felt that this was not enough and that there was a need to define additional attributes for "concept," "object," "event," and "place" so that they could be used in subject access points and authority records.

In FRAD the attributes for FRBR access roles, "name," "title," and "term," become entities in themselves with sets of attributes for types and their identifiers. For example, "name" has attributes such as "title," "corporate name," and "identifier", elements like "forename" and "surname," and additional elements like "scope," "language," and "dates of usage." Also, in FRAD the attributes for each of the FRBR entities were expanded by additional attributes which were needed for confirming the identity of the entity represented by the access point. So, for example, a work might need a "place of origin" or a manifestation a "sequence number." For the entities "person," "corporate body," and "family," corresponding attributes would be "place of birth," "gender," "citizenship," "location of head office," etc. In FRAD for "concept" only "type" is given as an attribute, while "object" has "type," "date of production," etc. The entity "event" had "date" and "place" as attributes while "place" had the attribute "co-ordinates" and other geographic terms. Thus, only the "type" attribute of "concept" and the "type" attribute of "object" could be useful in implementing the categorizations that are reflected in the facets and hierarchies defined in thesauri and classification schemes.

Relationships would also need extending. In FRBR there were two levels of relationships, those that worked at the highest level on down — work "is realized by" expression, person "is known by name," etc. and those that operated between specific instances of the same or different entity type — for example, work "has supplement." The relationship "has a subject" would have to encompass not just the expected features (like subject headings) but also links by genre, form, and possibly geographic and temporal categories. Also, provision for semantic relationships would be needed, between subject terms, narrower and broader, equivalent and related, associative, and chronological/geographical ranges. Delsey noted that associative relationships ("see also") would be the hardest to accommodate, as they were neither equivalent nor hierarchical but simply what did not fit into those two groups. There was a need to establish whether associative relationships only operated between instances of "concept" or did they operate as well between "place," "event," and "object" as defined in FRBR.

Delsey also attempted to check the FRBR/FRAD models at a high level to determine whether they encompassed all possible subjects by comparing them against a recognized universal model, Indecs. Indecs was the outcome of a project funded by the European Community Info 2000 initiative and commercial rights organizations (Rust & Bide, 2000). It defined "percepts" (things that the senses perceive), "concepts" (things that the mind perceives), and "relations," which are composed of two or more percepts and objects. At a lower level, percepts were divided into animates, "beings," and inanimates, "things," and relations into dynamic "events" and static "situations." The FRBR entity "object" was equated to Indecs "percepts", and "concept" is in both FRBR and Indecs. However, the FRBR entity "event" was equated to a subclass of "relation," while FRBR's "place" in Indecs was paired with "time" as in Indecs these two concepts together were needed to fix an "event" or "situation." "Person" in FRBR was a problem as it needed a subset of Indecs "beings," while FRBR's "corporate body" was a special instance of "group" (which included family, societies, etc.) which would go under either "object" or "concept" in Indecs. These were problems chiefly caused by FRBR's need to focus on distinct entities needed for bibliographic purposes, but the mismatch in the high-level classification of reality in the two models did raise serious doubt on the viability of the FRBR Group 3 entities.

Delsey also noted Buizza and Guerrini's approach in creating a new entity to represent the entire string or indexing terms forming a topic. He agreed that syntactic priorities for ordering the terms would still need to be applied within the string, so some system of assigning string roles and ordering was required. The challenge in creating such a system:

> lies in the wide and diverse range of such relationships .... Ideally the relationship types would be the same range of relationships but would do so at a higher level of generalization to which specific types in indexing languages could be mapped .... On a practical level it would also provide the basis for mapping syntactic relationships to generic categories to support subject across databases containing index strings constructed using different thesauri and subject heading lists (Delsey, 2005, p. 52)

3.5. The Arrival of FRSAD

The Working Group on the Functional Requirements for Subject Authority Data (FRSAD) was the third IFLA working group of the FRBR family. Formed in April 2005, it was charged with the task of developing a conceptual model of FRBR Group 3 entities within the FRBR framework as they relate to the "aboutness" of works.

It began by conducting two user studies. The first was a study of attendees at the 2006 Semantic Technologies Conference (San Jose, California, USA). The second was an international survey sent to information professionals throughout the world during the months of May–September 2007. In both, participants were asked to describe their work and their use of subject authority data in different contexts. The FRSAR five user tasks were based on the results (Zumer, Salaba, & Zeng, n.d.). Another objective was to redefine the FRBR/FRAD user-tasks toward "aboutness," so a new set was produced:

> Find one or more subjects and/or their appellations, that correspond(s) to the user's stated criteria, using attributes and relationships;

> Identify a subject and/or its appellation based on its attributes or relationships (i.e., to distinguish between two or more subjects or appellations with similar characteristics and to confirm that the appropriate subject or appellation has been found);
>
> Select a subject and/or its appellation appropriate to the user's needs (i.e., to choose or reject based on the user's requirements and needs);
>
> Explore relationships between subjects and/or their appellations (e.g., to explore relationships in order to understand the structure of a subject domain and its terminology). (FRSAD, 2010, p. 9)

The last one, "explore," is a new task not in FRBR/FRAD to enable users to browse subject resources.

Although "aboutness" is the focus, FRSAD also considers "of-ness" in terms of form, genre, and target audience as this concept overlaps with that of the pure subject search.

There seems to have been a general agreement that Group 3 entities should be "revisited." Alternative models, including the one discussed previously from Buizza and Guerrini, were considered. Delsey's approach of using other general models to examine the Group 3 entities was copied, and Indecs, and other general models, like Ranganathan's, were examined.

By 2007, the focus had shifted toward the development of a different conceptual model of Group 3 entities. What was proposed was a very new general model, based on "thema" and "nomen," whereby the former, defined as "any entity used as the subject of a work," was represented by the latter, defined as "any sign or sequence of signs." In general a "thema" could have many "nomens" and vice versa, while "works" could have many "thema" and one "thema" could apply to many works. A "nomen" was defined as any sign or sequence of signs (alphanumeric characters, symbols, sound, etc.) by which a thema was known by, referred to, or addressed as. For example, "indexing," or "025.4." These two entities enabled the task "to build a conceptual model of Group 3 entities within the FRBR framework as they relate to the aboutness of works" to be fulfilled, and the model resulting was very compact and generic. Any existing subject access scheme could be "represented" and examples were given in appendices.

Themas could vary substantially in complexity or simplicity. Depending on the circumstances (the subject authority system, user needs, the nature of the work, etc.) the aboutness of a work could be expressed as a one-to-one relationship between the work and the thema. In an implementation, themas could be organized based on category, kind, or type. The report did not suggest specific types, because they may differ depending on implementations.

Thema attributes were "type," the category to which a thema belonged in the context of a particular subject organization system and "scope note," text describing and/or defining the thema or specifying its scope within a particular subject organization system.

Nomen attributes were "type" (e.g., identifier, controlled term), "scheme," reference source, representation (e.g., ASCII), "language," "script", "script conversion," "form" (additional information), "time of validity" (of the nomen not the subject), "audience," and "status."

Finally, the "thema" and "nomen" conceptual model also matches well with schemas such as Simple Knowledge Organization System (SKOS), Web Ontology Language (OWL), and the DCMI Abstract Model, making it ideal for resource sharing and re-use of subject authority data (Zeng & Zumer, n.d.).

Although produced by IFLA, the reports have come from different groups over a long period of time, which has meant that their approaches and outcomes have differed. There is a significant conceptual mismatch between the reports in how far to go when proposing a new conceptual model. The FRSAD report is also different in that it reads more like an academic paper than a structure that lays the foundations for practical developments, which the earlier reports do.

However, by using such a simple model the aim "to provide a clearly defined structured frame of reference for relating the data that are recorded in subject authority records to the needs of the users of that data" is fulfilled on paper and in theory. What is needed is bridge into being able to apply FRSAD's abstract model using a tried and tested tool.

To try and move on, without revisiting work on FRSAD, it seems prudent to adopt the general model it proposes but actually use an existing system that is based on solid theory, congruent with that in FRSAD, that has been tried and tested and possesses the ability to form a structure that can both exist on its own and also can serve to interlink between other existing schemes, especially the dominant ones, Library of Congress Subject Headings (LCSH) and Dewey Decimal Classification (DDC). PRECIS is proposed for this role.

3.6. Implementing FRSAD with PRECIS

PRECIS is not a list of terms/codes. It is two sets of procedures, one syntactic using a general "grammar" of roles to generate one or more terms (a "string") to unambiguously represent a topic, the other semantic setting up permanent thesaural connections between terms where needed. It does not prescribe terms. PRECIS grew out of research into classification which produced its set of syntactic codes, known as "role operators" (Austin, 1974).

Implemented first by the British National Bibliography to streamline subject operations, each PRECIS string was given a unique Subject

Indicator Number (SIN). Added to the SIN were equivalents in DDC and LCSH. Once SINs were created, their reuse would save time and effort. Reference Indicator Numbers (RINs) performed a similar role for thesaural aspects (Austin, 1984). In its heyday, PRECIS was being used in bilingual Canada and its use in a number of languages was being investigated (Detemple, 1982; Assuncao, 1989). It was even given a trial at the Library of Congress (Dykstra, 1978). Subject data can be seen as more crucial to the growth of the Semantic Web than descriptive data. Austin (1982) attacked the early claims of machine retrieval. It is surely prudent to equip cataloguers as soon as possible with the tools to mount one more offensive.

Derek Austin joined the British National Bibliography (BNB) in 1963 as a subject editor, after having worked as a reference librarian for many years. He says in his memoirs (Austin, 1998) that:

> A hard pressed reference librarian quickly learns to distinguish among and evaluate everyday working tools such as indexes and bibliographies, and tends as a matter of course, to identify, possibly at a sub-conscious level, those features which mark one index, say, as more or less successful than another.

This practical experience was crucial to his utilitarian, rather than philosophical approach to subject retrieval. His job at BNB was checking the appropriateness and accuracy of Dewey Decimal Classification (DDC) numbers. In 1967, he was seconded to research work for the Classification Research Group (CRG).

At the time there was general dissatisfaction with the two main schemes used for subject access, DDC and the Library of Congress Classification (LCC) as their lack of a well-explained logical structure and inconsistencies in their sub-division made it hard to accommodate new subjects. However, critiques of existing schemes in themselves did not solve these issues, nor gave a basis for more solid approach. One potential route was offered by S.R. Ranganathan, whose facet analysis approach was based on the universal facets of place, material, energy, space, and time (PMEST).

At a conference of the CRG in London in 1963, as well as investigating the design of a new systematic arrangement of main classes within a new classification scheme, the citation order of components of compound subjects was also discussed. This was proposed as the basis for a "freely faceted" scheme, initially intended to provide open-ended extension capabilities for classification schemes.

Later work was funded by BNB and NATO. A general system of categories based on fundamental classes of ideas was produced. Things were distinct from Actions. Concrete things were different from Ideas. Concrete things were divided into naturally occurring and artificial. Types of relationship between categories were also defined: whole/part, genus/species, etc.

Categories and types were to supply the semantics of the subject representation scheme. No notation was added in order to avoid traps set by its form, for example decimal numbers only allowing up to 10 choices.

As well, work proceeded on handling compound topics:

> for example, a topic such as training of supervisors in Californian industries involves an *action/patient* relationship linking 'training' to 'supervisors', a whole/part relationship between 'supervisors' and 'industries' and a 'space/location' relationship which links 'industries' to California. A basic set of these *syntactical* relations was implicit in Ranganathan's PMEST and this had been expanded and modified by Vickery as the sequence: Things (Products), Kinds, Parts, Materials, Properties, Operations, Agents. (Austin, 1998, p. 31).

Using this sequence however would not remove all ambiguity. The CRG had tried to address this problem by using a set of role operators, single digit numbers in brackets, which not only determined the citation order of elements but also indicated their roles.

Also at this time the automated production of BNB was being upgraded and a project was set up to create a new indexing system for it, the existing alternatives all being ruled out. The job of generating this index was to be automated, so a system was created of strings of terms for each index entry, with lead term(s) indicated and the appropriate formatting and display of other terms. Unlike the previous chain indexing system, each entry would display the full set of terms in the entry. As well as index entries, *see* and *see also* references would also be automatically generated. Finally, unlike the old chain index system, which was bound to a classification system, the new system would use a set of role operators to identify and order concepts in an index entry and that the set of role operators and index terms used should be able to represent any subject.

To achieve this novel last goal, two innovations were made (Austin, 1986). One was the development of a generic set of role operators that were not tied to any existing scheme. They were to provide complete disambiguation of meaning in any string of indexing terms. To aid in this disambiguation, a new form for index entries was required.

Terms were ordered by the principle of context dependency in which terms set the context for following terms. Thus, in the topic "training of supervisors in Californian industries," "California" would come first to set the location for the remaining terms. In California are located "Industries," so this is the second term. In those industries are supervisers who are being trained, so "Supervisors" provides the context for "Training," the last term. So the final string of index terms would be:

California — Industries — Supervisors — Training

The above string is unambiguous, but if it shunted around to create entries for the other terms as in a KWIC index, then ambiguity reappears, for example, in:

Training — California — Industries — Supervisors

it is not clear whether the supervisors are being trained or giving the training. To solve this issue a multi-line entry format was developed, a lead term, followed by terms in a "qualifier" and under this line of terms were the remaining terms in a "display," for example:

California
    Training — Industries — Supervisors

Industries — California
    Supervisors — Training

Supervisors — Industries — California
    Training

Training — Supervisors — California — Industries

This "shunting" process produces a lead term set in its wider context (if any) by the "qualifier" and given more detail by the "display." To compress the index display, if different strings have the same lead and qualifier, then only their displays need to be shown. For example, suppose another string is:

Industries — California
    Technicians — Salaries

then combining its display with the previous example string would give:

Industries — California
    Supervisors — Training
    Technicians — Salaries

The driver of string creation was a set of primary operators denoting roles and identified by numbers, the most important being:

0 — Location
1 — Key concept
2 — Action/Effect of action
3 — Performer/Agent/Instrument

There were also secondary operators, the most commonly used being "p" for part or property. To code the example string would produce:

0 — California
1 — Industries
P — Supervisors
2 — Training

Note that in the above string, "Supervisers" are considered a part of "Industries." Strings had to contain a Key concept and an Action, else they would be rejected as being invalid. The best to build a string was to work out first the activity involved (the "2" Action) and then what the target of the action was (the "1" Key concept).

PRECIS was taken up by the Australian National Library and the National Film Board of Canada. It was used for back of the book indexing including the final edition of the PRECIS manual (Austin, 1984) and the IFLA *UNIMARC Manual* (Holt, 1987). The first edition of the manual has trials of PRECIS in other languages and suggests that PRECIS follows an underlying grammar (BNB, 1974). This grammar is not language itself, as attempts to teach PRECIS as a grammar failed. There is some similarity between the roles in PRECIS and grammatical categories, but there are significant differences. For example, sentences have verbs, but PRECIS strings contain only nouns or noun phrases. PRECIS seemed to work well in related languages like French and German as well as in different languages like Tamil and Telugu (Vencatachari, 1982).

Austin (1998) suggests that this generality in indexing capability comes from Chomsky's theory of transformational generative grammar (1965). He posits that here is a deep structure underlying language which is understood only innately and a surface structure which is comprehended by speakers. The same deep structure is common across languages, which accounts for their common form and functions, while their surface structures seemingly differ. People can innately understand deep grammar, which enables them to learn surface languages easily, since language acquisition and use is vital for human society. Other theorists support this approach and Longacre (1976) lists four basic elements common across different theorists: locative, agentive, instrumental, and patient/object. There is an obvious similarity between these and the role operators in PRECIS. PRECIS was tested for its application across languages, and while many trials were successful, there was pressure to expand the set of role operators to address particular issues with certain languages. For example, codes to handle Komposita in German were devised but never added to the core set. However, even if extra codes for special situations with certain languages had been added to PRECIS, these would never have complicated the majority of indexing which would have used the core operators.

3.7. What Future for FRSAD in Filling the Blanks in RDA?

This chapter has traced the development of the FRSAD model and suggested a mechanism, based on PRECIS, for putting into practice this model. Yet there seems to be a general denial of the FRSAD model. Rather than being incorporated into RDA, at the most recent meeting (November 2011) of the RDA's JSC, its existence appears not to have been mentioned.

According to a blog post by the ALA's JSC representative (Attig, 2011) there was a suggestion to:

> consider the "subject" entities [Concept, Object, Event, and Place] independent of their grouping in FRBR as Group 3 "subject" entities, but rather consider them as bibliographic entities and define whatever attributes and relationships seem appropriate to each entity. One implication of this is that entities should not be limited to the subject relationship, but considered more broadly within the context of bibliographic information. The JSC accepted this as a basis for further development and discussion.

which could be interpreted as a rethink leading up to the recognition and incorporation of FRSAD. However, one proposal which was passed seems to completely ignore FRSAD:

> There was tentative consensus that there should be a very general definition of the subject relationship; that the Concept and Object entities should be defined in RDA; and that further discussion was needed about the Event/Time/Place entities.

The JSC is not an organization tied to IFLA so it is not bound to recognize IFLA standards. However, it is strange that it is planning a revision of a now superseded structure. The literature review for this chapter found no fundamental criticisms of FRSAD, and its gestation seems to have been open and informed by the same processes that FRBR and FRAD went through. Its lineage back to work from Buizza and Guerrini, and from Tom Delsey, is clear. Yet, it is almost as though FRSAD itself has never appeared. The blanks in RDA will go though. From the same blog post:

> The suggestion was made that we delete the "placeholder" chapters from RDA outline — because they are so closely related to Group 3/Subject concepts — and rethink how we wish to define and document additional entities.

FRSAD seems to have come and gone in the night: a strange case indeed!

References

Assuncao, J. B. (1989). PRECIS em portugues: em busca uma adaptacao. *Revista da Escola Biblioteconomia da UFMG*, *18*(2), 153–365.

Attig, J. (2011). *Report of the meeting of the joint steering committee*. November 1, 2011. Retrieved from http://www.personal.psu.edu/jxa16/blogs/resource_description_and_access_ala_rep_notes/2011/11/report-of-the-meeting-of-the-joint-steering-committee-1-november-2011.html

Austin, D. (1974). The development of PRECIS: A theoretical and technical history. *Journal of Documentation*, *30*(1), 47–102.

Austin. (1982). Basis concept classes and primitive relations. *Universal classification: Proceedings of the fourth international study conference on classification research*, Index-Verlag, Augsburg, Germany, June 1982.

Austin, D. (1984). *PRECIS: A manual of concept analysis and indexing* (p. 397). London: British Library.

Austin, D. (1986). Vocabulary control and information control. *Aslib Proceedings*, *38*(1), 1–15.

Austin, D. (1998). Developing PRECIS, preserved context index system. *Cataloging and Classification Quarterly*, *25*(2/3), 23–66.

British National Bibliography. (1974). *PRECIS: A manual of content analysis and indexing*. London: British Library.

Buizza, P., & Guerrini, M. A. (2002). Conceptual model for the new "Soggettario": Subject indexing in the light of FRBR. *Cataloging & Classification Quarterly*, *34*(4), 31–45.

Chomsky, N. (1965). *Aspects of the theory of syntax*. Cambridge, MA: The MIT Press.

Delsey, T. (2005). Modeling subject access: Extending the FRBR and FRANAR conceptual models. *Cataloging and Classification Quarterly*, *39*(3/3), 49–61.

Detemple, S. (1982). PRECIS. *Bibliothek: Forschung und Praxis*, *6*(1/2), 4–46.

Dykstra, M. (1978, September 1). The lion that squeaked. *Library Journal*, *103*(15), 1570–1572.

Functional Requirements for Subject Authority Data (FRSAD). (2010). IFLA Working Group.

Holt, B.P. (1987). *UNIMARC manual*. London: British Library for IFLA.

IFLA Study Group on the Functional Requirements for Bibliographic Records. (2009). *Functional requirements for bibliographic records: Final report*. Retrieved from http://www.ifla.org/files/cataloguing/frbr/frbr_2008.pdf

IFLA Working Group on Functional Requirements and Numbering of Authority Records. (2009). *Functional requirements for authority data — A conceptual model*. Munich: Saur.

IFLA Working Group on the Functional Requirements for Subject Authority Records. (2010). *Functional Requirements for Subject Authority Data (FRSAD): A conceptual model*. Retrieved from http://www.ifla.org/files/classification-and-indexing/functional-requirements-for-subject-authority-data/frsad-final-report.pdf

Longacre. (1976). *An anatomy of speach notions*. Peter De Ridder Press.

Patton, G. (2005). *FRAR: Extending FRBR concepts to authority data.* Retrieved from http://archive.ifla.org/IV/ifla71/papers/014e-Patton.pdf

Rust, G., & Bide, M. (2000). *The <indecs> metadata framework: Principles, model and data dictionary.* Retrieved from http://www.doi.org/topics/indecs/indecs_framework_2000.pdf

U.S. RDA Test Coordinating Committee. (2011). *Report and recommendations of the U.S. RDA Test Coordinating Committee.* Retrieved from http://www.loc.gov/bibliographic-future/rda/rdatesting-finalreport-20june2011.pdf

Vencatachari, P. N. (1982). Application of PRECIS to Indian languages: A case study. In S. N. Agawhal (Ed.), *Perspectives in library and information science.* Lucknow, India: Printhouse.

Zeng, M. L., & Zumer, M. (n.d.). *Introducing FRSAD and mapping it with SKOS and other models.* Retrieved from http://www.ifla.org/files/hq/papers/ifla75/200-zeng-en.pdf

Zumer, M., Salaba, A., & Zeng, M. (n.d.). Functional Requirements for Subject Authority Records (FRSAR): A conceptual model of aboutness.

Chapter 4

Organizing and Sharing Information Using Linked Data

Ziyoung Park and Heejung Kim

Abstract

Purpose — The purpose of this chapter is to introduce the basic concepts and principles of linked data, discuss benefits that linked data provides in library environments, and present a short history of the development of library linked data.

Design/methodology/approach — The chapter is based on the literature review dealing with linked data, especially focusing on the library field.

Findings — In the library field, linked data is especially useful for expanding bibliographic data and authority data. Although diverse structured data is being produced by the library field, the lack of compatibility with the data from other fields currently limits the wider expansion and sharing of linked data.

Originality/value — The value of this chapter can be found in the potential use of linked data in the library field for improving bibliographic and authority data. Especially, this chapter will be useful for library professionals who have interests in the linked data regarding its applications in a library setting.

New Directions in Information Organization
Library and Information Science, Volume 7, 61–87

ISSN: 1876-0562/doi:10.1108/S1876-0562(2013)0000007008

4.1. Introduction

Tim Berners-Lee (2009), who introduced the concept of linked data as an extension of the semantic web, promoted the possibility of making myriad connections among data. His was a novel innovation because the majority of previous discussions had focused upon machine-readable or machine-understandable data that embody the semantic web through data structure or encoding methods. Broadly speaking, linked data is a part of the semantic web. However, as a more highly developed concept it emphasizes "link" as well as "semantic."

Various definitions of linked data are currently in use. The most common ones, cited by Bizer, Heath, and Berners-Lee (2009) state that "linked data is publishing and connecting structured data on the web" and "linked data is using the Web to create typed links between data from different sources" (pp. 1–2). The next most common approach is the concept of linked open data (LOD) that characterizes linked data as open to the public in terms of both its technology and its capacity for unlimited use and reuse. Although the core concepts in all of these definitions of linked data are the connection and extension of web data through linked information, the ultimate aim of linked data is to establish LOD.

In the library field, numerous standards and tools have been developed for the purpose of sharing and exchanging bibliographic data in order to solve the issues raised by Byrne and Goddard (2010), who wrote that "libraries suffer from most of the problems of interoperability and information management that other organization have, but we additionally have an explicit mandate to organize information derived from many other sources so as to make it broadly accessible." As a method, linked data can solve this kind of issue in the library field. Therefore, our discussion of linked data treats it as an opportunity within the information environment that is efficiently improving the ways in which secondary information is organized and shared.

4.2. Basic Concepts of Linked Data

4.2.1. From Web of Hypertext to Web of Data

The generally accepted understanding of linked data is that it is a structured method of storing data on the web (Wikipedia, 2011). However, because today's web is structured according to methods that may no longer be maximally useful, it is necessary to distinguish between "web of hypertext" and "web of data." Web of hypertext, currently the most common method, creates web links through hypertext and anchor tags. As shown in Figure 4.1, links based on hypertext connect web documents via specific information assigned by the web document creator as well as via hypertext included in the link itself.

In the web of data method (Figure 4.2), larger amounts of data in a web document are linked by additional identifiers. This approach allows identification and linkage per individual data units rather than to document units only. Data that possess the same identifier(s) are connected automatically, without the addition of web document creators' link information. Connected information across a web of data can lead users to unexpected information.

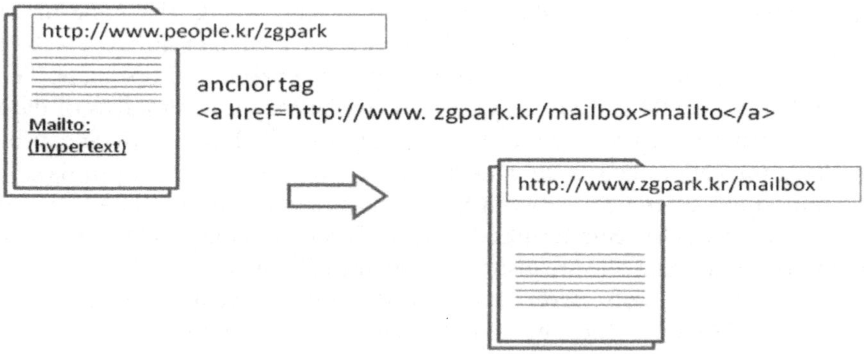

Figure 4.1: Web of hypertext: links using hypertext and anchor tag.

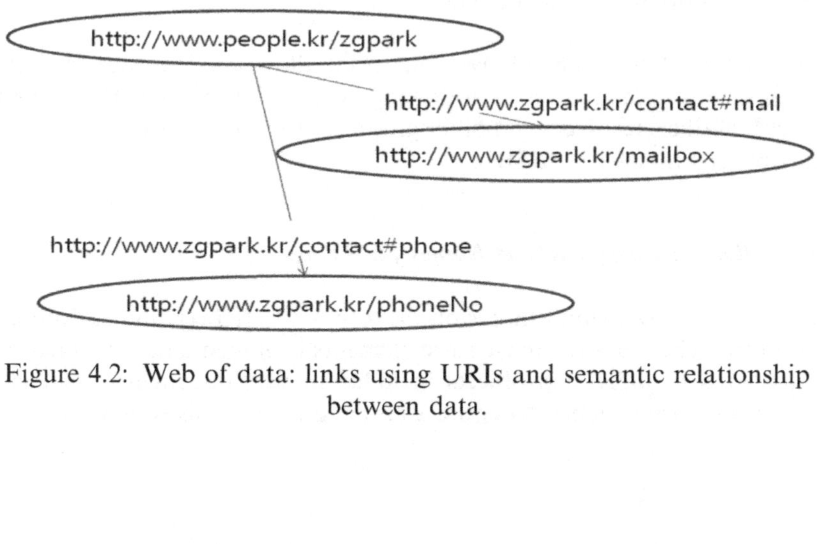

Figure 4.2: Web of data: links using URIs and semantic relationship between data.

4.2.2. From Data Silos to Linked Open Data

"Silo," a term that originally referred to a granary, in the context of the web means inaccessible data stored in a closed data system. Applied to an individual institution or person, using a silo means keeping and managing data in a closed condition that prevents exposure to the external information environment (Stuart, 2011). If channels such as APIs or methods of receiving raw data from external sources are not provided, high-tech applied data — regardless of its complexity — become data silos.

A broader definition of web of data is "data that is structured in a machine-readable format and that has been published openly on the web" (Stuart, 2011, p. x). A more detailed version calls it "data published according to Linked Data Principles" (Berners-Lee, 2009). These definitions differ in terms of the data structure or identification system that they are applied to data publishing; both, however, include the concept of "openness." In contrast to the use of separate, fortified data silos, the web of data that is built of linked data is based upon the premise of openness. The desirability of LOD is frequently used to emphasize the advantages of data sharing using linked data because the value of the web itself, which can be realized through linked data, is dependent on the inclusion of open data.

Important differences between information contained in a data silo and LOD can be seen by comparing Microsoft Excel and Google Docs. Because data presented in Excel spreadsheets is separated from external links as well as saved on the web server, its data structure prevents openness. The openness of Google Docs, by contrast, enables data sharing through APIs (Stuart, 2011).

4.3. Principles of Linked Data

According to Berners-Lee (2009), four rules allow maximization of linked data functions. Examples in the following explanations include DOI (Digital Object Identifier) resolvers and bibliographic information using an Resource Description Framework (RDF).

4.3.1. Rule 1: Using URIs as Names for Things

The first rule is to identify things on the web with URIs (Uniform Resource Identifiers). These are the most basic elements of linked data, in which they are assigned to individual objects included in web documents, instead of URLs which are assigned to entire web documents. This difference is that

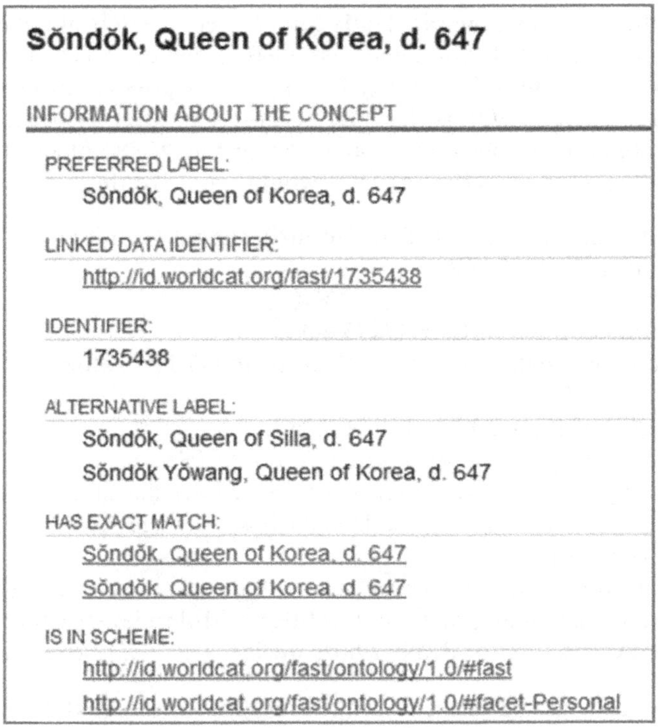

Figure 4.3: URI in FAST linked data.

data, not document, is the basic unit of identification and connection in the data-centered web.

For example, in Figure 4.3, FAST (Faceted Application of Subject Terminology) Linked Data, the web object "Sŏndŏk," Queen of Korea (d. 647) has a URI "http://id.worldcat.org/fast/173543" instead of the whole-page URL "http://experimental.worldcat.org/fast/1735438/." FAST is derived from LCSH (Library of Congress Subject Headings) and provided in linked data experimentally (OCLC, 2012). In FAST, each heading has a URI and headings can be linked to other web data using URIs.

4.3.2. Rule 2: Using HTTP URIs so that Users can Look Up Those Names

The second rule is to use HTTP protocols to approach URIs. In the data-centered web, URIs used for data identification cannot be accessed directly through the web; instead, a URI must be de-referenced using HTTP protocols. Currently so many kinds of URIs are being used that employing protocols other than HTTP will make it difficult to access specific URIs through the web. For example, DOIs can be used as URIs in linked data. A DOI is a unique identification code assigned to digital object, such as single articles within a scholarly journal. However, it is possible to search article information using a DOI as the URI because CrossRef has built metadata for 46 million DOIs as linked data. According to Summers (2011), an example of how to use URIs as DOI would look like this:

- Receiving an article's DOI from an institutional repository:
  - Doi: 10.1038/171737a0
- Constructing URL based on the DOI:
  - http://dx.doi.org/10.1038/171737a0
- Obtaining metadata from the URI using an HTTP protocol in structured form such as RDF:
  - <http://dx.doi.org/10.1038/171737a0>
    a <http://purl.org/ontology/bibo/Article>;
    <http://purl.org/dc/terms/title> "Molecular Structure of Nucleic Acids: A Structure for Deoxyribose Nucleic Acid" ... [the rest is omitted]
- Metadata transmitted to the structured data as above means that:
  - The document is an article, and its title is "Molecular structure of nucleic acids: A structure for deoxy ribose nucleic acid" ... [the rest is omitted].

This process can be verified on the CrossRef website (PILA, 2002). DOI Resolver (Figure 4.4) imports related metadata by converting DOIs to HTTP URIs. Metadata that can be identified through an input DOI are shown in Figure 4.5.

4.3.3. *Rule 3: When Looking Up a URI, Useful Information has to be Provided Using the Standards*

The third rule concerns data structure for reusing and sharing data. After accessing an object on the web through an HTTP URI, it should be

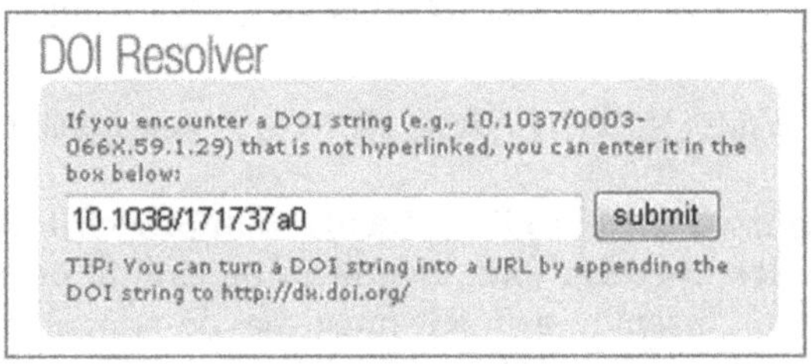

Figure 4.4: DOI Resolver at CrossRef, from http://www.crossref.org/.

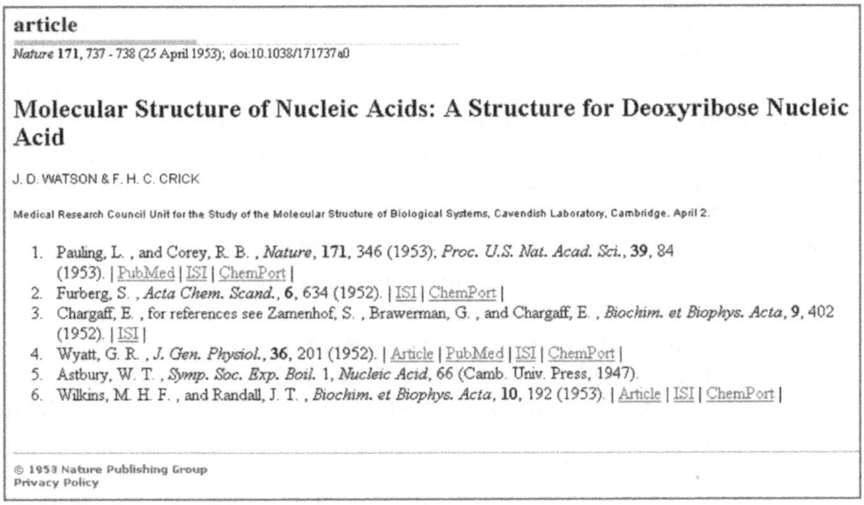

article

Nature **171**, 737 - 738 (25 April 1953); doi:10.1038/171737a0

Molecular Structure of Nucleic Acids: A Structure for Deoxyribose Nucleic Acid

J. D. WATSON & F. H. C. CRICK

Medical Research Council Unit for the Study of the Molecular Structure of Biological Systems, Cavendish Laboratory, Cambridge. April 2.

1. Pauling, L. , and Corey, R. B. , *Nature*, **171**, 346 (1953); *Proc. U.S. Nat. Acad. Sci.*, **39**, 84 (1953). | PubMed | ISI | ChemPort |
2. Furberg, S. , *Acta Chem. Scand.*, **6**, 634 (1952). | ISI | ChemPort |
3. Chargaff, E. , for references see Zamenhof, S. , Brawerman, G. , and Chargaff, E. , *Biochim. et Biophys. Acta*, **9**, 402 (1952). | ISI |
4. Wyatt, G. R. , *J. Gen. Physiol.*, **36**, 201 (1952). | Article | PubMed | ISI | ChemPort |
5. Astbury, W. T. , *Symp. Soc. Exp. Boil.* 1, *Nucleic Acid*, 66 (Camb. Univ. Press, 1947).
6. Wilkins, M. H. F. , and Randall, J. T. , *Biochim. et Biophys. Acta*, **10**, 192 (1953). | Article | ISI | ChemPort |

© 1953 Nature Publishing Group
Privacy Policy

Figure 4.5: Metadata from DOI, from http://www.nature.com/nature/journal/v171/n4356/abs/171737a0.html.

possible to import information through data that is structured according to classes and properties. That is, in order to share many data produced by applying semantic web technologies, a data standard such as RDF/XML, N3 (Notation 3), or Turtle (Terse RDF Triple Language) should be observed. Because the basic data structure provided through the linked data is RDF/XML, standards that can express information as triple types should be used.

The RDF model comprises subject, predicate, and object triple. This structure is useful in defining and connecting data in the web environment. For example, person A can be connected to person B because "A knows B." This can be expressed by assigning URI and relationship information to both A and B. In this case A is expressed as the subject; the relationship "know" is expressed as the predicate; and B is expressed as the object. Thus a relationship between person and bibliographic object could be connected (e.g., person C and scholarly article D) by assigning a URI to both C and D and by assigning the relationship "is author of" (Bizer et al., 2009).

However, data structuralization through RDFs should be differentiated from simple XML-based data or data that uses only a namespace. The examples below suggest three types of data structure. Of the first two, simple XML and XML syntax, only the second uses applied namespace; it also has the advantage of sharing attributes such as title or creator through namespace. A triple-structure RDF and a URI are assigned to the third, which is structuralized at a high level compared to the first two (Stuart, 2011, pp. 83–88).

(1) Bibliographic information expressed by a simple XML
  a. <book><title>Facilitating Access to the Web of Data</title>
  b. <author>David Stuart</author>
  c. <ISBN>9781856047456</ISBN></book>
(2) Bibliographic information expressed by an XML-applied namespace
  a. <book xmlns:dc="http://purl.org/dc/elements/1.1">
  b. <dc:title>Facilitating Access to the Web of Data</dc:title>
  c. <dc:creator>David Stuart</dc:creator>
  d. <dc:identifier>9781856047456</dc:identifier></book>
(3) Bibliographic information expressed in an XML format and RDF triple structure
  a. <rdf:RDF xmlns:rdf="http://www.w3.org/1999/02/22-rdf-syntax-ns#"
  b. xmlns:dc="http://purl.org/dc/elements/1.1">
  c. <rdf:description rdf:about="http://www4.wiwiss.fu-berlin.de/book-mashup/doc/books/9781856047456">
  d. <dc:title>Facilitating Access to the Web of Data</dc:title>
  e. <dc:creator>David Stuart</dc:creator>
  f. <dc:identifier rdf:resource="urn:ISBN:9781856047456"/>
  g. </rdf:description>
  h. </rdf:RDF>

Structuralized data can use the query language of SPARQL, which is appropriate for standardized data such as RDFs. In this way, users can structuralize web data just like data saved in a relational database. The example below shows a simple SPARQL query (W3C, 2008).

- Data: <http://example.org/book/book1><http://purl.org/dc/elements/1.1/title> "SPARQL Tutorial."
- Query: SELECT?title
  WHERE
  {
  <http://example.org/book/book1>
  <http://purl.org/dc/elements/1.1/title> ?title.
  }
- Query Result:

title
"SPARQL Tutorial"

As described by W3C (2008), "The query consists of two parts: the SELECT and WHERE. SELECT clause identifies the variables to appear in the query results, and the WHERE clause provides the basic graph pattern to match against the data graph. The basic graph pattern consists of a single triple pattern with a single variable (?title) in the object position."

4.3.4. Rule 4: Including Links to Other URIs so that Users can Discover More Things

Rule 4 is to assign link information between data that have been tagged according to the first three rules. By displaying link information, the semantic web data can support more wide-ranging discoveries. Semantic data that has been built up by applying standard such as RDFs cannot be regarded as linked data, if link information has not been assigned. There are three ways to connect individual data by triple structures into linked data (Bizer et al., 2009; Heath & Bizer, 2011):

i. *Relationship links* (a linkage method that uses triple RDFs). This is similar to linkage through an ontological relationship. For example, the subject is "Decentralized Information Group" (DIG) in MIT, identified by the URI http://dig.csail.mit.edu/data#DIG. The object is a person, "Berners-Lee," identified by the URI http://www.w3.org/People/Berners-Lee/card#i. The predicate represents the relationship between object and subject and is identified by the URI http://xmlns.com/foaf/0.1/member. In this relationship, Berners-Lee is a member of the DIG.

    - Subject: http://dig.csail.mit.edu/data#DIG
    - Object: http://www.w3.org/People/Berners-Lee/card#i
    - Predicate: http://xmlns.com/foaf/0.1/member

ii. *Identity links* (a linkage method using URI aliases). This method uses URI aliases that include "owl:sameAs." For example, the sameAs that appears next to the description of Abraham in Bibleontology shows that he is the same person as Abraham in DBpedia. Therefore, each subsequent description of this person can be merged (Cho & Cho, 2012).

    - <http://bibleontology.com/resource/Abraham><http://www.w3.org/2002/07/owl#sameAs><http://dbpedia.org/resource/Abraham>

iii. *Vocabulary links* (the use of equivalence relationships). This method, which uses relational terms such as "owl:eaquivalentClass" and "rdfs:subClassOf," is looser than sameAs. For example, the term "film," identified by the URI http://dbpedia.org/ontology/Film can be mapped with the term "movie," identified by the URI http://schema.org/Movie (DBpedia, 2012).

- <http://dbpedia.org/ontology/Film><http://www.w3.org/2002/07/owl#equivalentClass><http://schema.org/Movie>

These steps can be simplified as: (1) identify objects by URI (i.e., provide each URI) through HTTP protocol; (2), observe semantic web standards such as RDFs when writing documents; and (3) assign link information, after which linked data will be produced that enable the integrated use of related information beyond the boundaries of the managing institutions.

Figure 4.6 shows connections through the DOI on CrossRef, using "sameAs" link information, from the article "Molecular Structure of Nucleic Acids: A Structure for Deoxy Ribose Nucleic Acid" from the journal *Nature*, with the same article under the management of Data Incubator. Different metadata may exist for the same article because the procedures used by metadata management institutions may differ from those of CrossRef and Data Incubator. Because the two sets of metadata for this article are built by linked data, metadata from more than one institution can be merged and used together. The subject of this particular article is Biology. Therefore, through the LCSH "Biology," this article can be connected to other similar articles. LCSH is a controlled vocabulary of subjects that is mainly used by libraries. Figure 4.6 shows that LCSH is connected to the resources of the National Library of France. This connection is possible because LCSH is built up by linked data.

Another method, known as the "star scheme" (Berners-Lee, 2009), is dependent on the linked data level. (Figure 4.7). Data that is constructed

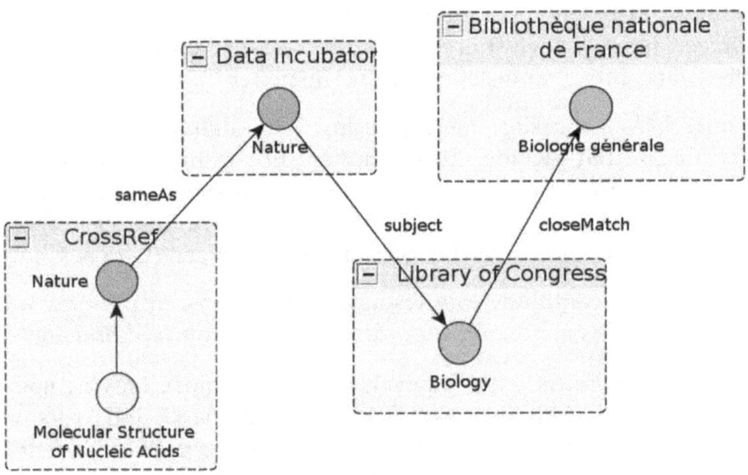

Figure 4.6: Data aggregation using link information (Summers, 2011).

★	Available on the web (whatever format) but with an open license, to be open data
★★	Available as machine-readable structured data (e.g., an Excel table instead of an image scan of a table)
★★★	As the one above plus non-proprietary format (e.g., CSV instead of Excel)
★★★★	All the above plus the use of open standards from W3C (RDF and SPARQL) to identify things, so that people can point at your data
★★★★★	All the above, plus the linkage of your data to other people's data to provide context

Figure 4.7: Five-star data scheme (Berners-Lee, 2009).

according to W3C standards such as RDF is fourth-level. Rule 4 (Link your data to other people's data) implies the fifth level of linked data.

4.4. Linked Data in Library Environments

Through the findings of the Library Linked Data Incubator Group, W3C offers sample applications of linked data in library fields and explains their advantages (W3C Library Incubator Group, 2011a–2011c). The group's mission was completed in August 2011, and its two-part final report and related documents were published in October 2011. The first part presents the benefits of utilizing linked data in libraries and related fields; the second part presents recommendations to overcome the limitations of utilizing linked data that arise from the peculiarity of current library fields.

4.4.1. Benefits of Linked Data in Libraries

The W3C final report sorted beneficiaries of linked data into four categories: (1) researchers, students, and patrons; (2) organizations; (3) librarians, archivists, and curators; and (4) developers and vendors (W3C Library Incubator Group, 2011b). These groups are classified broadly as final users, bibliographic data creation institutions, bibliographic data creators, and bibliographic data management program creators.

4.4.1.1. Benefits to researchers, students, and patrons The greatest benefit an end user can get from linked data is through a federated search, which means the collective results integrated searches of scattered related information in current libraries, museums, and archives. Linked information between web data, comprised of URIs and RDFs, provides much more efficient browsing functions than links between previous web documents that used URL, HTML, and Hypertext. This advantage is described as "toURIsm" because searching by linked data provides a seamless tour of various data from various origins.

4.4.1.2. Benefits to organizations The benefits of linked data to organizations include improved data quality and budgets through changed data creation methods. W3C defined the previous bibliographic data creation method as top-down, which means that libraries described their own holding resources individually and managed their own bibliographic records. These methods required from institutions to maintain large budgets in order to improve the quality of their catalogs. However, most institutions cannot afford this level of investment in cataloging process. By contrast, linked data is a bottom-up method in which creators produce metadata related to the same resources and connect them for general use within a single frame.

Linked data is not the technology that converts the contents or quality of data, but rather a data creation methodology that integrates scattered information and simplifies its presentation. This is called the "cloud-based" approach. Thus, the successful use of linked data does not necessitate finding solutions for the improvement of data per individual institutions. Instead, unlimited number of users and contributors can form partnerships among unlimited number of communities within the web.

4.4.1.3. Benefits to librarians, archivists, and curators Professional data management groups benefit hugely from the use of linked data. Individually, librarians, archivists, and curators can acquire broader metadata related to the resources they manage without having to contend with redundancy (i.e., metadata already assembled by other institutions). Instead, such information can be recycled through data sharing. In addition, meta-information can be created from the perspectives of the communities that manage and provide services related to that data. Instead of inputting information by each institution or sole community, inputting only data associated with each community and then linking them improves data creation efficiency as well as data quality.

4.4.1.4. Benefits to developers and vendors Current libraries use externally crafted programs to provide bibliographic records and services to users. However, the features of library-specific data formats such as Machine-Readable Cataloging (MARC) and library-specific protocols such as Z39.50

are complicated for database or library resource management program developers to manage. Moreover, difficulties are created by limitations on exchanging data from outside the library community with data that has been created according to the particular standards of an individual library. By contrast, linked data can be easily understood by general web developers and can be shared efficiently among users as well as source institutions. Therefore, library bibliographic data created as linked data confers benefits to entities outside the library community that need to cooperate/collaborate with libraries.

4.5. Suggestions for Library Linked Data

Libraries were making consistent efforts to connect and share information long before the appearance of the semantic web. These endeavors have been formalized into rules and tools that enable the use of information from a variety of media as well as from catalogs published by multiple libraries. Now, an analysis is needed to show how, within the library community, linked data can be more beneficial than the previous methods were.

Methods of integrated searching by using authoritative terms have already been developed in the library community. Linked data can enhance this strong point (Byrne & Goddard, 2010). Through their utilization of linked data, libraries can participate in linking hub functions that provide bibliographic information, subject authorities, name authorities, and holding information from their book and journal collections as well as other resources.

4.5.1. The Necessity of Library Linked Data

Within the library community there are two major perspectives about the desirability of linked data. One emphasizes the higher level of structure and greater credibility of bibliographic and authority data provided by libraries than in the uncontrolled contents that exist on the current web. From this perspective, although its quality is high, library data is a data silo that is hard to exchange beyond library borders. In order to build up library linked data, political decisions must be made about data openness and technical conversion processes.

The other perspective emphasizes libraries' weak points, particularly inconsistency and redundancy of data, and the improvements that will result from increased use of linked data. For example, the current methods of identifying bibliographic records by main headings and identifying authority records by authorized headings are not seen as efficient ways to identify objects. Furthermore, identifier such as ISBN or ISSN are considered unstable because various expressions or manifestations of the same work are difficult to collocate. Singer (2009) illustrated these problems by citing one well-known work that is available in many different forms:

- A monograph, *The Complete Works of William Shakespeare*
- An e-book version of *Romeo and Juliet* from Project Gutenberg
- CliffNotes, *Shakespeare's Romeo and Juliet*
- A DVD of the film "Romeo and Juliet" (1968, dir. Franco Zeffirelli)

Within current bibliographic data it is difficult to express that all of the above resources are based upon a play, *Romeo and Juliet*, by William Shakespeare. Singer also noted the difficulty of connecting related works, for example the Broadway musical *West Side Story*, because there is no way to express that the musical is a modern retelling of Shakespeare's original plot.

Although these two perspectives seem to be firmly opposed, they agree upon the necessity of linked data and the potential to improve certain limitations of current bibliographic and authority records. In addition, both agree that through linked data connections developed by external entities, abundant library data can be supplied to users. The first, however, places greater importance upon the connection of internal library data to external data through the use of linked data, whereas the second stresses the enhancement of library data quality by the use of linked data.

4.5.2. Library Data that Needs Connections

Singer (2009) suggested descriptive elements of bibliographical data that should be more closely connected:

- "work" (provided by a title or ISBN value)
- "creator" (provided by a statement of responsibility or author added headings)
- "publisher" (provided by publication information)
- "series" (provided by a series information)
- "subject heading" (provided by subject heading information)

These five elements can exist independently of a bibliographic record; moreover, the potential is great for related data to be created outside the library field. For example, information about an author can be found on a website belonging to an individual, an institution, or an SNS.

Other library data that can be connected to non-library communities are usage information related to circulation records. For such connections to be useful, however, closer cooperation will be needed between libraries and publishers. Other topics and issues that could benefit from such collaboration include CIP, legal deposits, and copyright payments. In this situation, publishers must recognize and act upon the necessity of connecting library holding and circulation information with publishing and sales information (Choi, 2011).

4.5.3. The Development of the FRBR Family and RDA

Many changes have occurred in libraries when linked data has been developed for the semantic web, that is, Functional Requirements of Bibliographic Records (FRBR), Functional Requirements of Authority Data (FRAD), and Functional Requirements of Subject Authority Data (FRSAD). The first draft of Resource Description and Access (RDA) seeks to revise the descriptive cataloging rules found in the second edition of Anglo-American Cataloging Rules Revision (AACR2R). Some parts that correspond to subject authority are not included; however, most of the functional models that correspond to bibliographic records and name authority records suggested by FRBR and FRAD are discussed.

These changes can be summarized as FRBR family and RDA. One feature of these new standards is that bibliographic record structures (e.g., description elements) have been adapted to entity-relational database model. This new approach, as well as the restructuring of records presented by MARC and based on FRBR and RDA, will make it much easier to assign URIs to each descriptive element included in bibliographic records and to express each object, attribute, and relationship by triple structure.

In fact, the basic elements suggested in FRBR and RDA models are already being expressed in linked data. Davis and Newman (2009) expressed the basic element of FRBR in RDF. Byrne and Goddard also observed this library trend and stated that libraries should actively promote RDA to maximize the use of RDF's strong points.

4.6. Current Library-Related Data

4.6.1. Linking Open Data Projects

Linking Open Data (LOD) projects are representative data sets that are built according to the five rules of linked data described above. Figure 4.8 shows an LOD cloud diagram of visualized linked data registered on

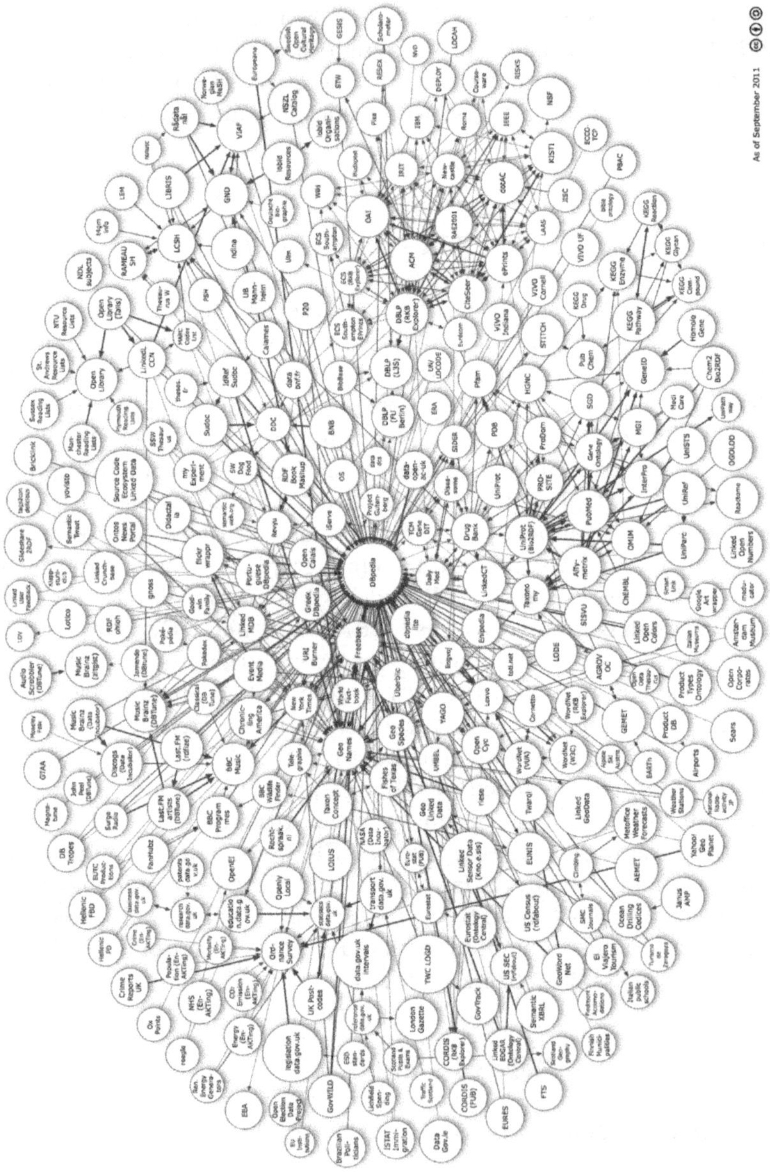

Figure 4.8: Linking open data cloud diagram (Cyganiak & Jentzsch, 2011).

the LOD site. The nodes, which are expressed as a circle, indicate individual linked data; arrows between nodes indicate link information between individual linked data. The size of a node indicates the size of the linked data. The width of the arrows shows the strength of the connections. Linked data which is related to the library community or bibliographic data such as BNB or LCSH are presented on the right.

Along with conforming to the linked data rules, the linked data represented in this diagram contain more than 1000 triples, more than 50 links that connect it to a previously established cloud diagram, and the ability (per whole data set) to crawl through the RDF format (if an SPARQL endpoint has not been provided). Of course, not all of the nodes in the LOD cloud diagram are completely opened data. Opened data, located in the centers of the largest circles, include DBpedia and BNB (British National Bibliography). Unopened data such as DDC (Dewey Decimal Classification) are farther from the middle of the diagram, within smaller circles. Some have been partly opened because they only provide limited queries using SPARQL endpoints (Linked Data Community, 2011).

4.6.2. Library Linked Data Incubator Group: Use Cases

As presented in this document (W3C, 2011c) use cases are focused on the linked data in library community and clustered according to eight categories:

- Bibliographic data. These are use cases related to bibliographic records, for example, AGRIS (International Information System for the Agricultural Sciences and Technology) Linked Data or Open Library data.
- Authority data. These are use cases related to controlled access points for "work," "persons," or "corporate bodies," for example, a VIAF (Virtual International Authority File) or FAO Authority Description Concept Scheme.
- Vocabulary alignment. These are use cases related to vocabulary control, for example, AGROVOC Thesaurus or Bridging OWL and UML.
- Archives and heterogeneous data. These are use cases related to archival community or cultural institutions, for example, Europeana or Photo museum.
- Citations. These are use cases related to references for published or unpublished data, for example, SageCite or Bibliographica.
- Digital objects. These are use cases related to the identification of digital objects, for example, NDNP (National Digital Newspaper Program or NLL (National Library of Latvia) digitized map archive.

- Collections. These are use cases related to resources which need collection level description, for example, AuthorClaim or Nearest physical collection.
- Social and new uses. These are use cases related to social network information, for example, Crowdsourced Catalog (i.e. Librarything), or Open Library Data.

Among the library linked data, the bibliographic data clusters contain data related to bibliographic records, including the conversion process used to update previous bibliographic data to linked data standards. In the bibliographic records cluster, tagging to bibliographic records is included, and annotation to bibliographic records by end users is allowed. This process also allows the development of metadata standards for the integration of many bibliographic data from a number of resources. One valuable resource for linked data conversion and utilization is AGRIS, which has provided bibliographic references such as research papers, studies, and theses from many countries as well as huge volumes of metadata related to agricultural information searches. A link that connects Google searches with combined search terms extracted from AGRIS is currently available, as well. Expanding this connection to other information resources will enable more efficient service. Below is an AGRIS use scenario (W3C, 2010a):

- The AGRIS center of Kenya sends a batch of bibliographical records to AGRIS.
- AGRIS compares the data elements to AGRIS standard vocabularies such as AGROVOC, NAL, and UNBIS and normalizes the element semantics to AGRIS standard element sets.
- AGRIS compares and disambiguates the content of the elements against the FAO Authority Description Concept Scheme (journals, authors, and conferences).

Another heavily utilized set of data clusters, authority data clusters, expand search results using authority data and integrate various types of authority data. This method, which allows consistent identification of concepts, is based upon the features of authority data that can control numerous representations of same object. A major example is FAO (Food and Agriculture Organization of the United Nations) authority, which is related to AGRIS. First, the multilingual FAO Authority Description Concept Scheme expresses concepts to URIs and assigns the relationships among each concept. A representative FAO use case scenario, self-archiving related to institutional repository, appears below (W3C, 2010b):

- A user wants to deposit a paper in his institutional open access document repository. The document to be deposited is a journal article.

- From the data entry interface, the user accesses the FAO Authority Description Concept Scheme web service that provides a list of international journals in agriculture and related sciences.
- After the user selects a journal from the list, the system invokes the URI and the labels in numerous languages. The system can even integrate information from web services such as ISSN.
- The user has now described the journal in which his article appears with consistent data.

4.6.3. Linked Data for Bibliographic Records

Linked data for bibliographic records is built up through conversion from national bibliography into linked data or through collaboration on the social web. An example of national bibliography linked data is British National Bibliography (BNB); an example of bibliography linked data created by web users is Open Library (OL).

4.6.3.1. British National Bibliography linked data BNB was built by the British National Library with a target of 260,000 bibliographic records; it is composed of about 80 million triples. Along with bibliographic information, BNB includes abundant link information for related external sources such as VIAF, LCSH, GeoNames, and DDC. Raw data from BNB, which is divided into separate models for books and serials, can be downloaded through BNB websites; a SPARQL endpoint is also provided (British Library Metadata Services, 2012) (Figure 4.9).

Figure 4.10 presents an example of BNB linked data, specifically the bibliographic data of *American Guerrilla* by Roger Hilsman. The book is identified by a URI, http://bnb.data.bl.uk/id/resource/006893251. Its classification number, 940.548673092, a DDC class number, is connected with the linked data targeted as DDC 21. Subject headings (Guerrillas–Burma, Biography, etc.) are connected with LCSH linked data. Bibliographic Resource and Book correspond to DCMI Metadata Terms and OWL vocabulary, respectively. Creator information (Hilsman, Roger) is connected with VIAF as well as with a BNB authority record. BNB, VIAF, and 1574886916 are connected with the German national bibliographic number for the same book. In this manner, BNB has not only converted its bibliographic data into linked data but has also provided qualitative linked data that supplies abundant linked information with external schemes.

4.6.3.2. Open Library linked data Open Library (OL) linked data has been built through Internet Archive, a wiki project to which users can append bibliographic records. For users without an account, the writer's

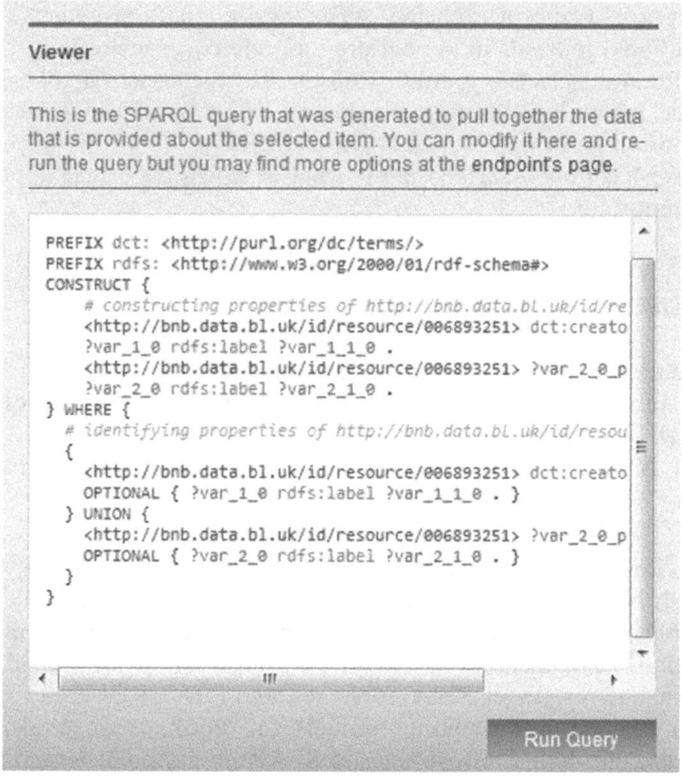

Figure 4.9: SPARQL endpoint for BNB linked data.

IP address is recorded (Internet Archive, 2012). Bibliographic data provided by OL follow the FRBR model to collect and present various editions of one work. Figure 4.11 shows an OL bibliographic record that clusters 82 editions of Edith Wharton's *The House of Mirth*. Users who click on the detailed bibliographic information for one edition can download the corresponding URI of both the bibliographic data and the RDF file.

4.6.4. Linked Data for Authority Records

4.6.4.1. VIAF linked data The Virtual International Authority File (VIAF) is a cluster of authority records built through the collaboration of many national libraries. VIAF provides not only basic types of authority files (e.g., personal name or corporate body) but also works and titles, all

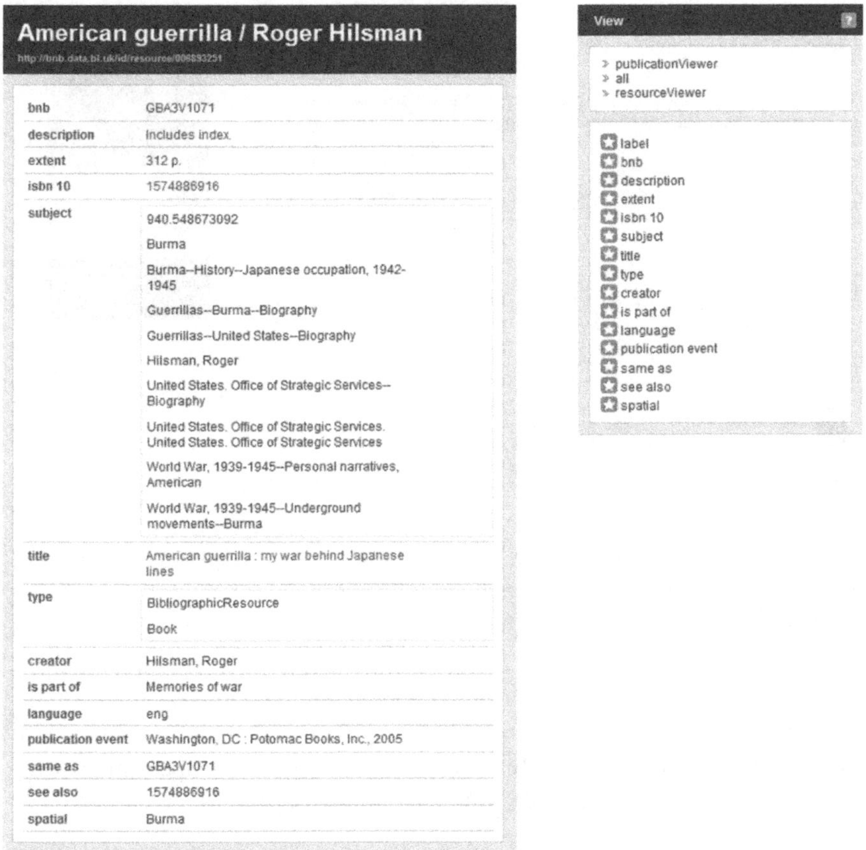

Figure 4.10: Bibliographic records example (user interface) from BNB Linked Data (http://bnb.data.bl.uk/doc/resource/006893251?_properties=creator.label).

expressed according to the FRBR model (Park, 2012, p. 239). Figure 4.12 shows part of a search result screen for *Harry Potter* books at VIAF.

For each entry, VIAF provides a permalink that corresponds to the URI (Figure 4.13). Using this information, an object (entity) can be uniquely identified and all information included in this data can be connected (Park, 2012, p. 239).

4.6.4.2. LC linked data service LC has built linked data for subject headings and name authority files and provides a search service as well (Library of Congress, 2012). Figure 4.14 shows a search result screen

Figure 4.11: Open Library bibliographic record (http://openlibrary.org/works/OL98587W/The_house_of_mirth).

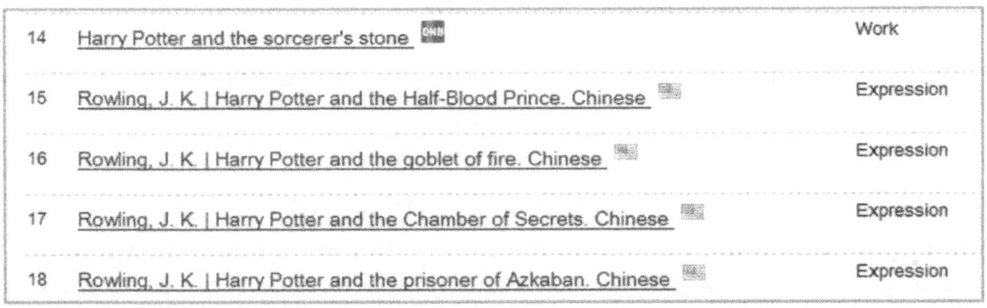

Figure 4.12: Example of a search result screen for "Harry Potter" at VIAF.

Figure 4.13: VIAF entity permalink.

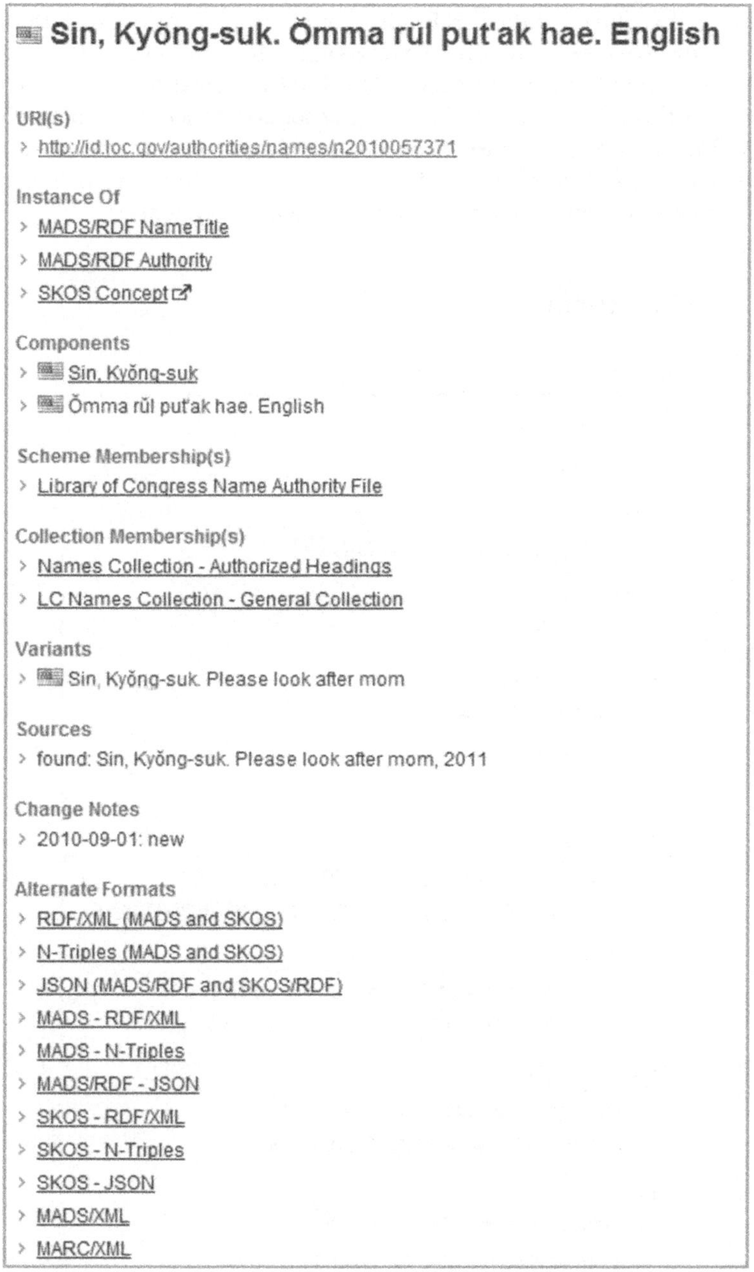

Sin, Kyŏng-suk. Ŏmma rŭl put'ak hae. English

URI(s)
> http://id.loc.gov/authorities/names/n2010057371

Instance Of
> MADS/RDF NameTitle
> MADS/RDF Authority
> SKOS Concept

Components
> Sin, Kyŏng-suk
> Ŏmma rŭl put'ak hae. English

Scheme Membership(s)
> Library of Congress Name Authority File

Collection Membership(s)
> Names Collection - Authorized Headings
> LC Names Collection - General Collection

Variants
> Sin, Kyŏng-suk. Please look after mom

Sources
> found: Sin, Kyŏng-suk. Please look after mom, 2011

Change Notes
> 2010-09-01: new

Alternate Formats
> RDF/XML (MADS and SKOS)
> N-Triples (MADS and SKOS)
> JSON (MADS/RDF and SKOS/RDF)
> MADS - RDF/XML
> MADS - N-Triples
> MADS/RDF - JSON
> SKOS - RDF/XML
> SKOS - N-Triples
> SKOS - JSON
> MADS/XML
> MARC/XML

Figure 4.14: LC linked data search result.

containing LC linked data for English bibliographic records of the novel *Please Look After Mom* by Sin, Kyong-suk, a Korean author (the title has been transliterated and romanized). The URI assigned to this entity is the channel for this information to link with other controlled vocabulary (VIAF or FAST). The book has also been described with semantic web standard form such as MADS/RDF (Metadata Authority Description Schema in RDF) or SKOS (Simple Knowledge Organization System).

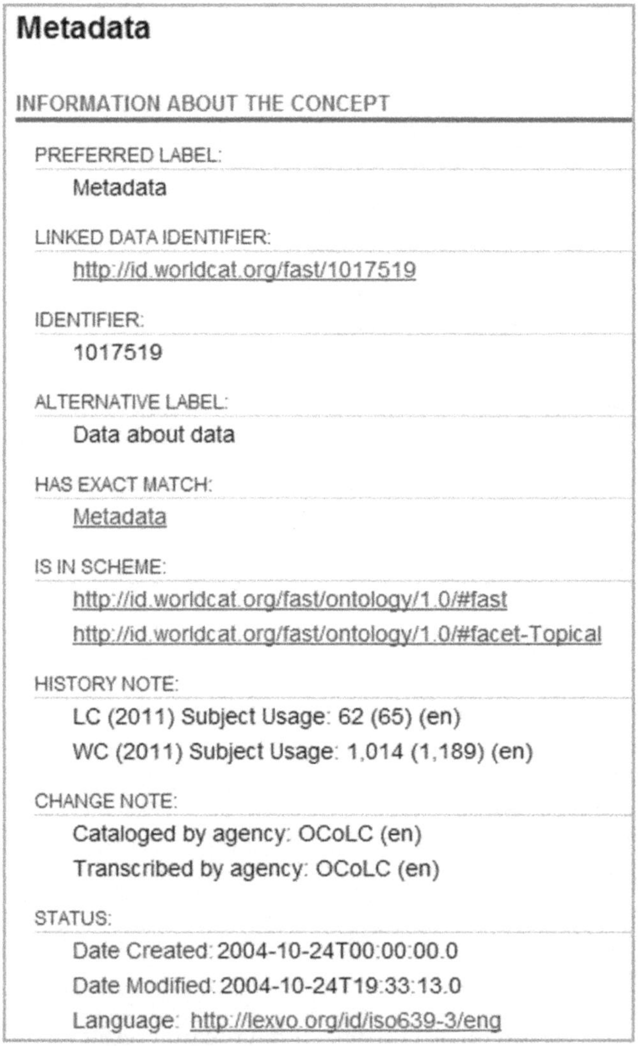

Figure 4.15: FAST linked data search result.

4.6.4.3. FAST linked data FAST (Faceted Application of Subject Terminology) is a simplified version of LCSH syntax, developed by the LC ALCTS subcommittee in 1998 to provide subject approach tools that can be used with Dublin Core metadata. Subjects from WorldCat Bibliographic Records were also included. One major feature of FAST is its ability to apply facets to LCSH. Broadly speaking, FAST can be divided into subject facets and form/genre facets. Subject facets include topic, place, time, event, person, corporate body, and title of work (Chan & O'Neill, 2010).

During the development of FAST, which involved OCLC, SKOS (Simple Knowledge Organization System) types were converted into linked data; the result is called FAST linked data. FAST is connected to LCSH and the links that are assigned are connected to the geographic database, GeoNames (OCLC, 2012). Figure 4.15 shows "information about the concept" part derived from the search result of "metadata" in FAST linked data. The result screen shows that identifiers of "metadata" are suggested as HTTP URI, which is shown in the linked data identifier. Because FAST targets the authority file, through "Alternative Label," variant forms that implies the same object also provided; through "has exact match," LCSH and related information are also provided. Because this information is LOD, it is a useful and efficient way to manage authority control of web data.

4.7. Conclusion

In this chapter we reviewed linked data, a newly developing way to share data through the web. To provide basic information about linked data, the basic concept and four governing rules were identified. Linked data projects that are well known to be part of LOD clouds were also introduced. General considerations for libraries that plan to utilize linked data were suggested. The final report of the W3C library linked data incubator group was specifically mentioned because of its comprehensive review of current trends within library linked data. Moreover, linked data currently developed in library field was introduced. Just like BNB linked data, there was vast linked data on the level of national bibliography, and also there was linked data which has potential for development such as Open Library linked data. Overall, linked data is still in its beginning stages, in numerous information communities as well as the library field. Therefore, in the current stage, we can't experience directly the possibilities that linked data possess. However, because of its huge potential, many issues must be resolved. We hope that the potential of linked data in the library field will be positively received in the future, and that applications of linked data to bibliographic data and authority data will increase and expand.

Acknowledgment

This research was financially supported by Hansung University.

References

Berners-Lee, T. (2009, June). *Linked data.* Retrieved from http://www.w3.org/DesignIssues/LinkedData.html

Bizer, C., Heath, T., & Berners-Lee, T. (2009). *Linked data — The story so far.* Retrieved from http://tomheath.com/papers/bizer-heath-berners-lee-ijswis-linked-data.pdf

British Library Metadata Services. (2012). *British National Bibliography (BNB) — Linked open data.* Retrieved from http://bnb.data.bl.uk

Byrne, G., & Goddard, L. (2010). The strongest link: Libraries and linked data. *D-Lib Magazine, 16*(11/12).

Chan, L. M., & O'Neill, E. T. (2010). *FAST: Faceted application of subject terminology: Principles and applications.* Santa Barbara, CA: Libraries Unlimited.

Cho, M., & Cho, M. (2012). *Bibleontology.* Retrieved from http://bibleontology.com/page/Abraham

Choi, S. (2011). *Korean Title [*Strategies for improvement of ISBN*].* Seoul: The National Library of Korea.

Cyganiak, R., & Jentzsch, A. (2011, September). *The linking open data cloud diagram.* Retrieved from http://richard.cyganiak.de/2007/10/lod/

Davis, I., & Newman, R. (2009, May). *Expression of core FRBR concepts in RDF.* Retrieved from http://vocab.org/frbr/core.html

DBpedia. (2012, August). Retrieved from http://dbpedia.org/ontology/Film

Heath, T., & Bizer, C. (2011). *Linked data: Evolving the web into a global data space.* San Rafael, CA: Morgan & Claypool.

Internet Archive. (2012). *The open library.* Retrieved from http://openlibrary.org/

Library of Congress. (2012). *LC linked data service: Authorities and vocabularies.* Retrieved from http://id.loc.gov/

Linked Data Community. (2011). *Linked data — Connect distributed data across the web.* Retrieved from http://linkeddata.org/

OCLC. (2012, July). *FAST linked data.* Retrieved from http://experimental.worldcat.org/fast/

Park, Z. (2012). Extending bibliographic information using linked data. *Journal of the Korean Society for Information Management, 29*(1), 231–251.

PILA. (2002). DOIs as linked data. *CrossRef.* Retrieved from http://www.crossref.org/

Singer, R. (2009). Linked library data now!. *Journal of Electronic Resources Librarianship, 21*(2), 114–126.

Stuart, D. (2011). *Facilitating access to the web of data: A guide for librarians.* London: Facet Publishing.

Summers, E. (2011, April). DOIs as linked data. *inkdroid web.* Retrieved from http://inkdroid.org/journal/2011/04/25/dois-as-linked-data/

W3C. (2008, January). *SPARQL Query Language for RDF*. Retrieved from http://www.w3.org/TR/rdf-sparql-query/

W3C. (2010a, October 19). *Use case AGRIS*. Retrieved from http://www.w3.org/2005/Incubator/lld/wiki/Use_Case_AGRIS

W3C. (2010b, October 15). *Use case FAO authority description concept scheme*. Retrieved from http://www.w3.org/2005/Incubator/lld/wiki/Use_Case_FAO_Authority_Description_Concept_Scheme

W3C Incubator Group. (2011a, October 25). *Library linked data incubator group: Datasets, value vocabularies, and metadata element sets*. Retrieved from http://www.w3.org/2005/Incubator/lld/XGR-lld-vocabdataset-20111025

W3C Incubator Group. (2011b, October 25). *Library linked data incubator group final report*. Retrieved from http://www.w3.org/2005/Incubator/lld/XGR-lld-20111025/

W3C Incubator Group. (2011c, October 25). *Library linked data incubator group: Use cases*. Retrieved from http://www.w3.org/2005/Incubator/lld/XGR-lld-use-case-20111025/

Wikipedia. (2011). *Linked data*. Retrieved from http://en.wikipedia.org/wiki/Linked_data

SECTION II: WEB 2.0. TECHNOLOGIES AND INFORMATION ORGANIZATION

Chapter 5

Social Cataloging; Social Cataloger

Shawne Miksa

Abstract

Purpose — This is an attempt to introduce proactive changes when creating and providing intellectual access in order to convince catalogers to become more social catalogers then they have ever been in the past.

Approach — Through a brief review and analysis of relevant literature a definition of social cataloging and social cataloger is given.

Findings — User contributed content to library catalogs affords informational professionals the opportunity to see directly the users' perceptions of the usefulness and about-ness of information resources. This is a form of social cataloging especially from the perspective of the information professional seeking to organize information to support knowledge discovery and access.

Implications — The user and the cataloger exercise their voice as to what the information resources are about, which in essence is interpreting the intentions of the creator of the resources, how the resource is related to other resources, and perhaps even how the resources can be, or have been, used. Depending on the type of library and information environment, the weight of the work may or may not fall equally on both user and cataloger.

Originality/value — New definitions of social cataloging and social cataloguing are offered and are linked back to Jesse Shera's idea of social epistemology.

New Directions in Information Organization
Library and Information Science, Volume 7, 91–106

ISSN: 1876-0562/doi:10.1108/S1876-0562(2013)0000007009

5.1. Introduction

Jesse Shera wrote in 1970 that "The librarian is at once historical, contemporary, and anticipatory" (p. 109). Our work takes us across many disciplines, time periods, and we have always sought to use best practices when working with an ever changing information landscape. Historically, cataloging librarians have sought to provide service through the careful construction of records representing the descriptive and subject features of information resources of all types so that people may find, identify, select, and obtain information. This is still a main objective but it is what we must anticipate that is the focus of this chapter. Shera believed a librarian could maximize his effectiveness and service to the public through an understanding of the cognitive processes of both the individual and society and in particular the influence knowledge can have on society. User information behavior studies are quite common in library and information sciences today and there is no question that studying the cognitive processes of users greatly informs our work. This is especially true in regards to how we organize information in library catalog systems although changes move slowly and not always with the greatest of ease or willingness on the part of catalogers. At times, it feels like the love of constructing records overshadows how we can make the records most useful for our clients.

In the past few years we have seen an increase in the amount of user-contributed content in our catalog systems in the form of social tags and user commentary funneled directly into the catalog records. This new content affords us the opportunity to see directly the users' perceptions of the usefulness and about-ness of information resources. From the perspective of the information professional seeking to organize information to support knowledge discovery and access we can call this a form of social cataloging. Social cataloging is defined in this chapter as the joint effort by users and catalogers to interweave individually or socially preferred access points in a library information system as a mode of discovery and access to the information resources held in the library's collection. Both the user and the cataloger exercise their voice as to what the information resources are about, which in essence is interpreting the intentions of the creator of the resources, how the resource is related to other resources, and perhaps even how the resources can be, or have been, used. Depending on the type of library and information environment, the weight of the work may or may not fall equally on both user and cataloger.

This new aspect of cataloging does present a bit of a conundrum. Social tagging systems, folksonomies, Web 2.0, and the like, have placed many information professionals in the position of having to counteract, and even contradict their training when it comes to descriptive and subject cataloging. This is especially true for subject analysis and subject representation in library information systems. It is the success and popularity of websites such as LibraryThing, which practices its own form of social cataloging, that bring this shift into focus. Some portion of that success undoubtedly comes from the negative experiences that people have had when using library catalogs. People may think the records are poor, the search capabilities of the system are limited, call numbers are indecipherable, etc. However, it is a practice rooted in the very fundamental idea that the library collection needs an interface — the library catalog — and that librarians are the intermediaries between the catalog and the users, and especially between the tools used to search the catalog. It is a practice that is steadily being challenged by modern practices such as social tagging and the evolution of information organization standards and information retrieval systems. Thus, a proactive change to that practice is a logical action to take.

Library catalogs are the communication devices that allow for this knowledge discovery and sharing to take place. Catalogers construct the representations of the graphic records of societies — the social transcript — and users search these representations in order to find something to satisfy their information needs. There is also some pride, and perhaps a sizeable chunk of romantic idealism, about a library. Cataloging, for many of us, is an extension of this romantic ideal. For example, take Mann's (1943) description from nearly 70 years ago:

> The cataloger … must dip into volume after volume, passing from one author to another and from one subject to another, making contacts with all minds of the world's history and entering into the society of mental superiors and inferiors. Catalogers find their work a realm as large as the universe. (p. 1)

Furthermore, she wrote that the cataloger should " … adopt a neutral stance between the reader and his books, giving emphasis to what the author intended to describe rather than to his own views" (Mann, 1943, p. 2). However, the neutral stance is now taking a bit of a hit. In my experience, some people dislike library catalogs because they dislike other people having control over how things are organized and the knowledge structures used to convey that organization. (As if saying "It is *my* collection, and I want *my* organizational scheme.") In that case, they may create their own catalog, as in LibraryThing.

Mann's words, though, still carry some legitimacy because they illustrate the fundamental job that library catalogers should do — to enable the user to find what they need by taking the information resources in hand and interpreting and representing the content so that it is useable by both the information system and the user. Now we have even better technology, allowing for a much broader spectrum of knowledge production and sharing and with this better technology we need updated practices.

Social cataloging can help us to further incorporate that broader spectrum by interweaving other interpretations of information resources within our own systems, especially as it concerns how resources should be organized and used. It is the library catalog as a communication system, with the cataloger in the position of having to capture and represent many interpretations of resources, not just of the author-creator, but of the users as well. Forty years ago, Shera wrote

> The communication process is a duality of system and message, of that which is transmitted as well as the manner of its transmission. Therefore, the librarian must see his role in the communication process as being more than a link in a chain; he must also concern himself with the knowledge he communicates, and the importance of that knowledge both to the individual and the society. (Shera, 1972, p. 110)

How then do we continue and maintain this communication process? As a potential new direction in information organization, an argument for social cataloging and social catalogers is presented here. This chapter starts with a discussion on the nature of social tagging and the intersection of the uncontrolled access points with controlled access points created through subject analysis. A summary of the characteristics of social tagging studies from 2006 to 2012 follows as a way to understand how and why social tags are created and used. It will conclude by presenting the argument that social epistemology, as defined by Shera, is the conceptual framework upon which this new practice of social cataloging should rest.

5.2. Background

It is not a question of if or when user-generated content will show up in library catalogs. The drip-drip-drip of user tags trickling down into library catalogs has been getting louder and faster in the last few years. Social tags are already being incorporated into various library information systems either directly or indirectly (e.g., LibraryThing's widget for importing tags into a catalog record, or catalogs that allows user to add tags and comments or ratings). It is hoped by many that including these tags would serve to enhance the effectiveness and value of systems to the spectrum of users. Spiteri (2012) effectively argues for the extension of the principle of user convenience in social discovery systems in support of cultural warrant.[1]

> User assigned tags and reviews can help members of the library community connect with one another via shared interests and connections that may not be otherwise possible via the catalogue record that is created and controlled solely by the cataloguer. Social discovery systems can thus provide cataloguers with a way to interact, if indirectly, with users, since cataloger's can observe user-created metadata. (p. 212)

Abbas (2010) contends that " … the folksonomies that are developed as a result of the tagging activities of its users, represent a potential means to supplement knowledge organization systems" (p. 176). Abbas also feels that because the phenomena are so recent there is still much to learn about potential uses.

Since the early 2000s there has been a substantial amount of research conducted on user contributed data such as tags and folksonomies. Many of the studies compare tagging and folksonomies to controlled vocabularies and classification systems respectively, as well the pros and cons of incorporating social tagging into information systems, especially library catalogs. I found these studies raised even more questions and issues in my mind: How will the potential of social tagging best be harnessed? How will social tagging and vocabulary control interact? How does the concept and practice of authority control butt up against its complete opposite? Furthermore, how can we deliberately lose control over a time-honored process of authority control? What is the overall effect of social tags on the catalog and how does it affect the cataloger's work? Does it aid in subject cataloging and in particular subject analysis? How does it affect the catalog user?

In order to explore any of these questions it is necessary to suspend use of the word "control" in terms of how the control is currently practiced in cataloging. Catalogers are trained to be objective when analyzing and assigning controlled terms to information resource records. This is also true when they perform the complicated process of governing the choice and form of subject terms and personal and corporate names. This practice is quite the opposite of the personal nature of social tagging. Most catalogers' have been educated quite differently. We are trained to apply Haykin's

---

1. As defined by Beghtol (2005): "Cultural warrant means that the personal and professional cultures of information seekers and information workers warrant the establishment of appropriate fields, terms, categories, or classes in a knowledge representation and organization system. Thus, cultural warrant provides the rationale and authority for decisions about what concepts and what relationships among them are appropriate for a particular system" (p. 904).

(1951) fundamental concept of "reader as the focus" (specifically he writes "the reader is the focus in all cataloging principles and practice") (p. 7) and adhere to Cutter's (1904) objectives of the catalog, and the subsequent interpretations of those objectives. The cataloger's own personal view is to be suspended in favor of reaching as broad an audience as possible, to allow the user to find what they need. Let the reader have her say; let the reader have a voice.

The introduction of the Internet and the Web to our professional world has leveled the field in such a way that the librarian is not the sole voice, but simply one among the many. How does this happen? If we place social tagging within the process of subject analysis and subject representation then might we simply equate social tagging to the brainstorming of an indexer or classifier during the initial stages of the subject analysis process? (cf. Tennis, 2006; Voss, 2007). Subject analysis and subject representation has been the standard in cataloging for most of the 20th century and into the 21st. As is currently practiced, the subject analytical process starts with examining a resource for keywords or phrases that represent the intellectual content. These terms are then translated into the language used in a controlled vocabulary. If this process can be aided by social tags, then how do we best take advantage of them? Alternatively, could we say that social tags are another species of indexing language in and of itself? Are the users doing our job for us and, if so, how well are they doing it?

Furthermore, how can information professionals formally trained to catalog curtail the control of assigning "sanctioned" terms? It is an interesting situation. It doesn't necessarily mean relinquishing all control, just a part of it. At the same time we can justly ask if the popularity of social tagging comes simply from the need or desire for simplicity of words and phrases interpretation or ease of use/least effort, or perhaps even as result of lack of understanding of how a catalog record is created and organized? Is it born out of frustration of trying to understand and navigate an information system's subject search mechanism, or can we assume it is simply a desire of the user to gloss over the details in favor of rapid scanning of keywords as a quicker end to the angst of an information need? Or, is it just a need to have an opinion? Is tagging a narcissistic act or an act of sharing knowledge? These are just question that I have found myself asking and that I feel are worthy of pursuing.

A good many studies over the years, some of which will be discussed here, have focused on tags as a mechanism for sharing knowledge. For example, as stated above subject analysis involves identifying underlying concepts within a resource in the hopes of bringing together information resources of a similar subject matter, in addition to providing subject access for the user. How do these particular goals figure into the popularity of an individual, untrained user assigning their own terms to the resource (i.e., is this her goal?) We are not all the same; we all have different reasons for wanting to find information and will most likely use it in different ways.

In many ways, we catalogers have clung too closely to our practices, which has consequences. Cutter (1904) wrote

> … strict consistency in a rule and uniformity in its application sometimes lead to practices which clash with the public's habitual way of looking at things. When these habits are general and deeply rooted, it is unwise for the cataloger to ignore them, even if they demand a sacrifice of system and simplicity. (p. 6)

A rethinking of the purpose and scope of cataloging, and in particular subject cataloging, is in order because the public's way of looking at things has changed greatly, at least in this country and at this time, and especially as it relates to the social nature of the current information environment.

5.3. Review of Literature/Studies of User-Contributed Contents 2006–2012

The bulk of studies of folksonomies and social tagging and the effects on traditional information organization practices started to gain momentum around 2006. Pre-2006 studies were broader and tended to focus on bookmarking or what was then simply called user-generated or user-created content or classifications within information systems. For example, Beghtol's (2003) article on naïve or user-based classification systems is quite illuminating. The idea of user-generated content is not entirely new to the library and information science field. Since the mid-1990s there have been collaborative and socially oriented website available on the Web, most having started in the early 2000s (Abbas, 2010). Trant (2009) offers a comprehensive review of studies and their methodologies, mainly published between 2005 and 2007, in which she outlines three broad approaches: *folksonomy* itself (and the role of user tags in indexing and retrieval); *tagging* (and the behavior of users); and the nature of *social tagging systems* (as socio-technical frameworks) (pp. 1–2). What follows is an overview of some of the literature relevant to this discussion of social cataloging.

5.3.1. Phenomenon of Social Tagging and What to Call It

Research specifically using terms such as "social tags" or "tagging" start around 2006 although tagging started showing up on websites earlier in the decade. Many of the studies look at the phenomenon alone, either from system perspective or the user's and cataloger's perspective. Comparatively, the study of social tags and tagging is similar to how the cataloging community reacted to "websites" in the mid- to late-1990s. The first instinct is to ask "What is it?" and then study the attributes, dissecting it — like a frog in biology class — in order to identify how best to define it, to compare it to the type, or species, of information resources that were already known and then follow with studying how it is used by people and systems either together or separately. As with all new phenomena, after identification there is discussion of what to call it (i.e., "folksonomies," social tagging, tags, etc.). Golder and Huberman (2006) wrote "a collaborative form … which has been given the name 'tagging' by its proponents, is gaining popularity on the Web" (p. 198). It is a practice "allowing anyone — especially consumers — to freely attach keywords or tags to content" (p. 198). Golder and Huberman go on to outline the types of tags they had found and to note the patterns of usage that tags are used for personal use rather than for all. Sen et al. (2006) point out that tagging vocabulary "emerge organically from the tags chosen by individual members" (p. 181). They suggest it may be "desirable to 'steer' a user community toward certain types of tags that are beneficial for the system or its users in some way" (p. 190).

As noted earlier, a common approach was to compare folksonomies, collaborative tagging, social classification, and social indexing to traditional classification and indexing practices. Voss (2007) stated that "Tagging is referred to with several names … the basic principle is that end users do subject indexing instead of experts only, and the assigned tags are being shown immediately on the Web" (p. 2). Tennis (2006) defined social tagging as " … a manifestation of indexing based in the open — yet very personal — Web" (p. 1). His comparison of indexing to social tagging showed that indexing is in an "incipient and under-nourished state" (p. 14). This comparison with a traditional subject cataloging process is characteristic of the studies following those that ask what is social tagging.

5.3.2. A Good Practice?

Questions arise as to whether or not the new practice is a good practice, if it is accurate, more efficient, etc. Spiteri (2007) concluded that weaknesses of folksonomy tags included " … potential for ambiguity, polysemy, synonymy, and basic level variation as well as the lack of consistent guidelines for choice and form" (p. 23). Other studies explored the possible uses of tagging and the possibility of replacing current practices, such as assigning subject headings. Yi and Chan (2008) sought to use LCSH to alleviate the "ambiguity and complexity caused by uncontrolled user-selected tags (folksonomy)" (p. 874). They concluded that "matching user-produced, uncontrolled vocabularies and controlled vocabularies holds great potential: collaborative or social tagging and professional indexing on the bases of controlled vocabularies such as LCSH can be thought of as two opposite indexing practices'' (p. 897). Similarly, Rolla (2009) found that ''a comparison of LibraryThing's user tags and LCSH suggest that while user tags can enhance subject access to library collections, they cannot replace the valuable functions of controlled vocabulary like LCSH'' (p. 182). On the other hand, Peterson (2008) felt that blending ''Web 2.0 features into library databases may not be correct'' (p. 4).

5.3.3. Systems Reconfigurations

Next, forays into reconfiguring information systems to take advantage of the interoperability of tags and controlled vocabulary come about, as well as studies looking at the general measuring and evaluation of the meaning of social tags and the usefulness of social tagging systems (cf. Lawson, 2009; Shiri, 2009). Shiri (2009), for example, categorized the features of social tagging system interfaces and found ''an increased level of personal and collaborative interaction that influences the way people create, organize, share, tag and use resources on these sites'' (p. 917). The increased collaboration detail has potential implications for catalog system interface redesign, and even further, enhancing catalog records to ensure more collaborative advantages for knowledge discovery. Lawson (2009) concluded that '' … there is enough objective tagging available on bibliographic-related websites such as Amazon and LibraryThing that librarians can use to provide enriched bibliographic records'' (p. 580). Lawson feels adding tags to the system allows for new services and support for users.

5.3.4. Cognitive Aspects and Information Behavior

Currently, the research is focused on both the cognitive aspects and information behavior of users when using tags and/or subject headings for information retrieval as well as user motivations for using tags for retrieval or description (cf. Kipp & Campbell, 2010; McFadden & Weidenbenner, 2010) and more technical aspects such as semantic imitation, or semantically similar tags (Fu, Kannampallil, Kang, & He, 2010), and leveraging, or increasing user motivation to contribute tags (Spiteri, 2011). McFadden and Weidenbenner (2010) point out that

> … many libraries are beginning to see tagging as a viable means of harnessing the wisdom of crowds (i.e., users) to shed light on popular topics and resources and involve users in collaborative, socially networked ways of organizing and retrieving resources. (p. 57)

Additionally, the authors note that tagging is "user-empowering" and will attract users back to the library catalog (p. 58). People have long felt at the mercy of the catalog, or out of sync with it.

There are also dimensions to social tags that provide food for thought when it comes to information behavior of the user. Two papers stand out in particular. First, Kipp and Campbell's (2010) study of people searching a social bookmarking tool that specialized in academic articles found that while the participants used the tags in their search process, they also used controlled vocabularies to locate useful search terms and links to select resources by relevance.

> This study examined the relationship between user tags and the process of resource discovery from the perspective of a traditional library reference interview in which the system was used, not by an end user, but by an information intermediary who try to find information on another's behalf. (p. 252)

A fact of particular note is that tags reveal relationships that are not represented in traditional controlled vocabularies (e.g., tags that are task-related or the name of the tagger). The authors write that the "inclusion of subjective and social information from the taggers is very different from the traditional objectivity of indexing and was reported as an asset by a number of participants" (Kipp & Campbell, 2010, p. 239). In terms of information behavior the study revealed that while participants had preferences for reducing an initial list of returns, or hits (e.g., adding terms, quick assessments, modify search based on results, scanning) they were willing to change their search behavior slightly based on number of results. There was evidence of uncertainty, frustration, pausing for longer periods of time, hovering, scrolling up and down, confused by differences between controlled vocabularies and tags. They state "It was fairly common for participants to use incorrect terminology to identify their use of terms when searching" (p. 249). For example, users may not see clicking on a subject hyperlink the same as searching using a subject term.

The second study of note is one based on theories of cognitive science. Fu et al. (2010) ran "a controlled experiment in which they directly manipulated information goals and the availability of socials tags to study their effects of social tagging behavior" (p. 12:4) in order to understand if the semantics of the tags plays a critical role in tagging behavior. The study involved two groups of users, those who could and those that could not see tags created by others when using a social tagging system. In brief, the researchers confirmed the validity of their proposed model. They found that "social tags evoke a spontaneous tag-based topic inference process that primes the semantic interpretation of resource contents during exploratory search, and the semantic priming of existing tags in turn influences future tag choices" (p. 12:1). In other words, users tend to create similar tags when they can see the tags that have already been created, and users who are given no previously created tags tend to create more diverse tags that are not necessarily semantically similar. This is particularly interesting when considering the practice of copy cataloging versus original cataloging and the number, quality, and depth of assigned subject headings depending on what type of record creation is taking place.[2]

Spiteri (2011) found that user contributions to library catalogs were limited when compared to other social sites where social tagging is prevalent and that it is lack of motivation that causes this limitation. She posits that perhaps it is peoples' outdated notions of the library catalog and catalogers that stands in the way and that research into user motivations is needed in order for librarians to make informed decisions about adding social applications to the catalog.

5.3.5. Quality

Just as there have been questions as to the quality and usefulness of social tagging there have also been questions of the quality of cataloging practices when compared to user-contributed content. For example, Heymann and Garcia-Molina (2009) question subject heading assignment by experts and report that " … many (about 50 percent) of the keywords in the controlled vocabulary are in the uncontrolled vocabulary, especially more annotated keywords" (p. 4). They suggest that when there is a disagreement then deferring to the user is the best course of action and that perhaps the experts have "picked the right keywords, but perhaps annotated them to the wrong books (from the users' perspectives)" (p. 1). This may be difficult for many catalogers to even come around to, even agree with. As pointed out earlier, catalogers are trained to be objective when analyzing and assigning controlled terms to resources, which is exactly the opposite of how social tagging is used. The reader applies words and phrases that result out of their personal interaction and interpretation of a resource, and not necessarily with the broader audience in mind. The latter of which is exactly how most catalogers' have been educated. Steele (2009), points out many of the same weaknesses of social tagging as Spiteri (2007), in that there is a lack of hierarchy, no guarantee of coverage, synonymy, polysemy (more than one meaning), user's intent, etc., but nonetheless contends that "one of the most

---

2. Šauperl's (2002) study of subject determination during the cataloging process touches on a similar issue and is highly recommended.

important reasons libraries should consider the use of tags is the benefits of evolution and growth ... patrons are changing and are expecting to be able to participate and interact online" (p. 70). More importantly, Steele asks if that if tagging is here to stay will patrons be willing to keep it up or if it is all "just a fad" (p. 71).[3] There is also the risk of "spagging," or spam tagging, coming from users with unsuitable intentions (Arch, 2007, p. 81).

This review of relevant literature pertaining to social tagging and library catalogs from 2006 to 2012 is selective and certainly not comprehensive. Reading Trant's (2009) study, as well as the relevant chapter in Abbas' (2010) book is suggested for a more thorough overview of the literature and history, as well as any subsequent literature reviews that are not addressed here. It serves mainly to provide an understanding of the current social information environment as viewed from the perspective of information organization in library catalogs.

5.4. Social Cataloging; Social Cataloger

In this chapter I am defining social cataloging and social cataloger based on the emerging trends in practice that I have observed. Social cataloging, as previously stated in the introduction, is the joint effort by users and catalogers to interweave individually or socially preferred access points, which can be both subject-based and task-based, with traditional controlled vocabularies in a library information system for the purpose of highly relevant resource discovery as well as user-empowerment. Both the user and the cataloger exercise their voice as to how information resources are related within the system.

A social cataloger is an information professional/librarian who is skilled in both expert-based and user-created vocabularies, who understands the motivations of users who tag information resources and how to incorporate this knowledge into an information system for subject representation and access.

Of course, these definitions may be too pat and not at all broad or deep enough. They also suppose that the cataloger and the user both understand and can perform subject analysis fairly well. Agreeing on the "about-ness" of any information resource is fraught with difficulties. Wilson (1968) wrote in a chapter entitled "Subject and a Sense of Position" that

3. An interesting piece of data: In April 2012, I asked a librarian at a public library that uses a catalog system from BiblioCommons how many tags have been added to their records — in the last 12 months around 3000 tags had been assigned, but almost 100,000 ratings had been completed. Perhaps giving an opinion is much more interesting than assigning keywords.

> … a single reader, trying by different means to arrive at a precise statement of the subject of a writing, might find himself with not one but three or four different statements. And if several readers tried the several methods, we should not be surprised if the same method gave different results when used by different people. Estimates of dominance, hypotheses about intentions, ways of grouping the items mentioned, notions of unity, all of these are too clearly matters on which equally sensible and perspicacious men will disagree. And if they do disagree, who is to decide among them? (p. 89)

This harkens back to an issue about control of subject headings and subject representation within a library catalog, and the idea of letting go of some of that control. Catalogers, and probably users too, tend to work in a state of uncertainty. This is not to say the point of exercising any type of control is useless, but rather there is most likely no one right answer.[4] At best we can lay out as many options as seem sensible when it comes to organizing information for knowledge discovery and access in uncertain information environments.

5.5. Social Epistemology and Social Cataloging

There is a possibility for a good foundation in which to lay social cataloging if we look at it through the lens of *social epistemology* as proposed by Jesse Shera. Shera (1972) wrote that

> The new discipline that is envisaged here (and for which, for want of a better name, Margaret Egan originated the phrase, *social epistemology*) should provide a framework for the investigation of the complex problem of the nature of the intellectual process in society — a study of the ways in which society as a whole achieves a perceptive relation to its total environment. (p. 112)

He spoke of the "social fabric" and the production, flow, integration, and consumption of thought throughout that fabric. I would not assume that social information activities on the Internet and Web constitute the whole of the social fabric, but it is certainly a large part of it in this day and age, especially when it comes to the great value that we put on being able to discover, access, and share information. Shera believed there existed an "important affinity" between librarianship and social epistemology and that librarians (read "information professionals") should have a solid mastery over "the means of access to recorded knowledge" (p. 113). Forty years later this is, I believe, still solidly true. Of course, I am taking some interpretive

4. Charles Cutter perhaps says it best — "… the importance of deciding aright where any given subject shall be entered in is inverse proportion to the difficulty of decision" (1904, p. 66).

license when it comes to Shera's vision of social epistemology but when he wrote that "the value system of a culture exerts a strong influence upon the communication of knowledge within a society and the ways in which that society utilizes knowledge" (p. 131) it seems logical to apply it to the cataloger's current need to shift focus and priorities when it comes to supporting that utilization.

Many of the studies mentioned earlier present conclusions that provide evidence for using social epistemology as a framework for social cataloging, and I feel that many of these can be attributed to user motivation. Spiteri (2007) urges librarians to provide better motivation so that users will contribute content to library catalogs as much as they do social applications such as LibraryThing and Amazon's encouraging user comments and ratings. This doesn't mean we have to commercialize library catalogs but rather we can provide more and better access to the library collection as well as more communication between the users of the catalog. Fallis (2006) wrote that "social institutions such as schools and libraries need to be aware of how social and cultural factors affect people's abilities to acquire knowledge" (p. 484). Tagging is a social process and the tags themselves are evidence of knowledge acquisition and sharing.

We need to attempt to address some of these broader ideas in the hopes of outlining a clearer process for the cataloger to follow when creating and providing intellectual access. Ultimately, I think it will convince catalogers to become more *social* catalogers then they have ever been in the past.

References

Abbas, J. (2010). *Structures for organizing knowledge: Exploring taxonomies, ontologies, and other schema*. New York, NY: Neal Schuman.

Arch, X. (2007, February). Creating the academic library folksonomy: Putting social tagging to work at your institution. *College & Research Library News*, *68*(2), 80–81.

Beghtol, C. (2003). Classification for information retrieval and classification for knowledge discovery: Relationships between "professional" and "naïve" classifications. *Knowledge Organization*, *30*, 64–73.

Beghtol, C. (2005). Ethical decision-making for knowledge representation and organization systems for global use. *Journal of the American Society for Information Science & Technology*, *56*(9), 903–912.

Cutter, C. A. (1904). *Rules for a dictionary catalog*. Washington, DC: Government Printing Office.

Fallis, D. (2006). Social epistemology and information science. In B. Cronin (Ed.), *Annual review of information science and technology* (Vol. 40, pp. 475–519). Medford, NJ: Information Today.

Fu, W., Kannampallil, T., Kang, R., & He, J. (2010). Semantic imitation in social tagging. *ACM Transactions on Computer-Human Interaction*, *17*(3), 12:3–12:37.

Golder, S. A., & Huberman, B. A. (2006). Usage patterns of collaborative tagging systems. *Journal of Information Science*, *32*(2), 198–208.

Haykin, D. J. (1951). *Subject headings, a practical guide*. Washington, DC: Government Printing Office.

Heymann, P. & Garcia-Molina, H. (2009). Contrasting controlled vocabulary and tagging: Do experts choose the right names to label the wrong things? In R. A. Baeza-Yates, P. Boldi, B. Ribeiro-Neto & B. B. Cambazoglu (Eds.), *Proceedings of the second international conference on web search and web data mining* (*WSDM'09*), Barcelona, Spain. (ACM, New York, NY). Retrieved from http://ilpubs.stanford.edu:8090/955/1/cvuv-lbrp.pdf

Kipp, M. E. I., & Campbell, D. G. (2010). Searching with tags: Do tags help users find things? *Knowledge Organization*, *37*(4), 239–255.

Lawson, K. G. (2009). Mining social tagging data for enhanced subject access for readers and researchers. *Journal of Academic Librarianship*, *35*(6), 574–582.

Mann, M. (1943). *Introduction to cataloging and the classification of books* (2nd ed.). Chicago, IL: American Library Association.

McFadden, S., & Weidenbenner, J. V. (2010). Collaborative tagging: Traditional cataloging meets the "Wisdom of Crowds". *Serials Librarian*, *58*(1–4), 55–60.

Peterson, E. (2008). Parallel systems: The coexistence of subject cataloging and folksonomy. *Library Philosophy & Practice*, *10*(1), 1–5.

Rolla, P. (2009). User tags versus subject headings: Can user-supplied data improve subject access to library collections? *Library Resources & Technical Services*, *53*(3), 174–184.

Šauperl, A. (2002). *Subject determination during the cataloguing process*. London: Scarecrow Press.

Sen, S., Lam, S. K., Rashid, A. M., Cosley, D., Frankowski, D., Osterhouse, J., … Riedl, J. (2006). Tagging, communities, vocabulary, evolution. *Proceedings of the ACM 2006 conference on CSCW*, Banff, Alberta, Canada (pp. 181–190). Retrieved from http://www.shilad.com/papers/tagging_cscw2006.pdf

Shera, J. H. (1970). *Sociological foundations of librarianship*. Mumbai: Asia Publishing House.

Shera, J. H. (1972). *The foundations of education for librarianship*. New York, NY: Becker and Hayes.

Shiri, A. (2009). An examination of social tagging interface features and functionalities: An analytical comparison. *Online Information Review*, *33*(5), 901–919.

Spiteri, L. (2007). The structure and form of folksonomy tags: The road to the public library catalog. *Information Technology & Libraries*, *26*(3), 13–25.

Spiteri, L. F. (2011). Using social discovery systems to leverage user-generated metadata. *Bulletin of the American Society for Information Science & Technology*, *37*(4), 27–29.

Spiteri, L. (2012). Social discovery tools: Extending the principle of user convenience. *Journal of Documentation*, *68*(2), 206–217.

Steele, T. (2009). The new cooperative cataloging. *Library Hi Tech*, *27*(1), 68–77.

Tennis, J. (2006). Social tagging and the next steps for indexing. In J. Furner & J. T. Tennis (Eds.), *Advances in classification research, Vol. 17: Proceedings of the 17th ASIS&T SIG/CR classification research workshop*, Austin, TX, November 4 (pp. 1–10). Retrieved from http://journals.lib.washington.edu/index.php/acro/article/view/12493/10992

Trant, J. (2009). Studying social tagging and folksonomy: A review and framework. *Journal of Digital Information North America*, *10*(1). Retrieved from http://journals.tdl.org/jodi/article/view/269

Voss, J. (2007). Tagging, folksonomy, & company — Renaissance of manual indexing? *Proceedings of the international symposium of information science* (pp. 234–254). Retrieved from http://arxiv.org/abs/cs/0701072v2

Wilson, P. (1968). *Two kinds of power; An essay on bibliographical control*. Berkeley, CA: University of California Press.

Yi, K., & Chan, L. M. (2008). Linking folksonomy to Library of Congress subject headings: An exploratory study. *Journal of Documentation*, *65*(6), 872–900.

Chapter 6

Social Indexing: A Solution to the Challenges of Current Information Organization

Yunseon Choi

Abstract

Purpose — This chapter aims to discuss the issues associated with social indexing as a solution to the challenges of current information organization systems by investigating the quality and efficacy of social indexing.

Design/methodology/approach — The chapter focuses on the study which compared indexing similarity between two professional groups and also compared social tagging and professional indexing. The study employed the method of the modified vector-based Indexing Consistency Density (ICD) with three different similarity measures: cosine similarity, dot product similarity, and Euclidean distance metric.

Findings — The investigation of social indexing in comparison of professional indexing demonstrates that social tags are more accurate descriptions of resources and reflection of more current terminology than controlled vocabulary. Through the characteristics of social tagging discussed in this chapter, we have a clearer understanding of the extent to which social indexing can be used to replace and improve upon professional indexing.

New Directions in Information Organization
Library and Information Science, Volume 7, 107–135

ISSN: 1876-0562/doi:10.1108/S1876-0562(2013)0000007010

Research limitations/implications — As investment in professionally developed web directories diminishes, it becomes even more critical to understand the characteristics of social tagging and to obtain benefit from it. In future research, the examination of subjective tags needs to be conducted. A survey or user study on tagging behavior also would help to extend understanding of social indexing practices.

6.1. Introduction

Libraries have a long history in organizing and providing access to resources. As networked information resources on the web continue to grow rapidly, today's digital library environments have led librarians and information professionals to index and manage digital resources on the web. Thus, this trend has required new tools for organizing and providing more effective access to the web. Subject gateways and web directories are such tools for Internet resource discovery. Yet, studies have shown that such tools based on traditional organization schemes are not sufficient for the web. Problems with current information organization systems for web resources via gateways and directories are: (1) they were developed using traditional library schemes for subject access based on controlled vocabulary and (2) web documents were organized and indexed by professional indexers. Although there have been efforts to involve users in developing information organization systems, they are not necessarily based on users' real languages. Accordingly, social tagging has received significant attention since it helps organize contents by collaborative and user-generated tags. Users' tags reflect their real languages because they allow users to add their own tags based on their interests. Several researchers have discussed the impact of tagging on retrieval performance on the web, but further discussion is needed to investigate the usefulness of social tagging in subject indexing and to determine its accuracy and quality. The main objective of this chapter is to study the issues associated with social indexing as a solution to the challenges of current information organization systems by investigating the quality and efficacy of social indexing. The following research questions are central to this topic:

- How consistent is professional indexing between two professionally indexed subject gateways? Are there various or alternative interpretations of the same web document between two groups of professionals?
- How consistent is tagging/indexing between Delicious taggers and Intute professionals?

Section 6.2 provides the key definitions of subject gateways and their general background as tools for organizing the Web in order to address how professionally indexed web directories are characterized. The following sections present the details of BUBL and Intute which are the main subject gateways of this research for a comparison with a social tagging site. Section 6.2.3 discusses advantages with controlled vocabulary which has been traditionally used for subject indexing, and points out challenges of controlled vocabulary for the web with the intention to emphasize the need for social tagging data as natural language terms.

Section 6.3 discusses several points related to the issue of social tagging since it is a core concept of this chapter. Section 6.3.1 provides the definitions of the terms social tagging and folksonomy with the aim to provide a good understanding of the concepts. Section 6.3.2 describes an exemplary social tagging site such as Delicious. Section 6.3.3 discusses the combination of controlled vocabulary and uncontrolled vocabulary. Section 6.3.4 illustrates social tagging in subject indexing in order to provide appropriate context for the subsequent discussion of related research which investigates tagging as a more accurate description of resources and reflection of more current terminology than controlled vocabulary.

Section 6.3.5 briefly summarizes criticisms of folksonomy which should not be ignored. Finally, Section 6.4 provides the conclusions of this chapter and also serves to identify future research directions.

6.2. Information Organization on the Web

Effective searching and navigation of web resources is at the forefront of issues related to the area of information organization. As networked information resources on the web continue to grow rapidly, the need for effective access to better organized information has received a lot of attention. Morville (2005) points out that findability is the most important issue in an information overload environment. Given the growing number of web resources, tools for organization and providing access to the web have been developed. Subject gateways and web directories are such tools, designed to provide access to quality resources selected and indexed by experts or information professionals. Subject gateways can range from "loosely collated commercial directories" such as Yahoo! subject categories, to "collections of quality assessed web resources compiled by the academic or research community" (University of Kent, 2009). In this chapter, I will refer to the concept of the latter for further discussion.

The subject gateways emerged in response to the challenge of "resource discovery" in a rapidly developing Internet environment in the early and mid-1990s. The term "subject gateway" was commonly used in the UK

Electronic Libraries Programme (eLib)[1] (Dempsey, 2000). Under the eLib project, Internet subject gateways were established to deal with Internet searching problems, such as finding good quality and relevant resources (Burton & Mackie, 1999). The EU project DESIRE[2] (Development of a European Service for Information on Research and Education) invented the term "subject-based information gateway (SBIG)" which looks like almost a synonym with the term "subject gateway" (Koch, 2000). Koch (2000) refers to "information gateways" by defining them as "quality controlled information services." Sometimes, subject gateways are termed "quality gateways," "subject directories," or "virtual libraries" (Bawden & Robinson, 2002).

Although there is no precise definition of subject gateways, they share several characteristics (Bawden & Robinson, 2002):

- a clearly expressed subject scope, defining what resources may be considered for inclusion,
- explicitly defined criteria of quality, used to select resources for inclusion,
- some form of annotation or description of resources,
- some categorization, classification, or indexing of the collection,
- clearly defined responsibilities for their creation and maintenance.

Subject gateways can be enumerated by the subject categories which they cover (University of Kent, 2009). For instance, Social Care Online (http://www.scie-socialcareonline.org.uk/) (professional development support portal), SocioSite (http://www.sociosite.net/) (the University of Amsterdam's social science information system), and SWAP (Social Policy and Social Work) (http://www.swap.ac.uk/) (subject portal providing resources to support teachers and lecturers in this subject) are subject gateways which provide resources in social science subjects. For a psychology subject area, there are CogNet (http://cognet.mit.edu/) (MIT portal for the brain sciences), PsychNet.UK (http://www.psychnet-uk.com/) (a comprehensive UK gateway to psychology information), and so on. Doctors.net.uk (http://www.doctors.net.uk/) (Peer led Internet resource for UK doctors) and HON (Health On the Net) (http://www.hon.ch/) (international Swiss initiative to make quality guidance about medical treatments and health information

1. eLib was a JISC-funded program of projects in 1996 (initially £15m over 3 years but later extended to 2001). Projects included Digitization, Electronic Journals, Electronic Document Delivery, and On-Demand Publishing (Hiom, 2006).

2. The DESIRE project (from July 1998 until June 2000) was a collaboration between project partners working at 10 institutions from four European countries — the Netherlands, Norway, Sweden, and the United Kingdom. The project focused on improving existing European information networks for research users in Europe in three areas: Caching, Resource Discovery, and Directory Services (DESIRE Consortium, 2000).

available to patients and public) are examples for health and medicine subjects. As examples of subject gateways covering various subject areas, there are BUBL Link (http://bubl.ac.uk/) and Intute (http://www.intute.ac.uk/). BUBL describes itself as "Free User-Friendly Access to selected Internet resources covering all subject areas, with a special focus on Library and Information Science" (Wikipedia). Intute is a free web service aimed at students, teachers, and researchers in UK further education and higher education (Wikipedia). In the following sections, more details about BUBL and Intute are presented.

6.2.1. BUBL

The BUBL Information Service is "an Internet link collection for the library and higher education communities, operated by the Centre for Digital Library Research at the University of Strathclyde, and its name was originally short for Bulletin Board for Libraries" (Wikipedia). Since 1993 the BUBL Information Service has been a structured and user-friendly gateway for web resources in order to direct librarians, information professionals, academics, and researchers (Gold, 1996).

Many subject gateways provide controlled vocabularies: either "home-made" or "standard library/information tools" such as classification schemes, subject headings, and thesauri (Bawden & Robinson, 2002). BUBL offers broad categorization of subjects based on the Dewey Decimal Classification scheme (BUBL Link Home) (see Figure 6.1). For each subject, subject specialists like librarians work on the maintenance and development of subject categories.

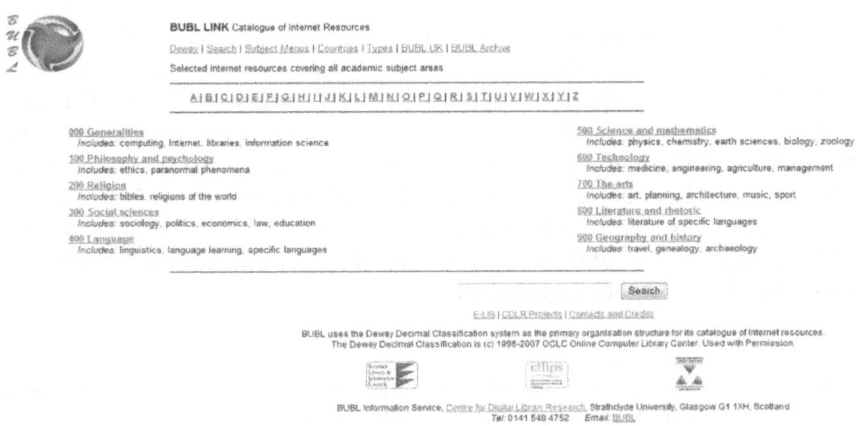

Figure 6.1: A screenshot of BUBL home page.

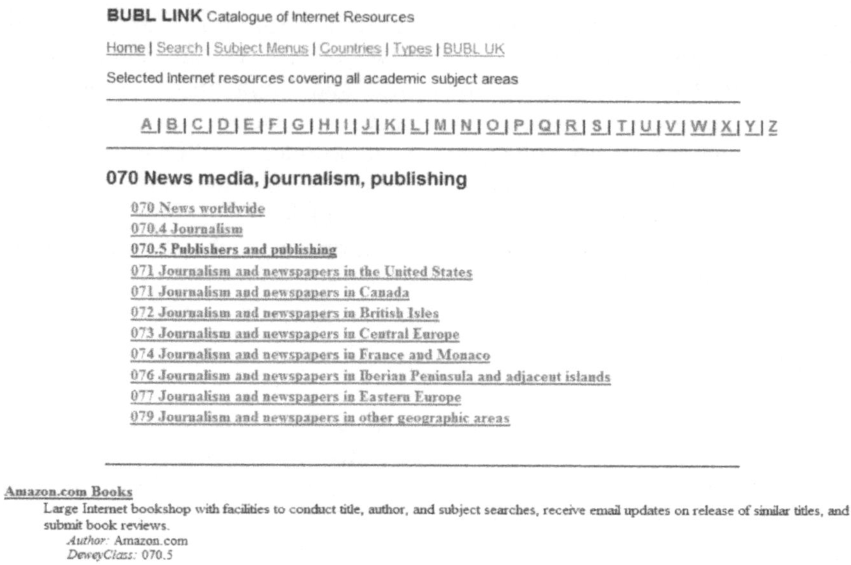

Figure 6.2: Amazon.com indexed at BUBL.

BUBL assigns each document a classification number based on DDC as shown in Figure 6.2. However, it has been noted that BUBL is no longer being updated as of April 2011 (BUBL Link Home), as support for BUBL was discontinued.

6.2.2. Intute

Intute is funded by the Joint Information Systems Committee (JISC) which supports "education and research by promoting innovation in new technologies and by the central support of ICT services" in the UK higher and further education sectors (JISC Home). Intute offers a searchable and browsable database of web resources that subject specialists select, evaluate, and describe (Joyce, Wickham, Cross, & Stephens, 2008) (see Figure 6.3).

Intute was formed in July 2006 after the Resource Discovery Network's (RDN)[3] eight hubs were merged. These hubs respectively serve particular academic disciplines (Wikipedia):

3. The Resource Discovery Network (RDN) is a JISC-funded national service. It is supported by the Economic and Social Research Council (ESRC) and the Arts and Humanities Research Council (AHRC), in order to provide quality internet service for the education community. The RDN originated in the Electronic Libraries (eLib) Programme (Hiom, 2006).

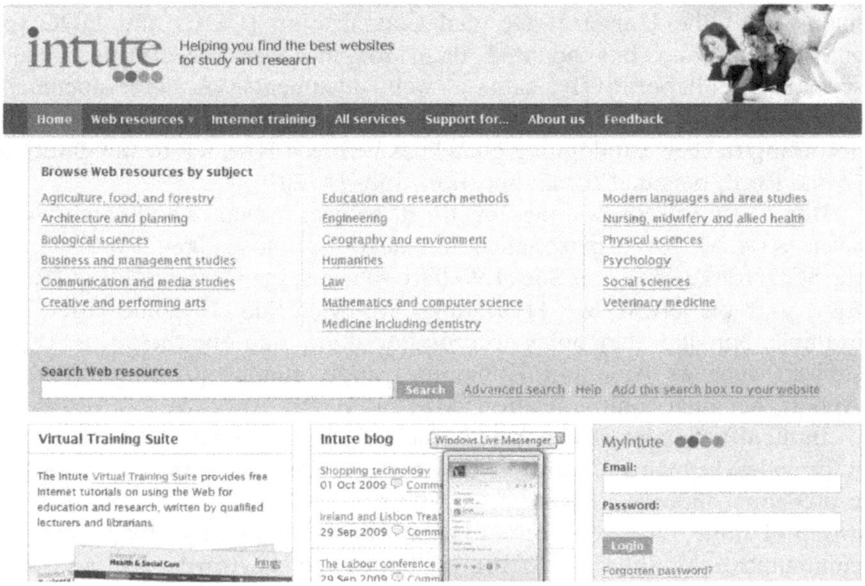

Figure 6.3: A screenshot of Intute home.

- Altis — Hospitality, leisure, sport, and tourism
- Artifact — Arts and creative industries
- Biome — Health and life sciences
- EEVL — Engineering, mathematics, and computing
- GEsource — Geography and the environment
- Humbul — Humanities
- PSIgate — Physical sciences
- SOSIG — Social sciences

Intute is created by a consortium of seven universities and its service is offered by staff at those seven locations, that is, University of Birmingham (Intute Social Sciences), University of Bristol (Intute Social Sciences and Intute Virtual Training Suite), Heriot-Watt University (Intute Science, Engineering and Technology), The University of Manchester (Intute Executive), Manchester Metropolitan University (Intute Science, Engineering and Technology), University of Nottingham (Intute Health and Life Science), and University of Oxford (Intute Arts and Humanities) (Intute Home).

The selection for inclusion of resources within the Intute collection considers the quality, relevance, and provenance of resources (Robert Abbott, personal communication, May 21, 2009). It is reported that Intute mainly uses the Universal Decimal Classification (UDC) and DDC for classification and has adapted them for in-house use. Intute subject specialists collaboratively catalog web documents. A web document cataloged by one indexer is passed to another specialist for checking it according to their cataloguing guidelines before it is added to the database (Anne Reed, personal communication, July 14, 2010).

Intute also uses several thesauri for its subject relevance and comprehensiveness (A. M. Joyce, personal communication, June 2, 2009). For instance, the SCIE for keywords of Social Welfare subjects, the Hasset, IBSS, LIR for Law, and the NLM MeSH headings for Medicine. In some cases, for example, Nursing, they index according to more than one thesaurus. Other subjects such as Arts and Humanities apply similar principles (Robert Abbott, personal communication, May 21, 2009).

Intute offers index strings based on classification schemes and sometimes it provides keywords (controlled or uncontrolled or both) generated by professional indexers (Figure 6.4). Allocated keywords are reviewed by a group of subject indexers for consistent keywording (Anne Reed, personal communication, July 14, 2010). Uncontrolled keywords are added if indexers can find no suitable word in the above thesauri. They choose the uncontrolled keywords from among terms occurring in the titles and descriptions they write for the resources. They tend to select the uncontrolled keywords from among the words that the web sites themselves use (A. M. Joyce, personal communication, June 2, 2009). Figure 6.4 shows how Intute indexes a document, *Amazon.com* and how they present several types of information about the document including description, controlled keywords, uncontrolled keywords, type, URL, and category paths of classification. However, it has been recently noted that support for Intute was discontinued.

These two main subject gateways, BUBL and Intute are summarized in Table 6.1 in terms of classification, keywords, subjects, and database.

6.2.3. Challenges with Current Organization Systems

As there are more and more resources available on the web, it has been pointed out that current organization systems such as subject gateways are not sufficient for the web. One of the problems with current organization systems is that they were developed using traditional library schemes for subject access based on controlled vocabulary. Nicholson et al. (2001) point out problems with controlled vocabularies including a lack of or excessive specificity in subject areas. Shirky (2005a) asserts that formal classification systems are not suitable for electronic resources. As Mai (2004a) notes, traditional classification schemes have difficulties with representing

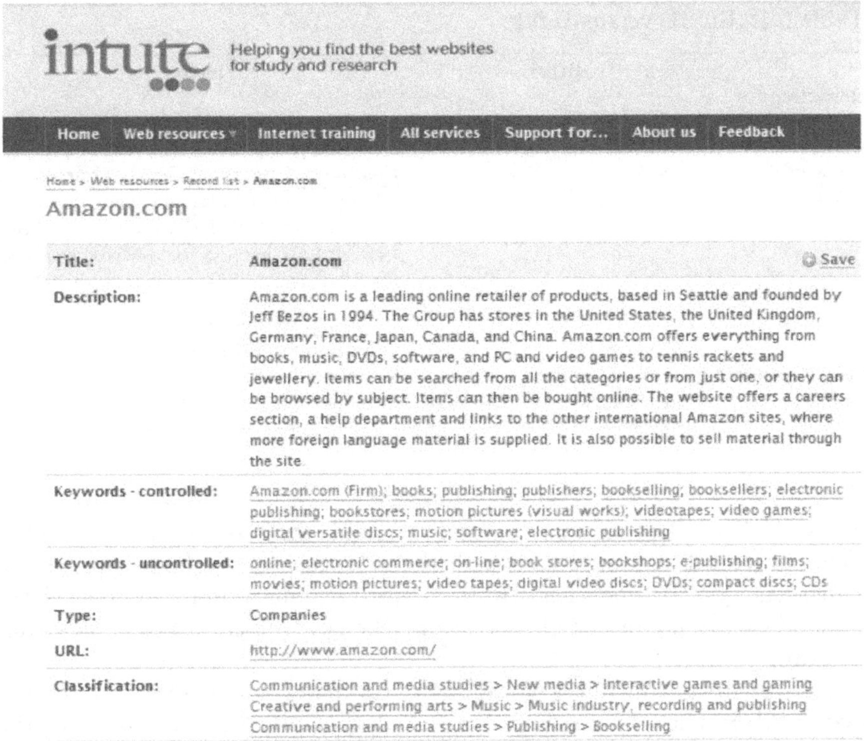

intute

Helping you find the best websites for study and research

Home | Web resources | Internet training | All services | Support for... | About us | Feedback

Home > Web resources > Record list > Amazon.com

Amazon.com

Title:	**Amazon.com**	Save
Description:	Amazon.com is a leading online retailer of products, based in Seattle and founded by Jeff Bezos in 1994. The Group has stores in the United States, the United Kingdom, Germany, France, Japan, Canada, and China. Amazon.com offers everything from books, music, DVDs, software, and PC and video games to tennis rackets and jewellery. Items can be searched from all the categories or from just one, or they can be browsed by subject. Items can then be bought online. The website offers a careers section, a help department and links to the other international Amazon sites, where more foreign language material is supplied. It is also possible to sell material through the site.	
Keywords - controlled:	Amazon.com (Firm); books; publishing; publishers; bookselling; booksellers; electronic publishing; bookstores; motion pictures (visual works); videotapes; video games; digital versatile discs; music; software; electronic publishing	
Keywords - uncontrolled:	online; electronic commerce; on-line; book stores; bookshops; e-publishing; films; movies; motion pictures; video tapes; digital video discs; DVDs; compact discs; CDs	
Type:	Companies	
URL:	http://www.amazon.com/	
Classification:	Communication and media studies > New media > Interactive games and gaming Creative and performing arts > Music > Music industry, recording and publishing Communication and media studies > Publishing > Bookselling	

Figure 6.4: An example of an indexed document in Intute.

knowledge, and the problems of describing the subject matter of web documents have not received sufficient attention. Mai (2004a) posits the following two main obstacles for applying bibliographic classification principles to the classification of the web:

a. the principles are tied to the paper-based environment and
b. the principles have been focused on organizing scientific or scholarly material.

The other problem with current approaches to organizing the web via gateways and directories is that web documents have been organized and indexed by professional indexers. Although there have been efforts to involve users in developing organization systems, they are not necessarily based on users' natural language.

On the other hand, although controlled vocabulary has been challenged due to its ability of dealing with a broad range of digital web resources, indeed, controlled vocabularies were developed and used for effective subject

Table 6.1: BUBL versus Intute.

Site characteristics	BUBL	Intute
Classification	DDC	UDC and DDC
Keywords	N/A	*Controlled*: Several thesauri for their subject relevance and comprehensiveness, e.g., SCIE for Social Welfare, the Hasset, IBSS, LIR for Law, and the NLM MeSH headings for Medicine *Uncontrolled*: terms from web sites' titles and descriptions Intute indexers provide
Subjects covered	Various subjects	Various subjects
Database	Searchable and browsable	Searchable and browsable

indexing. For effective indexing and retrieval, the indexing process needs to be controlled by using a so-called *controlled vocabulary* (Lancaster, 1972). Lancaster (2003) identifies three major manifestations of controlled vocabulary: bibliographic classification schemes, subject heading lists, and thesauri.

Furthermore, controlled vocabulary has many advantages. One of the major advantages of controlled vocabulary is that it can increase the effectiveness of retrieval by providing unambiguous, standard search terms with a control of polysemy, synonymy, and homonymy of the natural language (Golub, 2006; Muddamalle, 1998). Another benefit from controlled vocabulary is that it improves the matching process with its systematic hierarchies of concepts featuring a variety of relationships like "broader term," "narrower term," "related term," or "see" and "see also" (Golub, 2006; Olson & Boll, 2001).

However, as there are more and more resources available on the web, existing controlled vocabularies have been challenged in their ability to index the range of digital web resources. One of the major challenges of controlled vocabulary in the digital environment is the slowness of revision. Indexing web content requires an updated thesaurus, but usually subjects are rapidly evolving with new terminology, so it is hard to always keep up-to-date vocabulary (Muddamalle, 1998). Golub (2006) also addresses "improved currency" and "hospitality for new topics" as new roles which controlled vocabularies need to take. The other problem is that the construction of controlled vocabularies and indexing are labor-intensive and expensive (Fidel, 1991; Macgregor & McCulloch, 2006). The process of indexing is conducted by professional efforts requiring expert knowledge

(Olson & Boll, 2001). Another obstacle of controlled vocabulary is that it has been developed with a focus on physical and traditional library collections. Traditionally, controlled subject headings have been employed for indexing physical resources, so they need to be flexible or expandable in order to encompass web resources (Golub, 2006; Macgregor & McCulloch, 2006; Nowick & Mering, 2003). For instance, LCSH is designed to describe monographs and serials, so it might not be specific enough for describing web resources (Nowick & Mering, 2003). Furthermore, Nicholson et al. (2001) have discussed the problems with controlled vocabularies in indexing for describing online collections by identifying that "they have a lack of, or excessive, specificity in the subject areas." Last but not least, controlled vocabulary should be comfortable for users to use, and it should be able to meet the users' interests and their needs (Golub, 2006). Golub mentions "intelligibility, intuitiveness, and transparency" as new challenges for controlled vocabulary.

Accordingly, using free-text or natural language terms is one alternative to resolve identified problems with controlled vocabulary. Advantages of free-text terms are that they require only nonprofessional knowledge for searching techniques for users, and reflect up-to-date vocabulary (Dubois, 1987). Social tagging data is one example of natural language terms, that is, uncontrolled vocabulary assigned by users. In the next section, social tagging will be discussed in more detail.

6.3. Social Tagging in Organizing Information on the Web

6.3.1. Definitions of Terms

Social tagging is described as "user-generated keywords" (Trant, 2009). Since tags indicate users' perspectives and descriptions in indexing resources, they have been suggested as a means to improve search and retrieval of resources on the web. The term "social tagging" is frequently associated with the term "folksonomy" which was coined by Thomas Vander Wal from "folk" and "taxonomy" (Smith, 2004). Folksonomy consists of three elements: users, resources to be described, and tags for describing resources (Vander Wal, 2005a). Vander Wal (2007) describes "folksonomy" as "user-created bottom-up categorical structure development with an emergent thesaurus." Quintarelli (2005) defines folksonomy as "user-generated classification, emerging through bottom-up consensus." Examples of folksonomy sites include Flickr, Del.icio.us, and LibraryThing.

While Trant (2009) provides good reviews of the overall trends of research on social tagging and folksonomy, she distinguishes the two terms "social tagging" and "folksonomy" by providing short definitions:

- Tagging: "a process with a focus on user choice of terminology"
- Folksonomy: "the resulting collective vocabulary (with a focus on knowledge organization)"
- Social tagging: "a sociotechnical context within which tagging takes place (with a focus on social computing and networks)"

In addition, other terms have been used by several researchers like "social classification" (Furner & Tennis, 2006; Landbeck, 2007; Smith, 2004; Trant, 2006), "community cataloguing" and "cataloguing by crowd" (Chun & Jenkins, 2005), "communal categorization" (Strutz, 2004), and "ethnoclassification" (Boyd, 2005; Merholz, 2004). These terms describing this phenomenon are not well defined yet, and they have often been selected depending on focal points, for example, sociability, collaboration, and cooperation (Vander Wal, 2005a; Weinberger, 2006). Sometimes, these terms are also regarded as synonyms. For example, Noruzi (2006) notes folksonomy as a synonym of social tagging while describing its characteristics. "Social tagging" and "social indexing" can be considered as synonyms, but the latter can be understood with focus on behaviors or practices of describing about "topics" or "subjects" of a certain document.

6.3.2. An Exemplary Social Tagging Site: Delicious

Social tagging has been popularized by tagging sites such as Flickr, Technorati, and Deli.cio.us. Deli.cio.us is one of the most popular social bookmarking services, allowing users to add or share and organize tags. Deli.cio.us now redirects to the new domain, Delicious. The site was established by Joshua Schachter in 2003 and acquired by Yahoo! in 2005 (Wikipedia). Figure 6.5 shows how a web document is tagged by users at Delicious. Delicious provides "Top Tags" lists at the right side of the screen, and these ranked tags are not checked for variant spellings, synonyms, singular versus plural, etc. For instance, "costume" and "costumes" are both ranked.

Delicious has a broad coverage of web resources, not limited to scholarly documents (e.g., journal articles on CiteUlike.org) or specific types of resources (e.g., photos and videos on Flickr). According to Vander Wal's explanation of folksonomy, the broad folksonomy like Delicious has many people tagging the same object and every person can tag the object with their own tags in their own vocabulary while the narrow folksonomy such as

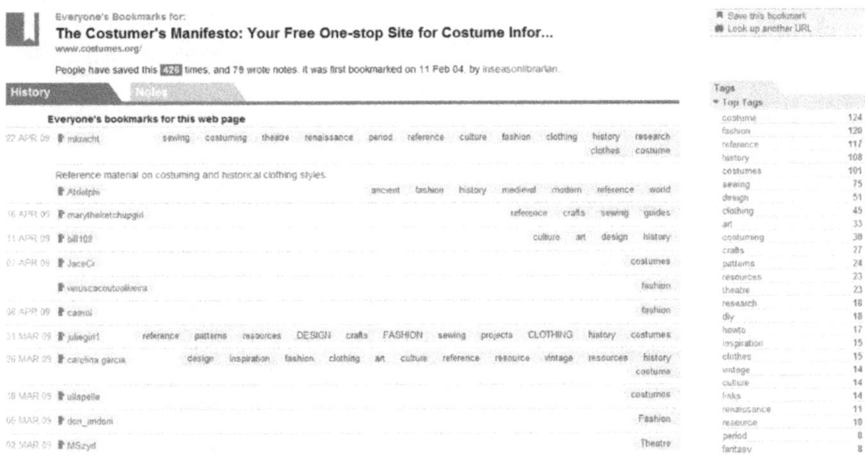

Figure 6.5: An example of Delicious tags.

Flickr is done by one or a few people providing tags that the person uses to get back to that information (Vander Wal, 2005b). He also claims that the tags in a narrow folksonomy tend to be singular, that is, only one tag with the term is used while many people assign the same tag in the broad folksonomy.

6.3.3. Combination of Controlled Vocabulary and Uncontrolled Vocabulary

Social tagging helps organize contents by collaborative and user-generated tags and users' tags reflect their language because they allow users to add their own tags based on their interests, so several researchers suggest the combination of both controlled vocabulary and uncontrolled vocabulary approaches since both may complement each other. Macgregor and McCulloch (2006) argue that it is obvious that controlled vocabularies and collaborative tagging systems will coexist: what they describe as "the dichotomous co-existence."

Knapp, Cohen, and Juedes's (1998) study illustrates that combining both approaches produced more effective retrieval performance rather than using only one approach. They conducted an experimental study to identify whether the free-text search terms could add supplementary relevant documents which are not retrieved by the controlled vocabulary. Their study allowed humanities scholars to search using both controlled vocabulary and free-text terms. Its results showed that when controlled vocabulary and free-text terms work together, more relevant records are retrieved.

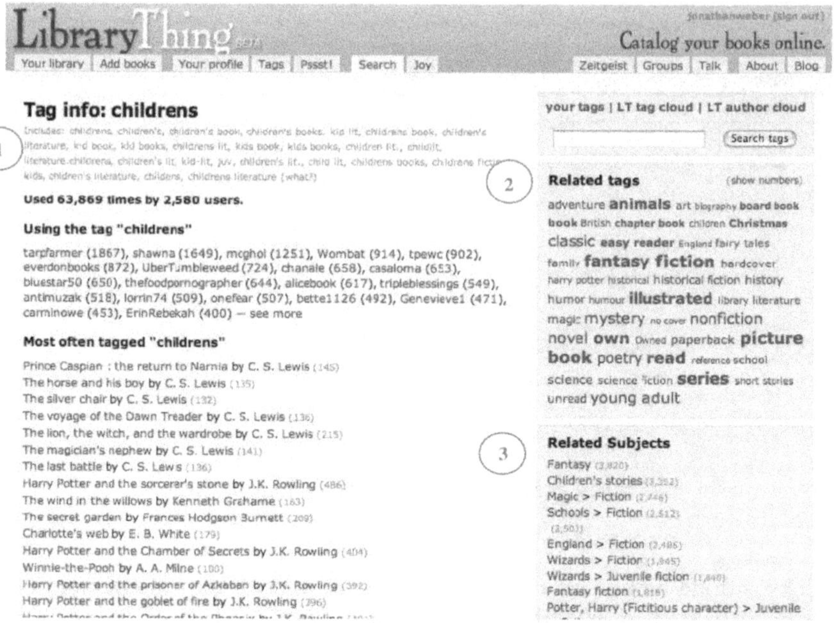

Figure 6.6: LibraryThing tag page for tag "childrens", showing (1) tag combinations, (2) related tags, and (3) related subjects. *Source:* Weber, 2006.

Weber's report (2006) on LibraryThing demonstrates that folksonomies and controlled vocabularies can harmoniously coexist: the combination of both would obtain benefits, and there are useful correlations between the two. Figure 6.6 illustrates that LibraryThing supplies tag combinations including multiple aspects of the tagged objects, links to statistically related tags, and subject headings.

6.3.4. Social Indexing

Several researchers have discussed the impact of tagging on retrieval performance on the web (Bao et al., 2007; Choy & Lui, 2006; Golder & Huberman, 2006; Heymann, Koutrika, & Garcia-Molina, 2008; Kipp & Campbell, 2010; Sen et al., 2006; Yanbe, Jatowt, Nakamura, & Tanaka, 2006). Choy and Lui (2006) have applied the statistical tool of Latent Semantic Analysis (LSA) to the evaluation of tag similarity by examining pairs of tags of singular and plural forms, and concluded that collaborative tagging has a great impact on retrieval. Yanbe et al. (2006) have explored an approach to enhancing search by proposing combining a link-based ranking metric with social tagging data, and investigated the utility of social bookmarking systems. Bao et al. (2007) have explored the use of social annotations to improve web search and stated that social annotations could be useful for web search by focusing on two aspects: similarity ranking (between a query and a web page) and static ranking. Kipp and Campbell (2010) have examined whether tags would be useful for information retrieval by limiting the scope of information to scholarly documents such as academic articles at CiteULike and PubMed online journal database.

On the other hand, the usefulness of social tagging for cataloging and classification has been discussed by examining the linguistic aspects of user vocabulary (Makani & Spiteri, 2010; Spiteri, 2007). Many researchers stress the need to add users to the development of controlled vocabularies for subject indexing (Abbott, 2004; Mai, 2004b; Quintarelli, 2005; Shirky, 2005b). Fidel (1991) asserts that online searchers use rules in an "intuitive way" to help their selection of search keys and these rules can be formalized. Furthermore, many researchers have suggested that social tagging has potential for user-based indexing (Golder & Huberman, 2006; Lin, Beaudoin, Bui, & Desai, 2006; Lu, Park, & Hu, 2010; Tennis, 2006). Lu et al. (2010) have investigated the difference between social tags and subject terms generated by professional cataloguers, and they have shown that social tags might be used to improve the accessibility of library collections. It can be recognized that the participation of users in building controlled vocabulary is being realized in a social tagging environment where users create or generate search keywords based on their intuitive principles.

Olson and Wolfram (2006) posit that social tagging could be utilized to index web resources by adding keywords which are being used by users. They also describe the concept of tagging as indexing performance in that people create and share their identified terms to describe contents of web documents. Lin et al. (2006) describe "emerging characteristics of social classification" and the relationship between tags and index terms. Voss (2007) also argues that it is more acceptable to see that tagging is a common means of manual indexing on the web. In addition, Trant (2009) asserts that a folksonomy can be studied in relationship to other indexing vocabularies since it provides additional access points to resources.

When considering the characteristics of social tagging such as low cost (since a great number of users from everywhere contribute to the creation of tags), social tagging seems to be a promising way to complement the disadvantages of professional indexing because it is low cost since a great number of users from everywhere contribute to the creation of tags. Users' tags might be alternate terms with additional entry points of retrieval which are not easily attained using controlled vocabularies (Hayman, 2007; Maltby, 1975; Quintarelli, 2005). Tags are generally much more current than controlled vocabulary since they are constructed in the process of "sensemaking" in that users share their experiences in subject terms reflecting their interests in various communities (Smith, 2007). Unlike hierarchical structures (broader and narrower terms) of controlled vocabularies, folksonomies are inherently flat which allows great flexibility in indexing terms (Smith, 2007).

There has been exploratory research investigating tagging as a more accurate description of resources and reflection of more current terminology. Smith (2007) has asserted that tagging is better than subject headings by investigating tags assigned in LibraryThing and the subject headings assigned by the Library of Congress Subject Headings (LCSH). LibraryThing is a website that allows users to manage a personal catalog with their own books (Wikipedia). Smith sampled five books including both fiction and nonfiction works published in the past five years. She analyzed the LCSH terms assigned to the book and the tag clouds and confirmed that the folksonomy has potential for augmenting subject analysis tools (see Table 6.2).

Smith hypothesized that LibraryThing would better represent the subject matter of fictional works whereas LCSH would be better at representing the subject of nonfiction works, and she concluded that LibraryThing is better at showing latent subjects when there are fewer synonym redundancies.

Table 6.2: Harry Potter tag cloud and subject headings.

LibraryThing	**LCSH**
Tags used to describe the book 2005(42) Adventure(36) **boarding school**(22) british(69) children(136) children's fiction(42) children's literature(69) childrens(361) england(41) **fantasy**(1,309) favorites(58) **fiction**(967) hardcover(35) **harry potter**(590) **Hogwarts**(36) juvenile(33) juvenile fiction(16) **magic**(306) novel(60) own(62) **potter**(19) read(139) **rowling**(56) school(33) series(145) unread(16) witches(31) **wizardry**(31) **wizards**(115) young adult(314) youth(19)	England > Fiction England > Juvenile fiction Fantasy fiction > Juvenile Good and evil > Juvenile fiction Hogwarts School of Witchcraft and Wizardry (Imaginary place) > Juvenile fiction Intergenerational relations > Juvenile fiction Magic > Fiction Magic > Juvenile fiction Maturation (Psychology) > Juvenile fiction Potter, Harry (Fictitious character) > Juvenile fiction Schools > Fiction Schools > Juvenile fiction Wizards > Fiction Wizards > Juvenile fiction

Source: Smith (2007).

She also noted that synonyms in the tag clouds allow for some natural language retrieval.

Choi (2010a, 2010b, 2011) has undertaken a study of indexing of a sample of 113 documents that are indexed in BUBL, Intute, and Delicious, drawing selected sites from each of 10 broad subject categories which BUBL provides as top-level categories using DDC numbers (see Figure 6.1). The study (Choi, 2011) compared indexing similarity between two professional groups, that is, BUBL and Intute, and also compared tagging in Delicious and professional indexing in Intute. The study (Choi, 2011) employed the method of the modified vector-based Indexing Consistency Density (ICD) with three different similarity measures: cosine similarity, dot product similarity, and Euclidean distance metric. The Inter-indexer Consistency Density (ICD) method, originally proposed by Wolfram and Olson (2007), measures indexing consistency based on the vector space traditional Information Retrieval (IR) model.

In today's social tagging environment, it has been acknowledged that traditional methods for assessing inter-indexer consistency need to be extended as a large group of users have been involved in indexing (Olson & Wolfram, 2006). Wolfram and Olson (2007) applied the concept of document space in the vector space model into the terms assigned by a group of indexers to a document, and defined an Indexer/Tagger Space. Thus, the Vector-based ICD method represents indexing spaces among indexers, so it is able to deal with consistency analysis among a large number of people such as social tagging users.

It has been demonstrated that indexing consistency between Delicious taggers and Intute professionals varied by subject area. For example, Sociology subject showed high indexing similarity between two professional groups (BUBL and Intute) (Figure 6.7), but indicated low similarity between taggers and professionals (Delicious and Intute) (Figure 6.8).

High indexing similarity on Sociology subject between BUBL and Intute explained that both BUBL and Intute located most documents in that subject into "Social sciences" or "Sociology" categories (Table 6.3). Thus most documents on that subject were simply located in the existing categories.

Also, regarding Literature subject, there was low similarity between Delicious taggers and Intute professionals. Low similarity in Sociology and Literature between Delicious taggers and Intute professionals could be attributed to tags that included additional access points with many newly coined terms such as ebook, online, web, web 2.0, e-guides, e-learning, and cyberspace which reflect more accurate descriptions of the web documents (Table 6.4).

In addition, the Technology subject showed low consistency due to different levels of indexing between Intute indexers and Delicious taggers (Figure 6.8). For example, regarding the document 610 *Medical sciences*,

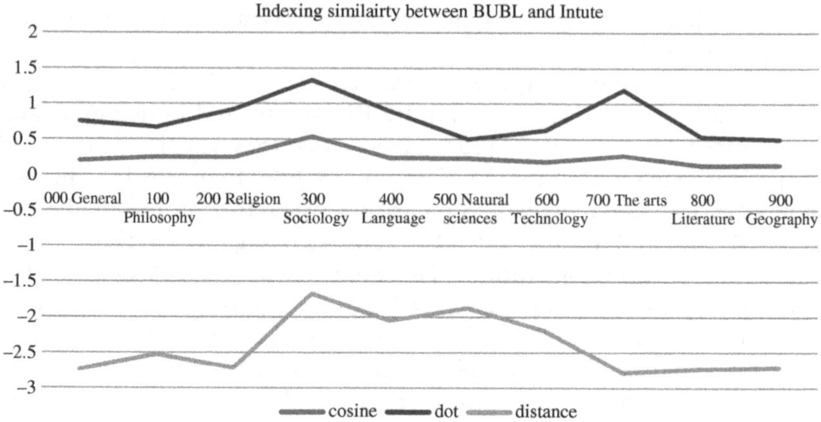

Figure 6.7: Indexing similarity between BUBL and Intute professionals. Since the similarity as measured by the Euclidean distance metric (Kohonen, 1995) is inversely proportional to the Euclidean distance, in the study, sign minus one (– 1) was put in front of the formula to make this metric proportional to the similarity (for more details, see Choi, 2011).

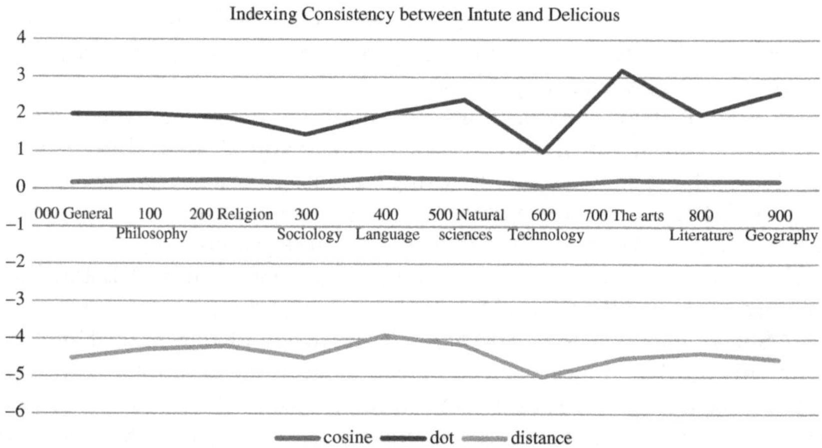

Figure 6.8: Indexing consistency for Intute professionals and Delicious taggers.

medicine, Intute keywords tend to be broader terms, that is, "disease" and "patient education," but Delicious tags consist of terms in various semantic relationships, for example, broader terms or narrower terms (Table 6.5). As shown in Table 6.5, tags on the document 610 *Medical sciences, medicine*

Table 6.3: Indexing on Sociology between BUBL and Intute.

Social sciences subject	Title	BUBL	Intute
301 Sociology: general resources	Sociological Tour Through Cyberspace, www.trinity.edu/~mkearl/index.html	Social sciences, Sociology	Social sciences, Sociology
310 International statistics	IDB Population Pyramids, International Data Base (IDB) — Pyramids, http://www.census.gov/ipc/www/idb/pyramids.html	Social sciences, Statistics	Social sciences, Statistics, data, Population
330 Economics: general resources	History of Economic Thought, http://cepa.newschool.edu/het/	Social sciences, Economics	Social sciences, Economics, Sociology
355 Military science: general resources	DOD Dictionary of Military Terms, http://www.dtic.mil/doctrine/dod_dictionary/	Social sciences, Military science	Social sciences, Government policy, Military science

Table 6.4: Indexing on Sociology and literature (Intute vs. Delicious).

Subject	Title	Intute	Delicious
Sociology (301 Sociology: general resources)	Sociological Tour Through Cyberspace, www.trinity.edu/~mkearl/index.html	death, euthanasia, families, homicide, mass media, time	sociology, links, resources, research, culture, web, science, resource, cyberspace, technology, web2.0, writing, social, internet, politics, reference, statistics
Sociology (370 Education)	Excellence Gateway, http://excellence.qia.org.uk/	numeracy, learning, key_skills, literacy	resources, education, e-learning, qia, teaching, learning, learning_resource, agency, elearning, quality, materials, jobs, qia_excellence, resource, e-guides, curriculum
Literature 808.8 Literature: general collections	Google Book Search, http://books.google.com/	writers, authors, books, search engines	books, google, search, ebooks, reference, book, library, research, tools, literature, search engine, web2.0, education, reading, resources, online, web, database
Literature 820 English, Scottish, and Irish literature	Cambridge History of English and American Literature, http://www.bartleby.com/cambridge/	literature, poetry, fiction, drama, Renaissance, Restoration, English, American, poets, poems, Anglo_Saxon, plays, writings, encyclopedias, history	literature, history, reference, encyclopedia, ebooks, books, humanities, research, language, reading, criticism, academic, writing, resources, information, englishliterature

Table 6.5: Indexing on technology (Intute vs. Delicious).

Technology	Title	Intute	Delicious
610 Medical sciences, medicine	MedicineNet, http://www.medicinenet.com/script/main/hp.asp	Disease, Patient_Education	health, medical, medicine, reference, drugs, information, education, news, research, healthcare, dictionary, science, search, resources, doctors, diseases, biology
630 Agriculture and related technologies	AgNIC: Agriculture Network Information Center, http://www.agnic.org/	agricultural_sciences, agriculture, agricultural_education, information_centres,	agriculture, research, food, information, statistics, environment, plants, farming, libraries, international, database, library, agnic, science, associations, produce, portal, horticulture
660 Chemical engineering	American Institute of Chemical Engineers, http://www.aiche.org/	young_engineers	engineering, chemistry, chemical, aiche, organization, professional, associations, society, engineers american, education, institute, chemicalengine, job, research, science, work, usa

include "health," "medical," "medicine," "drugs," "healthcare," etc. In the Library of Congress Subject Heading (LCSH), two terms "health" and "medical" are represented as "narrower terms" of that term "medicine." The term "healthcare" does not exist in the LCSH, but an alternative term "medical care" is represented as a narrower term of the term "health."

On the other hand, Natural Sciences showed relatively low similarity between two professional groups BUBL and Intute which demonstrated relatively higher similarity between Delicious and Intute. Table 6.6 illustrates that while Delicious and Intute are including many common terms between them, for some terminology, Delicious tags also additionally supply users' preferred or up-to-date terms. Examples are "bioinformatics" and "biotech" for the term "biotechnology" and "cheminformatics" for "chemistry."

This section has discussed the quality of social tags as a more accurate description of resources and reflection of more current terminology. As investment in professionally developed subject gateways and web directories diminishes (support for BUBL and Intute subject gateways have been discontinued as described in Section 6.2.1 BUBL and 6.2.2 Intute), it becomes even more critical to understand the characteristics of social tagging and to obtain benefit from it.

6.3.5. Criticisms of Folksonomy

Although social tagging or folksonomy has shown potential for improving the indexing and retrieval for web resources, its problems also have been pointed out by several researchers. Folksonomy has been criticized with its ambiguity of terms, a large number of synonyms, a lack of hierarchy, unstable term specificity, and variations of spelling, etc. (Quintarelli, 2005; Spiteri, 2005). Merholz (2004) also describes drawbacks of tags as synonyms and inaccuracy, and emphasizes the contribution of the traditional classification and vocabulary control. Peterson (2006) criticizes folksonomy in that it has an intrinsic defect caused by its inability to produce the accuracy of formal classification.

Therefore, social tags need to be preprocessed through normalization and checked for spelling, acronyms, or singular and plural forms before they are utilized in any way. This step includes removing misspelled terms and integrating terms which have different forms of words such as noun, adjective, adverb, and gerund. Choi (2011) preprocessed the social tags through normalization and set up five rules for specifying an exact match between two terms, based on discussion by Lancaster and Smith (1983):

- Exactly corresponding including singular/plural variations
  Ex) aurora to auroras, language to languages

Table 6.6: Indexing on Natural Sciences (Intute vs. Delicious).

Natural Sciences	Title	Intute keywords	Delicious top ranked tags
500 Natural sciences: national centres	National Science Foundation, http://www.nsf.gov/	science-policy, USA	science, research, education, government, nsf, funding, reference, technology, news, grants, academic, foundation, usa, biology, national, information, resource
540 Chemistry	Linux4Chemistry, http://www.redbrick.dcu.ie/~noel/linux4chemistry/	software, Linux, computational_chemistry	linux, chemistry, software, science, visualization, simulation, reference, opensource, research, cheminformatics, bioinformatics, chemical, physics, modeling, tools, python, quantum, links, java
570 Life sciences, biology	BBSRC: Biotechnology and Biological Sciences Research Council: http://www.bbsrc.ac.uk/	research_support, research_institutes, biology, Biological_sciences, Research, Great_Britain, Biotechnology	research, science, biotechnology, funding, biology, uk, education, work, bioinformatics, bioscience, development, bbsrc, research, councils, research_councils, postgraduate, news, academic biotech, biological, researchcouncil
580 Plants, general resources	Botanical Society of America Online Image Collection: http://images.botany.org/	Botany, Plants	images, botany, plants, biology, science, research, photos, pictures, media, collection, horticulture, gardening, multimedia, flowers, botanica, biologyguide

- Variant spellings
  Ex) organization to organisation
- Word forms (adjectival, noun, or verbal forms)
  Ex) medicine to medical
- Acronyms or abbreviations and full terms
  Ex) National Center for Biotechnology Information to NCBI, biotechnology to biotech
- Compound terms
  Ex) human/body to humanbody to human_body to human, body etc.

Generally, social tagging sites do not have the feature of adding a space between two tags for a compound term. So, the consideration of compound terms is important. For example, if there is a dash, slash, or underscore between two terms, or if two terms are found at the same time in the list of tags from a tagger, those two tags can be regarded as a compound term.

6.4. Conclusions and Future Directions

This chapter examined user-generated social tags in the context of subject indexing in order to see how they could be used to organize information in a digital environment. The chapter discussed the challenges of current information organization systems using controlled vocabulary with the intention to emphasize the need for social tagging data as natural language terms. The chapter mainly discussed the patterns and tendency of social indexing in comparison to professional indexing. Regarding subject areas which showed low indexing similarity between taggers and professional indexers, this chapter examined the quality of social tags as a more accurate description of resources and reflection of more current terminology (i.e., newly coined terms, users' preferred, or up-to-date terms).

Through the characteristics of social tagging discussed in this chapter, we have a clearer understanding of the extent to which social indexing can be used to replace (and in some cases to improve upon) professional indexing. This is particularly critical given the decline in support for professional indexing at the same time that web resources continue to proliferate and the need for guidance in their discovery and selection remains.

On the other hand, in terms of the characteristics of social tags, Sen et al. (2006) categorized social tags as factual (people, places, or concepts), subjective (e.g., good, worth, etc.), and personal tags (myDaughter, forSon, etc.). Since tags in the subjective category often would not be considered as terms for indexing subjects or topics of document, several research studies have tended to exclude those subjective tags in studying the properties of social indexing. However, subjective or emotional tags could also be crucial metadata describing important factors represented in the document. For example, tags such as resources, learning, teaching, and job imply user's intent to use documents for particular purposes. In future research, therefore, the examination of subjective tags needs to be conducted. In addition, a survey or user study on tagging behavior would help to extend understanding of social indexing practices.

Acknowledgments

This chapter derives from my University of Illinois doctoral dissertation entitled "Usefulness of Social Tagging in Organizing and Providing Access to the Web: An Analysis of Indexing Consistency and Quality." I am deeply grateful to my dissertation committee. Dr. Linda C. Smith was the chairperson of that committee, which included Dr. Allen Renear, Dr. Miles Efron, and Dr. John Unsworth. Linda C. Smith also reviewed the draft of this chapter and provided guidance in revising it. I wish to express my deepest respect and gratitude to her.

References

Abbott, R. (2004). Subjectivity as a concern for information science: A Popperian perspective. *Journal of Information Science*, *30*(2), 95–106.

Bao, S., et al. (2007). Optimizing web search using social annotations. *Proceedings of the 16th international conference on World Wide Web*. Retrieved from http://www2007.org/papers/paper397.pdf

Bawden, D., & Robinson, L. (2002). Internet subject gateways revisited. *International Journal of Information Management*, *22*(2), 157–162.

Boyd, D. (2005). Issues of culture in ethnoclassification/folksonomy. *Many-to-Many*. Retrieved from http://www.corante.com/many/archives/2005/01/28/issues_of_culture_in_ethnoclassificationfolksonomy.php

Burton, P., & Mackie, M. (1999). The use and effectiveness of the eLib subject gateways: A preliminary investigation. *Program: Electronic Library & Information Systems*, *33*(4), 327–337.

Choi, Y. (2010a). Traditional versus emerging knowledge organization systems: Consistency of subject indexing of the web by indexers and taggers. *Proceedings of the 73th annual meeting of the American Society for Information Science*, Pittsburgh, PA, October 22–27.

Choi, Y. (2010b). Implications of social tagging for digital libraries: Benefiting from user collaboration in the creation of digital knowledge. *Korean Journal of Library and Information Science*, *27*(2), 225–239.

Choi, Y. (2011). *Usefulness of social tagging in organizing and providing access to the web: An analysis of indexing consistency and quality*. Doctoral Dissertation, University of Illinois, Urbana, IL.

Choy, S. O., & Lui, A. K. (2006). Web information retrieval in collaborative tagging systems. *Proceedings of the IEEE/WIC/ACM international conference on web intelligence*, December 18–22, Hong Kong (pp. 353–355).

Chun, S., & Jenkins, M. (2005). Cataloguing by crowd: A proposal for the development of a community cataloguing tool to capture subject information for images (a professional forum). *Museums and the Web 2005*, Vancouver. Retrieved from http://www.archimuse.com/mw2005/abstracts/prg_280000899.html

Dempsey, L. (2000). The subject gateway: Experiences and issues based on the emergence of the resource discovery network. *Online Information Review*, *24*(8), 8–23.

Dubois, C. P. R. (1987). Free text vs. controlled vocabulary: A reassessment. *Online Review*, *11*(4), 243–253.

Fidel, R. (1991). Searchers' selection of search keys: II. Controlled vocabulary or free-text searching. *Journal of the American Society for Information Science*, *42*(7), 501–514.

Furner, J., & Tennis, J. T. (2006). *Advances in classification research, Volume 17: Proceedings of the 17th ASIS&T classification research workshop*, Austin, TX.

Gold, J. (1996). Introducing a new service from BUBL [Libraries of Networked Knowledge]. *The Serials Librarian*, *30*(2), 21–26.

Golder, S., & Huberman, B. A. (2005). *The structure of collaborative tagging systems*. Retrieved from http://www.hpl.hp.com/research/idl/papers/tags/tags.pdf

Golub, K. (2006). Using controlled vocabularies in automated subject classification of textual web pages, in the context of browsing. *IEEE TCDL Bulletin*, *2*(2), 1–11. Retrieved from: http://www.ieee-tcdl.org/Bulletin/v2n2/golub/golub.html

Hayman, S. (2007). Folksonomies and tagging: New developments in social bookmarking. *Ark group conference: Developing and improving classification schemes*, June 27–29, Rydges World Square, Sydney (p. 18). Retrieved from http://www.educationau.edu.au/jahia/webdav/site/myjahiasite/shared/papers/arkhayman.pdf

Heymann, P., Koutrika, G., & Garcia-Molina, H. (2008). Can social bookmarking improve web search? *Proceedings of the 1st international conference on web search and data mining*. February 11–12, Stanford University, CA.

Hiom, D. (2006). Retrospective on the RDN. *Ariadne*, Issue 47. Retrieved from http://www.ariadne.ac.uk/issue47/hiom/

Joint Information Systems Committee (JISC). Retrieved from http://www.jisc.ac.uk/

Joyce, A. M., Wickham, J., Cross, P., & Stephens, C. (2008). Intute integration. *Ariadne*, Issue 55, April. Retrieved from http://www.ariadne.ac.uk/issue55/joyce-et-al/

Kipp, M. E., & Campbell, D. G. (2010). Searching with tags: Do tags help users find things? *Knowledge Organization*, *37*(4), 239–255.

Knapp, S. D., Cohen, L. B., & Juedes, D. R. (1998). A natural language Thesaurus for the humanities: The need for a database search aid. *The Library Quarterly*, *68*(4), 406–430.

Koch, T. (2000). Quality-controlled subject gateways: Definitions, typologies, empirical overview. *Online Information Review*, *24*(1), 24–34.

Kohonen, T. (1995). *Self-organizing maps*. Berlin: Springer-Verlag.

Landbeck, C. (2007). Trouble in paradise: Conflict management and resolution in social classification environments. *Bulletin of the American Society for Information Science and Technology*, *34*(1), 16–20.

Lancaster, F. W. (1972). *Vocabulary control for information retrieval*. Washington, DC: Information Resources Press.

Lancaster, F. W. (2003). *Indexing and abstracting in theory and practice* (3rd ed.). Champaign, IL: University of Illinois.

Lancaster, F. W., & Smith, L. C. (1983). *Compatibility issues affecting information systems and services*. Paris: United Nations Educational, Scientific, and Cultural Organization.

Lin, X., Beaudoin, J. E., Bui, Y., & Desai, K. (2006). Exploring characteristics of social classification. *Advances in classification research* (Vol. 17): *Proceedings of the 17th ASIS&T classification research workshop*, Austin, TX.

Lu, C., Park, J., & Hu, X. (2010). User tags versus expert-created metadata: A comparison between LibraryThing tags and Library of Congress subject headings. *Journal of Information Science Journal of Information Science*, *36*(6), 763–779.

Macgregor, G., & McCulloch, E. (2006). Collaborative tagging as a knowledge organization and resource discovery tool. *Library Review*, *55*(5), 291–300.

Makani, J., & Spiteri, L. F. (2010). The dynamics of collaborative tagging: An analysis of tag vocabulary. *Journal of Information and Knowledge Management*, *9*(2), 93–103.

Maltby, A. (1975). *Sayers' manual of classification for librarians* (5th ed.). London: Andre Deutsch.

Mai, J.-E. (2004a). Classification of the Web: Challenges and inquiries. *Knowledge Organization*, *31*(2), 92–97.

Mai, J.-E. (2004b). Classification in context: Relativity, reality, and representation. *Knowledge Organization*, *31*(1), 39–48.

Merholz, P. (2004). *Metadata for the masses, adaptive path*. Retrieved from http://www.adaptivepath.com/ideas/e000361

Morville, P. (2005). *Ambient findability: What we find changes who we become*. Cambridge: O'Reilly.

Muddamalle, M. R. (1998). Natural language versus controlled vocabulary in information retrieval: A case study in soil mechanics. *Journal of the American Society for Information Science*, *49*(10), 881–887.

Nicholson, D., et al. (2001). *HILT: High level Thesaurus project: Final report*. Retrieved from http://hilt.cdlr.strath.ac.uk/Reports/Documents/HILTfinalreport.doc

Noruzi, A. (2006). Folksonomies: (Un) controlled vocabulary? *Knowledge Organization*, *33*(4), 199–203.

Nowick, E. A., & Mering, M. (2003). Comparisons between Internet users' free-text queries and controlled vocabularies: A case study in water quality. *Technical Services Quarterly*, *21*(2), 15–32.

Olson, H. A., & Boll, J. J. (2001). *Subject analysis in online catalogs* (2nd ed.). Englewood, CO: Libraries Unlimited.
Olson, H., & Wolfram, D. (2006). Indexing consistency and its implications for information architecture: A pilot study. *IA Summit*, Vancouver, British Columbia, Canada.
Peterson, E. (2006). Beneath the metadata: Some philosophical problems with folksonomy. *D-Lib Magazine*, *12*(11). Retrieved from: http://www.dlib.org/dlib/november06/peterson/11peterson.html
Quintarelli, E. (2005). Folksonomies: Power to the people. *Proceedings of the 1st international society for knowledge organization* (ISKOI), UniMIB Meeting, June 24, Milan, Italy. Retrieved from http://www.iskoi.org/doc/folksonomies.htm
Sen, S., et al. (2006). Tagging, communities, vocabulary, evolution. *Proceedings of the 2006 20th anniversary conference on computer supported cooperative work*. Retrieved from http://www.grouplens.org/papers/pdf/sen-cscw2006.pdf
Shirky, C. (2005a). *Ontology is overrated: Categories, links and tags*. Shirky.com, New York, NY. Retrieved from http://shirky.com/writings/ontology_overrated.html
Shirky, C. (2005b). *Semi-structured meta-data has a posse: A response to Gene Smith, you're it!* A blog on tagging. Retrieved from http://tagsonomy.com/index.php/semi-structured-meta-data-has-a-posse-aresponse-to-gene-smith/
Smith, G. (2004). *Folksonomy: Social classification*. Atomiq/information architecture [blog]. Retrieved from http://atomiq.org/archives/2004/08/folksonomy_social_classification.html
Smith, T. (2007). *Cataloging and you: Measuring the efficacy of a folksonomy for subject analysis*. In J. Lussky (Ed.), *Proceedings of the 18th workshop of the American Society for Information Science and Technology Special Interest Group in Classification Research*, Milwaukee, WI. Retrieved from http://dlist.sir.arizona.edu/2061
Spiteri, L. F. (2005). Controlled vocabularies and folksonomies. Presentation at Canadian Metadata Forum, Ottawa, ON, September 27, p. 23. Retrieved from http://www.collectionscanada.ca/obj/014005/f2/014005-05209-e-e.pdf
Spiteri, L. F. (2007). The structure and form of folksonomy tags: The road to the public library catalog. *Information Technology and Libraries*, *26*(3), 13–25.
Strutz, D. N. (2004). *Communal categorization: The folksonomy*. INFO622: Content Representation.
Tennis, J. T. (2006). Social tagging and the next steps for indexing. In J. Furner & J. T. Tennis (Eds.), *Proceedings 17th workshop of the American Society for Information Science and Technology Special Interest Group in Classification Research*, Austin, TX.
Trant, J. (2006). Social classification and folksonomy in art museums: Early data from the steve.museum tagger prototype. *Advances in classification research* (Vol. 17. p. 19). *Proceedings of the 17th ASIS&T classification research workshop*, Austin, TX.
Trant, J. (2009). Studying social tagging and folksonomy: A review and framework. *Journal of Digital Information*, *10*(1). Retrieved from: http://journals.tdl.org/jodi/article/viewDownloadInterstitial/269/278

University of Kent. (2009). *Library services subject guides*. Retrieved from http://www.kent.ac.uk/library/subjects/healthinfo/subjgate.html

Vander Wal, T. (2005a). *Folksonomy definition and wikipedia*. Off the Top. Retrieved from http://www.vanderwal.net/random/entrysel.php?blog=1750

Vander Wal, T. (2005b). *Explaining and showing broad and narrow folksonomies*. Retrieved from http://www.personalinfocloud.com/2005/02/explaining_and_.html

Vander Wal, T. (2007). *Folksonomy coinage and definition*. Retrieved from http://www.vanderwal.net/folksonomy.html

Voss, J. (2007). Tagging, folksonomy & co — Renaissance of Manual Indexing? *Proceedings of the international symposium of information science* (pp. 234–254). Retrieved from http://arxiv.org/PS_cache/cs/pdf/0701/0701072v2.pdf

Weinberger, D. (2006). *Beneath the metadata* — A reply. Joho the Blog [blog]. Retrieved from http://www.hyperorg.com/blogger/mtarchive/beneath_the_metadata_a_reply.html

Weber, J. (2006). *Folksonomy and controlled vocabulary in LibraryThing*. Unpublished final project, University of Pittsburgh.

Wolfram, D., & Olson, H. A. (2007). A method for comparing large scale interindexer consistency using IR modeling. *Proceedings of the 35th annual conference of the Canadian Association for Information Science*, May 10–12, McGill University, Montreal, Quebec.

Yanbe, Y., Jatowt, A., Nakamura, S., & Tanaka, K. (2006). Can social bookmarking enhance search in the web? *Proceedings of the 7th ACM/IEEE-CS joint conference on digital libraries*, Vancouver, Canada.

Chapter 7

Organizing Photographs: Past and Present

Emma Stuart

Abstract

Purpose —The chapter aims to highlight developments in photography over the last two centuries, with an emphasis on the switch from analog to digital, and the emergence of Web 2.0 technologies, online photo management sites, and camera phones.

Design/methodology/approach —The chapter is a culmination of some of the key literature and research papers on photography, Web 2.0, Flickr, camera phones, and tagging, and is based on the author's opinion and interpretation.

Findings — The chapter reports on how the switch from analog to digital has changed the methods for capturing, organizing, and sharing photographs. In addition, the emergence of Web 2.0 technologies and camera phones have begun to fundamentally change the way that people think about images and the kinds of things that people take photographs of.

Originality/value — The originality of the chapter lies in its predictions about the future direction of photography. The chapter will be of value to those interested in photography, and also to those responsible for the future development of photographic technology.

New Directions in Information Organization
Library and Information Science, Volume 7, 137–155

ISSN: 1876-0562/doi:10.1108/S1876-0562(2013)0000007011

7.1. Introduction

Images are embedded into our lives so intricately that we are often barely even aware of them (Jörgensen, 2003, p. ix). Walk through any public space, whether it is a high street, a museum, a shopping mall, or a government building, and you will be confronted with images at every step. Billboards, posters, wayfinding signage, information leaflets: all compete for our attention, trying to get us to buy certain products, follow a specific route, or think a certain way. Yet it is the images that we keep at home that we prize the most: our photographs. Photographs hold a special place in our hearts due to their symbiotic relationship with memory and our sense of identity. They are a way of communicating information about ourselves, both to ourselves and to future generations (Chalfen, 1987), and they are often quoted as being the most important thing that people would want to save from a house fire (Van House, Davis, Takhteyev, Ames, & Finn, 2004).

Both photographic equipment and the content of photographs themselves have changed dramatically since the first cameras were introduced into society, and whilst it is technological advancements in cameras (from analog to digital), which have fundamentally transformed the physical way in which images are both taken and subsequently organized, it is thanks to technological advancements in both the Internet and mobile phones that have truly revolutionized the ways in which we think about taking and organizing images, and even the kinds of things we photograph.

This chapter will discuss the changes that have taken place in the way photographs have been captured, organized, and shared over the last two centuries. The terms photograph and image will be used interchangeably and the discussion will center on the use of amateur vernacular photography, that is, photography centered on leisure, personal, and family life, rather than photography used in a serious amateur or professional capacity or for monetary gain. The switch from analog to digital will be discussed, as well as the emergence of Web 2.0 technology and online photo management sites, tagging, camera phones, the proliferation of apps, and how all of these things have changed the way we organize and share photographs.

7.2. From Analog to Digital

When photography was first introduced to society in 1839, only wealthy people were able to buy cameras, and they were cumbersome and difficult to use (Sontag, 1977, p. 7). They also required long exposure times in order to produce crisp and blur-free images, and this limited the kinds of things that could be photographed. Hence, the prevalence of the formal Victorian portrait image, as portraits were an ideal setting where people could be held still in front of the camera. In 1888, Kodak began to change the practice of photography with the development of a small compact camera that could be easily mass produced, hence making it cheap and therefore something that was within the reach of most classes of society. Amateur photography was born, and thanks to the new portability and simplicity of the camera, it began to be used in more varied settings and went from strength to strength with the development of tourism (Sontag, 1977, p. 9). Whilst the formal portrait shot began to decline in favor of more informal scenarios, the camera was still nonetheless used as an instrument for capturing idealized moments of daily life. Vernacular photography would rarely show family members engaged in an argument or ill. The camera was used as a way of constructing a perfect contrived visual moment that would serve as an *aide memoir* in the future to trigger a happy memory from the past, even if it wasn't necessarily happy at the time (Seabrook, 1991). Cameras came to represent a way of generating happy memories, and constructing a positive self and family identity whilst "systematically suppressing life's pains" (Milgram, 1977). It is for these reasons that photographs have come to hold such a valuable place within the human psyche and the practice of vernacular photography has only continued to grow as technology has advanced. In 1975, Kodak produced the first prototype of a digital camera, although digital photography did not become mainstream until the turn of the twenty-first century. However, digital cameras started outselling analog cameras in the United States in 2003, and worldwide by 2004 (Weinberger, 2007, p. 12). By 2011, 71% of UK households claimed to have a digital camera (compared to 51% in 2005) (Dutton & Blank, 2011, p. 13).

7.2.1. Organization

The organization of analog (print) photographs tends to consist of grouping together images based on spatial or temporal likeness such as dates and locations (e.g., "Christmas 1985" or "Trip to Russia"). This method of grouping photographs is an obvious practice due to the fact that people usually use a whole roll of photographic film(s) for a specific event, and then have the film developed (usually in a processing lab) quite soon afterwards, meaning that a natural grouping of images occurs based around the theme of the images from the roll of film, which tends to be tied to a specific date and location. Photographs are then usually placed in a display album based around the chosen grouping, or perhaps just left in the paper wallet that they came in if the whole roll of film naturally relates to the same thematic grouping. People often write on the back of photographs, jotting down the date, location, and perhaps a few notes about who is in the image and albums or wallets of photographs tend to be organized and stored chronologically within the home (Frohlich, Kuchinsky, Pering, Don, & Ariss, 2002).

Due to their physicality, analog photographs can only exist in one place at any one time as it is unlikely that more than one copy of the same photograph is printed unless it is singled out to perhaps go in a frame, or if extra copies are being given to friends or family. So, grouping images together based on date and location (e.g., Christmas, 1985) means that all of the images containing a specific family member (e.g., Uncle John) are split into all of the respective Christmases and events that he was present at (e.g., Christmas, 1985, Christmas, 1986, Bill & Kath's Wedding, etc.), rather than all images of him being in the same place. However, people tend to take a lot fewer photographs with analog cameras due to the restriction of 24/36 shots per film and the cost of having lots of films processed. Also, seeing as photographs cannot be viewed until the film has been processed and developed, there is often a more heightened sense of anticipation in seeing the final images, and in then reliving the moments afterwards when the images are being viewed. People are therefore quite familiar with what analog photographs they have.

However, with digital cameras there has come a newfound freedom in image taking. People no longer have to worry about running out of film before the end of their holidays as camera memory cards can hold a previously unimaginable number of images, and so people have become less conservative about the amount of images they take. The LCD screen built into digital cameras allows for captured images to be viewed straight away, meaning that people can continue taking images until they have captured the one they perceive to be "just right." People have also found freedom in the fact they do not have to pay to have all of the images they capture printed, only a selection of the best ones need be printed (if any at all), and this has further added to people's liberal image taking, leading to what is often referred to as "digital overload."

7.2.2. New Found Freedoms

However, aside from the fact that people can take many more images with a digital camera, to begin with, people still tend to upload images from their camera's memory card onto a computer hard drive quite soon after a specific event (e.g., a holiday or trip). Digital cameras tend to store images in a "folder" with the date as the name of the folder, and so it is quite easy for people to drag and drop these folders onto their computers, perhaps renaming the folder by adding in the name/location of an event, but otherwise leaving the date in the format that has been generated by the camera (Kirk, Sellen, Rother, & Wood, 2006). Therefore in its early stages, digital organization very much reflects that of analog organization. However, free from the constraints of the physical album where a photo can only exist in one place at any one time, photos can now digitally exist simultaneously in a number of different locations, meaning that they can be organized on the basis of a number of different facets. For example, as well as the temporal and spatial affiliations of an image, images can also be organized based on their content, so the same photograph containing Uncle John eating his Christmas dinner can exist simultaneously in the folders: "Christmas 1985," "Uncle John," and "Food." As the old proverb goes, "a picture is worth a thousand words," and so digital organization and its allowance for files to exist in more than one place could be said to be perfectly suited to that of image organization, allowing photographs to be organized on the basis of multiple different meanings. Although, in an investigation of 11 families use of analog and digital photos, Frohlich et al. (2002) found that very few of the families he investigated systematically organized their image collections on their PC and as a result had many "miscellaneous" folders containing sequences of numbered photos that were all uploaded to the PC in the same session.

With digital photography there also came a new playfulness in people's image taking habits. Whereas previously, people may have thought that the shots on a roll of film needed to be used sparingly so that there were always shots left for capturing important scenes, such as key family moments and events, without the constraints of the finite roll of film, people are free to experiment more with the kinds of images they capture, without the fear that they will run out of film just at the moment their child takes their very first steps. People have begun to take more photos of things that interests them outside of the family setting (e.g., images relating to hobbies), or they capture images to document things that might be useful to them, and this has begun to shift organization away from temporal and spatial groupings, and encourage more cognitive categorization based on what images are "of" and "about." Shatford-Layne (1994) explains the difference between *of* and *about* by using the example of an image depicting a person crying; whilst the image is *of* a person crying, the image is also *about* the concept of sorrow. Shatford-Layne (1994) goes on to explain that an image can also be simultaneously *generic* and *specific* depending on the terminology used to categorize it. For example, an image of St Paul's Cathedral in London could be useful to someone looking specifically for an image of St Paul's Cathedral, and it could also be useful to someone just looking for generic images of cathedrals.

Pulling together the concepts of *generic* and *specific* and *of* and *about*, and in light of a series of psychological experiments carried out in the 1970s, Eleanor Rosch (a professor at the University of California) proposed three levels of description that people tend to use when they want to place objects into categories that are linguistically useful. Take for example an image of Albert Einstein. The image could be described (and hence organized) using the words:

- *Person* — this would be classed as a superordinate level of description category. No subject-specific knowledge is needed to suggest this category of description.
- *Man* — this would be classed as a basic level of description. Slightly more knowledge is needed to make this distinction and a familiarity with the differences between males and females.
- *Albert Einstein* — this would be classed as a subordinate level of description as specific knowledge is needed to be able to determine *who* exactly the image of the man is.

Whilst Rosch's categories are primarily aimed at linguistic categorization (e.g., categorizing words in a sample of text), and do not therefore have to be tied to visual elements such as describing the meaning of a photograph or what it is about (e.g., theory of relativity/$E = mc^2$), they nonetheless closely reflect the work of the art historian Erwin Panofsky (1983) who proposed three levels of interpretation for analyzing the meaning in a work of art (pre-iconographic, iconographic, and iconological) and Rosch's three levels of description closely align to those of Panofsky's.

People have also begun to see the possibilities for categorizing photographs based on what Jörgensen (2003) describes as low-level visual features, such as: color, texture, and shape.

As previously mentioned, the newfound freedoms that have come with digital photography means that people have begun to accumulate a multitude of images, on camera memory cards, computer hard drives, and CDs, with many being of the same object, scene, or person, merely taken from a slightly different angle (Kirk et al., 2006). Also, because people can store hundreds of images on a memory card before it reaches its full capacity, people soon become overwhelmed by the number of images they have to sort through when they do get around to transferring and uploading their images. The prospect of sorting through all of the images in order to delete the ones that aren't worth keeping can become a burdensome task due to the sheer amount and the time that is needed to do it. A report in 2010 by IDC (a global market intelligence firm) predicted that by 2013, the number of photos printed per year will dip to 42 billion, which is one-third fewer than the 63 billion that were printed in 2008 (Evangelista, 2010).

7.3. Web 2.0: Photo Management Sites

The last decade has seen the emergence of a technology platform that has inadvertently provided ways for people to begin to deal with the problem of digital image overload: Web 2.0 technologies. Web 2.0 technology refers to a turning point for the web, characterized by a change in site content and creation (O'Reilly, 2005). The most notable of the changes in site content and creation has been the bringing together of the small contributions of millions of people (Grossman, 2006); that is, user-generated content, and the emergence of sites such as YouTube, Wikipedia, MySpace, and Delicious, where it is the users of the sites that upload the videos, articles, music, references, and various content. More specifically in relation to this chapter on photography, the last decade has seen the emergence of Web 2.0 photo management and sharing applications such as: Flickr, Picasa, Photobucket, SmugMug, Shutterfly, and Photoshelter. Sites such as these act as an online space where people can upload their digital images, and on sites such as Flickr, Picasa, and Shutterfly they can perform basic editing tasks such as cropping, red-eye reduction, adding filters, increasing the sharpness, etc. of images, if they so choose. They can decide to keep their images private and treat the site as an online storage/archival space or as a place for personal reflection (akin to a diary); or they can share their images with friends, family, or the public. They can create sets, collections, and groups based on whatever concepts they like; they can initiate competitions or discussions based on photographic practices or ideas; or they can treat the site as an online portfolio — a place where they can showcase their best images and access them from wherever without having to carry around a physical portfolio of their work. There is also the option to have some images as private, and others as public, so a person could use such a site as a combination of a personal storage space as well as a publicly accessible portfolio if they wanted.

These sites generally allow users to arrange their images into groups, sets, collections, or galleries (each site has slightly different options and uses different terminology). Flickr is classed as one of the earliest examples of a Web 2.0 site (Cox, Clough, & Marlow, 2008), and as such there has been more research and articles written about Flickr than any of the other photo management sites. Flickr is regarded as the most community orientated of the photo management sites (Remick, 2010) and the fact that users are for the most part motivated to use a site such as Flickr for social incentives such as the opportunity to share and play (Marlow, Naaman, Boyd, & Davis, 2006) has begun to alter the way that people think about organizing their images. Rather than grouping photographs based on their personal meaning to the photographer or the photographer's family and friends, users are thinking in a wider context and are interested in making their images findable to the whole user community. Social organization around photos and topics of interest occurs in the development of Flickr groups (Liu, Palen, Sutton, Hughes, & Vieweg, 2008), which are one of Flickr's flagship features (Negoescu, Adams, Phung, Venkatesh, & Gatica-Perez, 2009). Groups contain photos that all relate to a specific theme or topic as specified by the group administrator. Negoescu et al. (2009) describes that groups can be based on: geographical features (e.g., images relating to a particular city, mountain, or event); themes (e.g., macro photography, landscapes, transport); social (e.g., bringing together people with specific commonalities); and groups can also be based on exposure and awards, which often praise photographs that have been deemed to be of exceptional quality, or images that have received high view counts, etc. Negoescu et al. (2009) also point out that, "users often share the same photo with a number of groups," consolidating the digital photograph's ability to exist in more than one place at the same time. Photographs can also be organized based on equipment used such as the make and model of camera, lens used, exposure time, etc., and this can be seen as a particularly useful way for people who are looking to buy a new camera to research the pros and cons of particular cameras.

However there has been no research to date that has specifically analyzed the typology of images on Web 2.0 photo management sites, and so it could be the case that users tend not to make images public if they are overly personal (e.g., of family events), which could explain for the most part why users are happy to engage in such a social form of organization. Also, with such a mix of people using online photo management sites for a range of different purposes, the boundaries between amateur and professional are becoming more difficult to differentiate (Murray, 2008), and hence such sites could predominantly contain images from users who class themselves as serious amateur or professional photographers, rather than the vernacular form of photography that this chapter is concerned with.

7.3.1. Tagging

A key feature of many Web 2.0 sites and photo management sites in particular, is the ability to be able to tag the content (i.e., the photos) that are uploaded. Tagging is the assigning of freely chosen keywords that refer to the photo in some way, the objective of which is to describe and organize photos for the purposes of recovery and discovery (Xu, Fu, Mao, & Su, 2006). As tags are freely chosen, they do not have to follow any conventions, and so image tags can relate to: words describing who or what is in the image; words describing what the image is about; tags may relate to naming the event/date/location affiliated with the image; tags may relate to aspects surrounding image creation such as make and model of the camera used, type of lens, exposure time, technique, or the tags may even refer to the person who took the photograph. The person who uploads the photo assigns tags, and there is also the possibility that photos can be socially or collaboratively tagged. This is where other users of the system (either known or unknown to the person whom the image belongs to) can also add tags to public photos. People may do this if they feel they have something important to add, such as being able to name a particular person/street/building in the image. However, the practice of social/collaborative tagging is not that widespread on Flickr, and this is thought to be due to the fact people feel it is rude and an invasion of one's space (Cox et al., 2008; Marlow et al., 2006).

Research suggests that tagging on a site such as Flickr is carried out for one of four main reasons (or a combination thereof): self-organization (tagging to categorize images to aid with subsequent search and retrieval for oneself in the future); self-communication (tagging for purposes of personal reflection and memory, akin to keeping a diary); social organization (tagging to aid with other users of the system being able to search for and retrieve images); and social communication (tagging to express emotion or opinion, or to attract attention to the images the tags have been assigned to) (Ames, Eckles, Naaman, Spasojevic, & Van House, 2010; Nov, Naaman, & Ye, 2009a, 2009b; Van House, 2007; Van House et al., 2004; Van House, Davis, Ames, Finn, & Viswanathan, 2005).

Tag usage is seen as being highly dependent on a user's motivation for using the system (Marlow et al., 2006). For instance someone who is uploading their images to such a site so that they can be found and viewed by other people (i.e., social organization) is more likely to invest the time in tagging their images. Whereas someone who is using such a site as an online backup system (i.e., self-organization) is perhaps more likely to arrange their photos into collections or sets and just add titles and descriptions as a form of image narration, but perhaps not bother with actually tagging the images. However, in keeping with the social- and community-based aspect of Flickr, research has found that a lot of tagging is carried out in order to draw attention to a user's photographs as a way of then gaining feedback on the images (Cox et al., 2008), and research carried out by Angus and Thelwall (2010) found that social organization and social communication were the two most popular factors for the tagging of images on Flickr. However as image retrieval in Flickr can be achieved via serendipitous browsing, or via text in titles and descriptions, tagging is not the only way of drawing attention to one's images and many users see it as a boring or annoying task (Cox et al., 2008; Heckner, Neubauer, & Wolff, 2008; Heckner, Heilemann, & Wolff, 2009; Stvilia, 2009).

Another new way of organizing images on a site such as Flickr is via the use of geotagging. Geotagging is the act of attaching geographical identification to an image. Any location on earth can be found using a set of two-number coordinates: latitude and longitude (Bausch & Bumgardner, 2006). These coordinates can be used to create geotags in order to pinpoint the exact location that a photo was taken. Geotags can be automatically added to images that are taken by cameras or camera phones with inbuilt GPS tracking, or the tags can be found and attached at a later date using online maps.

7.3.2. Sharing

Thanks to digital communication and Web 2.0 technology the methods available to people for the sharing of their photos have evolved in new and unexpected ways since the days of analog photography.

Previously, if people had wanted to share images with others they would have had to do so in person, perhaps with everyone huddled around a physical album or with photos being passed around the room or displayed on a slide projector, as the proud photographer would describe what was happening in each and every photo. If other people wanted copies of any images then extra prints would need to be made from the negatives, or the chosen images could be photocopied. With the advent of digital cameras and free email accounts, people began to upload digital images onto computers and then either burn selected images onto a CD in order to give to friends or family, or email images as attachments. However, free email accounts tend to stipulate attachment limits of around 25 MB per email, and with a typical 12 megapixel point and shoot compact digital camera producing images between 2.5 and 5 MB, this allowance is soon used up when emailing digital photographs unless the person uses editing software to first of all reduce the file sizes before sending. Even if a selection of photographs were to be split and sent via a number of different emails, a recipient's inbox would soon become clogged and no longer able to accept more emails. There is also less scope for narrative or descriptions to be included with photos sent via email and unless the images sent are of a mutually shared event, then they can often seem out of context to the receiver who is viewing them; without the descriptions and verbal accompaniment to help hook in the viewer the images are often thought of as too abstract and viewing them in isolation on a computer is not an enjoyable experience (Van House et al., 2004).

Sites such as Flickr and Picasa allow people a place where they can upload their photos and also add accompanying details; they can give images a title, add descriptions to go with them, and assign keywords (i.e., tags). This means that the verbal narrative that used to go along with the physical nature of sharing analog photographs doesn't necessarily have to be lost if people take the time to add descriptions and tags to the photographs they upload. Uploading can even be done as a batch process so that a large number of images can be uploaded at the same time thus reducing the time-consuming nature of having to upload each image separately. Batch processes also allow for the same title/set of tags/descriptions to be added to all of the images within the batch at the same time and this can be useful for a selection of images all relating to a specific event or theme.

Uploading images to Web 2.0 sites used to be achieved by first of all transferring the images onto a computer hard drive and then browsing and uploading the images to the site via an Internet connection. Today, uploading images for both sharing and printing can be achieved directly from the camera itself. Fujifilm, Casio, Samsung, and Panasonic currently have a range of Wi-Fi enabled cameras, meaning that images can be uploaded online directly from the camera when there is a Wi-Fi connection. This eliminates the need to first of all connect the camera to a computer in order to upload images. The Panasonic FX90 has a dedicated "Wi-Fi button" on the camera for easy connection, and through Panasonic's "Lumix club" accounts on sites such as Flickr, Facebook, and Picasa, etc. can be connected to the camera and images can be shared simultaneously to all of the connected Web 2.0 sites at once. Nikon's COOLPIX S50c compact digital camera is connected to a service called COOLPIX CONNECT, whereby images can be sent to the service via a Wi-Fi connection, and an email notification can then be sent (direct from the camera) to alert friends and family that there are new images online for them to view. There is also a Picture Bank service that backs up the images in case the camera is lost.

7.4. Camera Phones: A New Realm of Photography

Whilst the shift from analog to digital and the emergence of Web 2.0 has dramatically changed how images are captured, stored, organized, and shared, the last decade has seen the emergence of new technology that has once again changed the practice of photography. Alongside changes in web technology, mobile phones have also gone through a big transition period in the last decade, and devices that were once merely a means of being able to talk and text on, have now transformed into devices that act as digital cameras, media players, pocket video cameras, GPS navigation units, and web browsers, aka smartphones.

It is the camera component of the smartphone that this chapter will focus on. Camera use on mobile phones was slow to gain acceptance from users at first. The early cameras were usually inferior to that of stand-alone compact digital cameras and so people did not like to rely on their camera phones for taking images at important events (Delis, 2010). Taking images to send via MMS (multimedia messaging service) to other people in a user's address book, was again slow to gain acceptance due to the fact that more people used to have pay as you go phones, and an MMS tended to cost slightly more to send than a normal text message so this deterred people from the service. There was also the problem of phone compatibility, as some MMS pictures could only be received if recipients had the same type of phone as the sender (*TheEconomist*, 2006). Yet by 2007, 83% of mobile phones came with an inbuilt digital camera (Terras, 2008) and in 2010, 50% of all mobile phone sales in the United States were predicted to be smartphones (White, 2010). This change has had subtle yet profound ramifications for photography. The fact that most smartphones now come with a high-quality inbuilt camera means that people are now happier to use their camera phones in place of stand-alone digital cameras. It was predicted that camera phone use would increase significantly when camera quality reached 4–5 megapixels; some camera phones currently on the market now have a 12 megapixel inbuilt camera (Clairmont, 2010). As such, people now carry a camera (i.e., a camera phone) with them everywhere they go and have it ready at hand to capture any "photo-opportunity." This has meant that rather than reserving image taking for special occasions such as parties, holidays, family gatherings, days out, etc., people now take images on a more daily basis, of the everyday things, items, and people that they come across. As Ames et al. (2010) point out, "more pictures of more kinds are taken in more settings that are not frequently seen with other cameras." The fact that such images are captured on a mobile phone means that they are often taken with the intent to share with friends, family, or loved ones in a communicative way; perhaps as a way of saying "I love you" or "I am thinking of you," through to the sharing of emotions such as "I am bored," or "I found this funny." For example, someone who takes a photo of a rose they pass in a flower garden on their way to work can send it to a loved one to let them know they are thinking of them; or someone taking a photo at a music concert can send it to a friend who wasn't able to attend so that they can at least partially share the experience with them. People are also taking more photos of the interesting and unusual things they come across in their daily lives, for example, humorous signage, a new beer they are about to drink, or an odd shaped cloud; people enjoy visually documenting their encounters and this has led to an emergent social practice in photography whereby people are capturing the fleeting, unexpected, and mundane aspects of everyday life (Okabe, 2004), often referred to as "ephemera photography" (Murray, 2008).

Coupled this with, more phone users now have monthly contracts rather than pay as you go packages, and this means that phone users often have data plans that allow them a substantial amount of time for connecting to the web. This has meant that rather than having to send MMS messages to contacts in one's phone address book to share images, people are now able to seamlessly upload images taken on their camera phones direct to sites such as Facebook, Twitter, Flickr, etc. so that they can share them with a group of people at the same time rather than having to send images individually to people. The fact that tags can be added to such images using the phone at the time of upload has further added to the "social-communication" genre of motivation as discussed earlier, and tags therefore often reflect the emotional or communicative intent that the image was taken with. For instance, an image taken of a blank computer screen in an office setting could be uploaded online and tagged with "bored," or "is it 5 o'clock yet?" or an image of an empty seat on an airplane tagged with "miss you," or "why aren't you with me?" Such tags reflect the emotional state of the image taker, rather than the content of the image, although the two don't necessarily have to be mutually exclusive.

However as well as taking images with the intent to share with specific friends and family, a smartphone's ability to interact with the web means that people are also taking images on their camera phones with the intention of sharing with the world at large.

7.4.1. Citizen Journalism

Linked to the area of social communication and the smartphone's ubiquity, its ability to connect easily to the web has led to the emergence of citizen journalism and the use of camera phones during times of tragedy and civil unrest. When a tragedy first unfolds, it is not always possible to send photojournalists to document the scene, such as was the case with the London Underground bombings in 2005. It was therefore the camera phone images taken by innocent people caught up in the tragedy that were sent via smartphones to news desks, which were then beamed around the world. During times of crisis, people often take photos to "document and make sense of these events … sharing photos in such situations can be informative, newsworthy, and therapeutic" (Liu et al., 2008). Images uploaded to sites such as Twitter also have the ability to go viral very quickly as there is a certain belief in the "truthfulness" of amateur photographs (Chalfen, 1987, p. 153).

Although many of these images are not necessarily being organized in a formal or structured way, they are nonetheless being socially organized, via the retweets and likes they receive on social networking sites, and it is the online community at large who will decide if an image is worth taking notice of.

7.4.2. Apps

As well as phones being able to connect with Web 2.0 platforms such as Facebook, Twitter, and Flickr, the emergence of the phone application (app) has also added a new element of playfulness and sociality to the taking of images. Apps are software programs that can "interrogate a web server and present formatted information to the user" (White, 2010). Apps are specifically developed for small handheld devices such as Personal Digital Assistants (PDAs), tablet computers, or mobile phones (although some apps do have web versions). Many phones now come with a selection of preinstalled basic apps that allow tasks and functions such as checking the weather, finding your position on a map, or quickly connecting to sites such as Facebook to be easily carried out at the touch of a button or screen icon. Apps are perhaps most synonymous with Apple's iPhone, as it was the Apple company that really created and marketed the concept of the app, but apps can be downloaded from a range of application distribution platforms, which are usually tied to a specific mobile operating system. There are currently six main platforms:

1. The Apple App Store (for Apple iPhones, iPod Touch, and the iPad)
2. Blackberry App World (for Blackberry Phones)
3. Google Play (for phones and tablet devices using an Android operating system)
4. Windows Phone Marketplace (for phones using a Windows operating system)
5. Amazon App Store (for Google Android phones and Kindle ebook readers)
6. Ovi Store (for Nokia phones)

App developers are always trying to think of new and innovative ideas and there are a whole host of apps that can be downloaded to assist with all aspects of daily life from grocery shopping, checking live travel information, finding out where the nearest ATM machine is, through to organizing a holiday, or playing a game. The area of photography is no exception, and there are a number of popular photography apps that have helped to further cement the notion of everyday vernacular photography and to also aid with the sharing of images. The two most notable instances in the genre of photography apps are Instagram and Hipstamatic.

Whilst Instagram is available on both Apple and Android platforms, Hipstamatic is only available for Apple devices. The apps pay homage to a recent resurgence in analog photography centered on the use of old Russian cameras that were badly made and hence produced grainy and unpredictable photos with light leaks and vignetting. The name given to this new cult trend is lomography. The Instagram and Hipstamatic apps seek to mimic the effects of lomographic cameras and allow the user to apply filters to images taken with the phone's camera; these filters give the image a look and feel reminiscent of the kind of images produced by the old Russian cameras, and the new lomographic analog cameras that seek to replicate them. The apps are marketed as producing vintage and retro looks, and borders can also be added to make images look like old Polaroid photographs. Once the user is happy with the filters and effects they have applied to their image, they can instantly upload them to sites such as Flickr, Twitter, Tumblr, Foursquare, and Posterous, as well as them being displayed on the app's homepage for other users of the app to see. When uploading an image from Instagram directly to Flickr, Tumblr, and Posterous, automatic tags are added to the image to indicate what app the image has been created with, and what filter has been applied to it. When uploading an image directly to Foursquare (a location based social networking website for mobiles), users can tag their images with a specific venue location, and venues are suggested based on the latitude and longitude of the phone's location. Such tags create useful groupings of images for people who want to search for images either of a specific location or of images taken with a specific app.

As mentioned previously, as well as the images produced via these apps being shared both privately and publicly with others (via MMS or Web 2.0 sites), they have also begun to be admired as stand-alone images with aesthetic worth as photographs in their own right, so much so that there have even been exhibitions at renowned London galleries for photos taken exclusively by these apps (see http://www.orangedotgallery.co.uk/hipstamatics-clippings/ and http://londonist.com/2011/09/my-world-shared-the-uk%E2%80%99s-first-instagram-exhibition-east-gallery-brick-lane.php). The third place prize in the 2011 "Pictures of the Year International" photojournalism contest was also an image taken with the Hipstamatic app (Buchanan, 2011).

However there is a certain cyclical nature surrounding these apps, as whilst their residence on mobile technology has created a new genre of photography in terms of subject matter, one of the primary aims of the apps is to transform "mundane everyday" images into ones that are more aesthetically pleasing via the use of filters and effects that often give the images a more vintage and age old quality. So whilst we are moving forward into a new genre of photography on the one hand, we are also anchoring ourselves to the past on the other hand, reluctant to truly let go of older forms of photography.

7.5. Conclusion

The organization of analog photographs was largely based on temporal and spatial groupings attached to the location and date surrounding when and where an image was taken. Digital technology changed the way people took, organized, and stored photographs, and due to the fact it became possible for an image to exist in more than one place at a time, images could be grouped according to a number of different cognitive facets in addition to their temporal and spatial affiliations, such as what an image was *of* or *about*, as well as low-level visual features such as shapes and colors contained within the image.

Whilst the initial switch from analog to digital caused concern that people's photographs would become lost in a digital abyss on ageing computer hard drives, web and mobile technology have provided new and novel ways in ensuring that people's photographs continue to be organized, and shared with both friends and family, and the world at large. Web 2.0 photo management sites such as Flickr have provided a new way for people to manage their photographs regardless of whether their intention is to create a private archive for themselves and future family members or a public portfolio for the world to see. Photographs can be socially organized via the use of tags and groups and the community aspect of Web 2.0 sites are a driving force behind people's motivation for uploading and sharing their images.

Advancements in mobile technology have added a new dimension to the ever changing photography landscape and camera phones have begun to alter the core subject matter of what is deemed as photo-worthy, a subject matter that has remained largely unchanged since the early days of photography. The ubiquity of the camera phone and its coupling with Web 2.0 technology has led to a new form of everyday photography, one that is keen to capture the mundane and fleeting aspects of daily life. Such images are often captured for their capacity to convey personal and shared meaning (i.e., via the use of MMS) and this in turn has led to images being organized based on emotional and communicative aspects relating to the reason behind image capture as well as the content of the image itself.

The future organization of photographs will be largely dependent on the technology that is available, and it is the technology that will be the driving force behind both the kinds of images we capture, and how we store, organize, and share them.

References

Ames, M., Eckles, D., Naaman, M., Spasojevic, M., & Van House, N. (2010). Requirements for mobile photoware. *Personal and Ubiquitous Computing*, *14*(2), 95–109.

Angus, E., & Thelwall, M. (2010). Motivations for image publishing and tagging on Flickr. Paper presented at the 14th international conference on electronic publishing, Hanken School of Economics, Helsinki.

Bausch, P., & Bumgardner, J. (2006). *Flickr hacks: Tips and tools for sharing photos online*. Sebastopol, CA: O'Reilly Media Inc.

Buchanan, M. (2011). Hipstamatic and the death of photojournalism. *Gizmodo*, February 10. Retrieved from http://gizmodo.com/5756703/is-hipstamatic-killing-photojournalism. Accessed on March 28, 2011.

Chalfen, R. (1987). *Snapshot versions of life*. Bowling Green, OH: Bowling Green State University Popular Press.

Clairmont, K. (2010). PMA data watch: Camera phone vs. digital camera use among U.S. households. *PMA Newsline*, June 7. Retrieved from http://pmanewsline.com/2010/06/07/pma-data-watch-camera-phone-vs-digital-camera-use-among-u-s-households/. Accessed on June 7, 2010.

Cox, A., Clough, P. D., & Marlow, J. (2008). Flickr: A first look at user behaviour in the context of photography as serious leisure. *Information Research 13*, 1. Available at http://InformationR.net/ir/13-1/paper336.html

Delis, D. (2010). Wireless photo sharing: The case for cameras that make calls. *PMA Magazine*, February 12.

Dutton, W. H., & Blank, G. (2011). *Next generation users: The internet in Britain*. Oxford internet survey 2011. Oxford, UK: Oxford Internet Institute, University of Oxford.

Evangelista, B. (2010). Photo site sees growth through social media. *SF Gate* (*San Francisco Chronicle*), April 10. Retrieved from http://articles.sfgate.com/2010-04-10/business/20843725_1. Accessed on April 13, 2010.

Frohlich, D., Kuchinsky, A., Pering, C., Don, A., & Ariss, S. (2002). Requirements for photoware. Paper presented at the Computer Supported Cooperative Work Conference '02, November 16–20, New Orleans, LA.

Grossman, L. (2006, December 13). *Time's person of the year: You*. Retrieved from http://www.time.com/time/magazine/article/0,9171,1569514,00.html. Accessed on January 8, 2007.

Heckner, M., Heilemann, M., & Wolff, C. (2009). Personal information management vs. resource sharing: Towards a model of information behaviour in social tagging systems. Paper presented at the third international conference for weblogs and social media, May 17–20, San Jose, CA.

Heckner, M., Neubauer, T., & Wolff, C. (2008). Tree, funny, to_read, google: What are tags supposed to achieve? A comparative analysis of user keywords for different digital resource types. Paper presented at the conference on information and knowledge management '08, October 26–30, Napa Valley, CA.

Jörgensen, C. (2003). *Image retrieval: Theory and research*. Lanham, MD: The Scarecrow Press Inc.

Kirk, D. S., Sellen, A. J., Rother, C., & Wood, K. R. (2006). Understanding photowork. Paper presented at the Conference on Human factors in Computing Systems, April 22–27, Montréal, Canada.

Liu, S. B., Palen, L., Sutton, J., Hughes, A. L., & Vieweg, S. (2008). In search of the bigger picture: The emergent role of on-line photo sharing in times of disaster. In F. Fiedrich & B. Van de Walle (Eds.), *Proceedings of the 5th international ISCRAM conference*, May, Washington, DC.

Marlow, C., Naaman, M., Boyd, D., & Davis, M. (2006). Position paper, tagging, taxonomy, flickr, article, toread. Paper presented at the collaborative web tagging workshop at WWW 2006, May, Edinburgh, Scotland.

Milgram, S. (1977). The image freezing machine. *Psychology Today*, January, p. 54.

Murray, S. (2008). Digital images, photo-sharing, and our shifting notions of everyday aesthetics. *Journal of Visual Culture*, *7*(2), 147–163.

Negoescu, R., Adams, B., Phung, D., Venkatesh, S., & Gatica-Perez, D. (2009). Flickr hypergroups. Paper presented at the ACM international conference on multimedia, October 19–24, Beijing, China.

Nov, O., Naaman, M., & Ye, C. (2009a). Analysis of participation in an online photo-sharing community: A multidimensional perspective. *Journal of the American Society for Information Science and Technology*, *61*(3), 555–566.

Nov, O., Naaman, M., & Ye, C. (2009b). Motivational, structural and tenure factors that impact online community photo sharing. *Proceedings of AAAI international conference on weblogs and social media (ICWSM 2009)*, May, San Jose, CA.

Okabe, D. (2004). Emergent social practices, situations and relations through everyday camera phone use. Paper presented at the 2004 international conference on mobile communication, October 18–19, Seoul, Korea.

O'Reilly, T. (2005). *What is Web 2.0: Design patterns and business models for the next generation of software*. Retrieved from http://www.oreillynet.com/pub/a/oreilly/tim/news/2005/09/30/what_is_web_20.html. Accessed on April 13, 2007.

Panofsky, E. (1983). *Meaning in the visual arts*. Singapore: Peregrine Books.

Remick, J. (2010). *Top 20 photo storage and sharing sites*. Retrieved from http://web.appstorm.net/roundups/media-roundups/top-20-photo-storage-and-sharing-sites/. Accessed on February 13, 2011.

Seabrook, J. (1991). My life in that box. In J. Spence & P. Holland (Eds.), *Family snaps: The meaning of domestic photography*. London: Virago Press.

Shatford-Layne, S. (1994). Some issues in the indexing of images. *Journal of the American Society for Information Science*, *45*(8), 583–588.

Sontag, S. (1977). *On photography*. London: Penguin Books.

Stvilia, B. (2009). User-generated collection-level metadata in an online photo-sharing system. *Library & Information Science Research*, *31*, 54–65.

Terras, M. M. (2008). *Digital images for the information professional*. Hampshire: Ashgate Publishing Limited.

The Economist. (2006). Lack of text appeal. *The Economist*, *380*(8489), 56.

Van House, N. (2007). Flickr and public image-sharing: Distant closeness and photo exhibition. Paper presented at the conference on human factors in computing systems, April 28–May 3, San Jose, CA.

Van House, N., Davis, M., Ames, M., Finn, M., & Viswanathan, V. (2005). The use of personal networked digital imaging: An empirical study of cameraphone photos and sharing. Paper presented at the conference on human factors in computing systems, April 2–7, Portland, OR.

Van House, N. A., Davis, M., Takhteyev, Y., Ames, M., & Finn, M. (2004). *The social uses of personal photography: Methods for projecting future imaging applications*. Retrieved from http://people.ischool.berkeley.edu/~vanhouse/photo_project/pubs/vanhouse_et_al_2004b.pdf

Weinberger, D. (2007). *Everything is miscellaneous: The power of the new digital disorder*. New York, NY: Times Books.

White, M. (2010). Information anywhere, any when: The role of the smartphone. *Business Information Review*, *27*(4), 242–247.

Xu, Z., Fu, Y., Mao, J., & Su, D. (2006). Towards the semantic web: Collaborative tag suggestions. *Proceedings of the collaborative web tagging workshop at the WWW*, May, Edinburgh, Scotland.

SECTION III: LIBRARY CATALOGS: TOWARD AN INTERACTIVE NETWORK OF COMMUNICATION

Chapter 8

VuFind — An OPAC 2.0?

Birong Ho and Laura Horne-Popp

Abstract

Purpose — The chapter aims to present a case study of what is involved in implementing the VuFind discovery tool and to describe usability, usage, and feedback of VuFind.

Design/methodology/approach — The chapter briefly documents Western Michigan University (WMU) and University of Richmond's (UR) experience with VuFind. WMU Libraries embarked on a process of implementing a new catalog interface in 2008. UR implemented VuFind in 2012. The usability result and usage of Web 2.0 features are discussed.

Findings — The implementation processes at WMU and UR differ. At WMU, users' input was not consistent and demanded software customization. UR strategically began with a very focused project management approach, and intended the product as short-term solution. The usability and feedback from several sites are also presented.

Practical implications — The benefits of using open source software include low barrier and cost to entry, highly customizable code, and unlimited instances (libraries may run as many copies of as many components as needed, on as many pieces of hardware as they have, for as many purposes as they wish). With the usability studies presented, VuFind is proved to be a valid solution for libraries.

New Directions in Information Organization
Library and Information Science, Volume 7, 159–171

ISSN: 1876-0562/doi:10.1108/S1876-0562(2013)0000007012

Originality/value — The chapter provides a unique account of library's experience providing an alternative catalog interface using open source software. It also uniquely reports on VuFind usability and initial testing results and evaluation.

8.1. Introduction

Library online public access catalogs (OPACs) have been relatively the same for years. OPACs continue to display Machine Readable Cataloging (MARC) records much as the information looked when libraries used print card catalogs. This continuity in display has proven less useful over the years, particularly as online search engines changed the nature of searching. It was no longer necessary for a user to have an understanding of controlled vocabulary as full-text searching replaced subject heading searches. Libraries have attempted to improve the searching features of their OPACs to mimic the search results of search engines; however, users are generally not satisfied with the results they get from OPACs. The look of OPACs has improved, but users are still frustrated by the un-intuitive library catalog interfaces that can't handle searches that start with articles, that don't enable easy discovery of similar items and that don't allow for interaction with the library records.

Web 2.0 features added to OPACs have attempted to reduce the limitations of traditional library catalog searches (Antelman, Lynema, & Pace, 2006; Breeding, 2010, 2007). Again, developers have looked to search engines to enable more successful searches in library catalogs. Web 2.0 OPAC features make use of the single search box along with "did you mean?" suggestions in the event the search isn't successful (usually due to misspellings). There have also been attempts to create relevancy rankings in OPACs that work as well as search engines. Another Web 2.0 technology hallmark is the ability for users to interact with the records, such as comments or tagging items for personal information management. Interacting with records in a library catalog has been of interest to academic libraries as a beneficial feature for researchers and scholarly communication. Faceted searching is another key feature of Web 2.0 OPACs (Fagan, 2010; Hearst, 2008). Librarians have long dreamed of better ways to utilize subject and authority headings from search results. Faceting has been the promise that users would be able to narrow their results from the myriad of search results listed from keyword searching. Licensed academic databases have been offering this for a number of years with great success; traditional library catalogs have not. Many studies of user information behavior have shown that library catalogs aren't the first place people begin their research (Head & Eisenberg, 2009; Xuemei, 2010; Yu & Young, 2004). Likely this shift is due to the library OPACs' inability to provide underlying sophistication to users' searches. If Web 2.0 OPACs can provide the sophistication and ease of use needed by the average searcher, then it may be possible to bring users back to the library catalog as a starting point.

8.2. Choosing a Web 2.0 OPAC Interface

By 2008, many libraries using Ex Libris' Integrated Library System (ILS), Voyager, and its OPAC, WebVoyage, were frustrated. WebVoyage failed to keep pace with the state of web development, including Web 2.0 trends. Version 6.5.3 had significant deficiencies, such as the continued inability to handle initial articles in keyword searching. (A title search for "the old man and the sea" yielded no results. Libraries were required to implement a "title keyword" search to allow usage of initial articles with any search results). Ex Libris released Voyager 7.0 in 2008 including a new version of WebVoyage with a more modern look and feel. However, WebVoyage 7 still relied on Voyager's inflexible user searching indexes. This hampered ability to improve relevancy searching and make use of facets.

At the 2008 Ex Libris Users of North America (ELUNA) conference, the company stated its strategy to commit resources to Primo, a search and discovery product, using the new Unified Resource Management (URM) concept (Rochkind, 2007). Ex Libris continued releasing refined versions of Voyager and its components while it developed Primo, yet clearly determined URM as its main emphasis for future development. At the 2012 ELUNA conference, Ex Libris restated its strategy to commit resources to Primo and ALMA (formally known as URM). This left Voyager libraries with several choices: continue using WebVoyage that would no longer be supported, use Primo (a very expensive tool) as its OPAC or implement an open source OPAC with Web 2.0 features. Many libraries went with implementing an open source product for their library catalog, it was the most feasible and affordable choice.

From 2007 to 2012, a variety of search and discovery tools became available to libraries (Yang & Hofmann, 2010; Yang & Wagner, 2010). There are now new URM products such as ALMA. There have been open source ILS systems developed such as Evergreen, Koha, Open Library Environment (OLE) Project and eXtensible Catalog. These newly developed systems require libraries to completely replace their technological systems. Many libraries could not implement these due to cost of the system or a lack of technological expertise. A new bevy of "discovery tools" was developed enabling users to search a library catalog along with licensed databases. The three major discovery tools have been Serial Solutions' Summon, EBSCO Discovery and Ex Libris' *Primo*. These discovery tools have gained popularity, but again are prohibitively expensive for many libraries. Many academic libraries have taken to waiting to see which product will develop into the most robust and supported system possible in order to plan for the costs of such a system.

Libraries unable, or not ready, to implement an URM, a discovery tool or a new open source ILS project, had the option of implementing software that could improve the OPAC. In 2006, North Caroline State University deployed Endeca and in 2007 OCLC introduced WorldCat Local. Other licensed OPAC interfaces became available such as Innovative Interfaces' Encore, Ex Libris' Primo, and AquaBrowser. There have been a handful of open source OPAC interfaces with Blacklight and VuFind being the best known.

Vufind was developed as a library discovery tool seeking to replace the weakest link in the traditional ILS, the database structure (Katz & Nagy, 2012). VuFind placed index-based searching on top of Voyager's database. VuFind became a viable option for libraries needing to implement a Web 2.0 OPAC due to its lack of fees, its low hardware costs, and its server maintenance (Houser, 2008; Nagy & Garrison, 2009; Seaman, 2012). Emanuel (2011) illustrated the cost factor and discussed the VuFind implementation at the Consortium of Academic and Research Libraries in Illinois (CARLI) libraries. VuFind's low implementation costs are offset with the requirement for substantial technological expertise, particularly in programming. Western Michigan University (WMU) compared the various search and discovery tools available in 2008 to determine the product to implement and chose VuFind (see Table 8.1).

Table 8.1: WMU local analysis of OPAC replacement products ca. 2008.

Search/discovery tool	Cost considerations	Technical/other issues
WorldCat Local	Expensive ($50,000+)	Showed OCLC's metadata, not local
Endeca	Prohibitively expensive	Very low install base
Primo	$30,000+ startup plus maintenance	
AquaBrowser		Busy interface, few our size to compare
Encore		Doesn't work well with Voyager
WebVoyage 7, 8		Inflexible indexes and interface
VuFind	Open source	Designed to work with Voyager

8.3. Implementation of VuFind

Because VuFind is an open source-based OPAC, there are different versions. Most libraries have adopted different versions of the VuFind "Stable Version" (1.0–1.3) and provided substantial local customization of the code. Many of these local customizations have focused on different search functions and on location facets. WMU's implementation started with version 1.0 and migrated to version 1.0.1.

VuFind is a flexible system that requires programming expertise. It was designed to run on Apache Solr, an open source platform that enables full text searching and facet searching. A program called SolrMARC is used to index MARC record fields into a Solr index. The MARC records reside in the Voyager server, while the Solr index and SolrMARC program are on a separate server dedicated to VuFind. The WMU Library technical systems team modified some configurations that import MARC metadata into the SolrMARC program. This was done to create specific indexes needed for searches such as publisher numbers and OCLC record numbers.

By default, VuFind is limited to one configuration per library. This can be an issue for libraries with multiple branch locations. WMU has five branch locations in four buildings. Therefore, a location limit was introduced to VuFind as a facet in the results page to help users reduce hits to specific buildings and collections as necessary. This ability to limit results to specific locations was done by extracting holdings information from Voyager and importing the information daily into VuFind. University of Michigan and CARLI libraries developed another way to limit to different branch libraries by having users select the specific library at the beginning of a search.

WMU made other customizations in the catalog records to aid users. Links to the Michigan eLibrary Catalog (MeLCat) and to OCLC Worldcat were added to expediate interlibrary loan requests. Also, a link to Google Books was added to individual records in order to provide users more information about an item. WMU improved the retrieval response time of cover images and reviews from Syndetic Solutions by implementing a customized programming algorithm. As with all of WMU's locally written and modified code, these improvements were shared with the VuFind. This was implemented in release 1.0.

VuFind has had a number of releases and a strong user community who work together on developing improvements to the code and functionality of VuFind. Customizations are routinely shared and incorporated in updates. Libraries in the VuFind community stay in contact to get programming assistance as well as share their solutions. There are also commercial companies that help libraries with customizing and supporting their own iterations of VuFind.

8.4. Usability, Usage, and Feedback of VuFind

A number of libraries that implemented VuFind have conducted usability studies to determine users' satisfaction with its features. The University of Michigan did a Mirlyn Search Satisfaction Survey of users in 2011 (Desai et al., 2011). The survey demonstrated that undergraduate students and graduate students rated high levels of satisfaction of the university's VuFind implementation (89% of undergraduates and 87% of graduate students gave high ratings to the OPAC). Interestingly, the Mirlyn survey documented that students in the survey conducted more known item searching than subject searching. Students in the survey rated higher satisfaction with the known item searching in VuFind than subject searching. The survey also captured user feedback about display features in Mirlyn. Respondents did not ask for major changes to the search features or display, but researchers thought modifications to the subject search would raise user satisfaction from "moderately high" to high.

Another usability study was done at Columbia College Chicago of the CARLI VuFind implementation in 2009 (CCC Library, 2009). The study consisted of 30 student participants who performed a series of tasks in the OPAC to determine the success of the implementation and provide feedback. Participants were asked to interpret holdings' information, locate the "Show all libraries" link, and create a login to the shared CARLI system. The 30 participants highly praised the CARLI VuFind interface. The participants made two recommendations regarding the VuFind OPAC: first, to make this iteration of the CARLI catalog the default display of the library website. Second, some participants desired more customization of the CARLI VuFind implementation. In particular, participants wanted the multiple status information to be removed from the search results' list, to move the faceted search from the right of the webpage to the left, and add text above the login box to prompt users to create an account if it was the first time using the VuFind OPAC. Both the University of Michigan and the Columbia College Chicago studies of their VuFind implementations demonstrated high satisfaction from users.

From 2008 to 2009, WMU conducted several usability studies at different stages of the library's VuFind implementation (Ho, Kelley, & Garrison, 2009). Phase I of the study included 10 undergraduate students in 2008. The WMU web team repeated the questions used in Yale's usability study of VuFind (Bauer, 2008). In Phase I, participants provided comments on the search experience they expected in an OPAC, constantly referring to

Google: "Google is the standard," "It should be like Google — type in whatever and tons of stuff comes up," "Google brings instant results, maybe a lot I don't need, but a result is somewhere," and "Everyone knows how to use Google" (Ho & Bair, 2008; Ho et al., 2009). These comments reinforced the need for a good search algorithm promised in VuFind's indexing. The web team used the Phase I participants' feedback on search experiences to tweak their beta VuFind implementation.

In 2009, WMU performed Phase II of the usability study. The number and variety of participants increased, including 10 undergraduates, 10 graduate students, and 10 faculty members. The participants were from the Central, East, and Engineering campuses. This phase of the study focused on both searching and the features of VuFind. This phase asked participants to perform different types of searches and search limits. Participants also examined features unique to VuFind such as the search suggestion box, facets, and "search within." Phase II participant search results were far better than those in Phase I. All Phase II participants succeeded in their searches, due to refinements of the Solr search parameters done by the web team after the Phase I usability study. Phase II participants showed high levels of satisfaction.

Through the usability studies at WMU, it was evident that participants saw VuFind as a major improvement to the catalog, particularly in searching and narrowing results. The WMU web team wanted to determine if users were making use of the newer Web 2.0 features available in VuFind, particularly the tagging and comments features. Over the period of 2009–2010, 489 users created 5940 tags at WMU in the VuFind interface (Ho, 2012). Twenty-four percent of those who used the tagging feature used it once (117 users). Another 24% of users tagged at least two records (115 users). Twenty-two users at WMU used the tags 20–100 times and there were some outlier users who tagged 400–500 tags (see Chart 8.1). Some of the tag usage was the result of bibliographic instruction. Instruction in tagging seemed beneficial. The WMU web team noticed many VuFind users clicked on the tag link but didn't add any tags. This feature requires the user to log into a personal VuFind account, which may confuse users or be deemed too onerous.

The University of Richmond (UR) implemented VuFind in the fall of 2012, making use of the new Library Systems Librarian's experience with VuFind at WMU. UR did not perform usability studies, but tag-usage information of VuFind in the six months of implementation was available. In the several months of VuFind going live at UR, there were 359 tags created by 316 users. Ninety percent of users created a tag once (284 users). Seventeen users created two tags, roughly .05% of tag users. Twelve users tagged a VuFind record four to seven times, about .03% of taggers. There was one user who used tags 15 times and another who used tags 16 times.

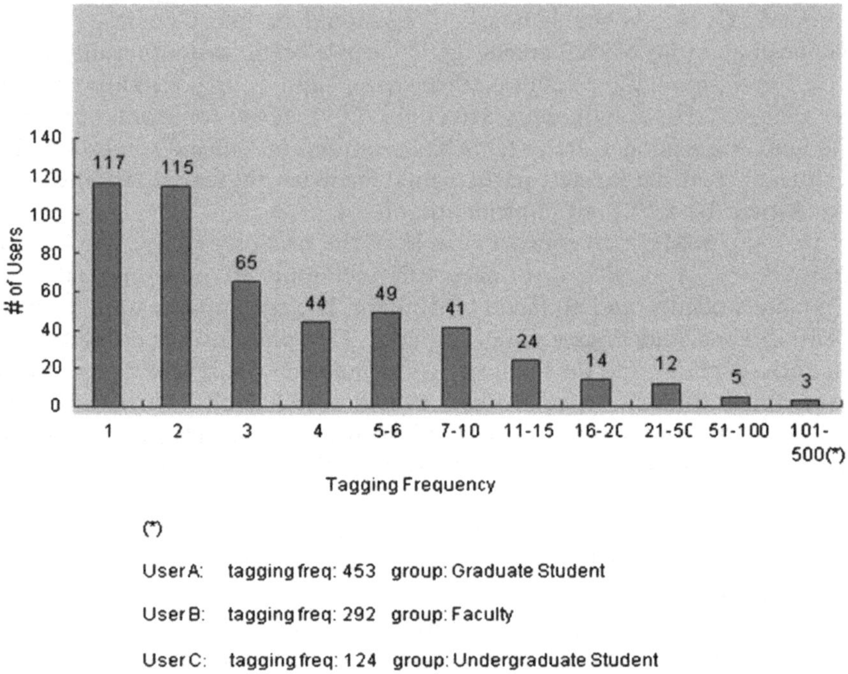

Chart 8.1: Tagging usage at WMU (2009–2010).

The highest user of tags (at 20 tags) was the Library Systems Librarian as the feature was being tested (see Chart 8.2). This may seem like rather small numbers, but it must be remembered that VuFind has only been live for several months and UR is a small liberal arts university with roughly 3,800 students. UR requires library research instruction in its first year seminars. The research librarians involved in each seminar provided instruction on the new VuFind interface, including the ability to use tags and comments. It is assumed the 90% of users who tagged a record once were predominately exploring this feature in these instruction sessions.

The minimal usage of tags at WMU and UR coincides with other usage studies of VuFind. Bauer (2008) noted users ranked the tagging feature last of possible features in VuFind or other library interface. It appears that using tags in VuFind will need to be encouraged. Reference librarians can demonstrate these in their instruction and subject liaisons can demonstrate the value of tags and comments to faculty departments, such as tagging-related subject books into one tag to be used as their reading list for their classes.

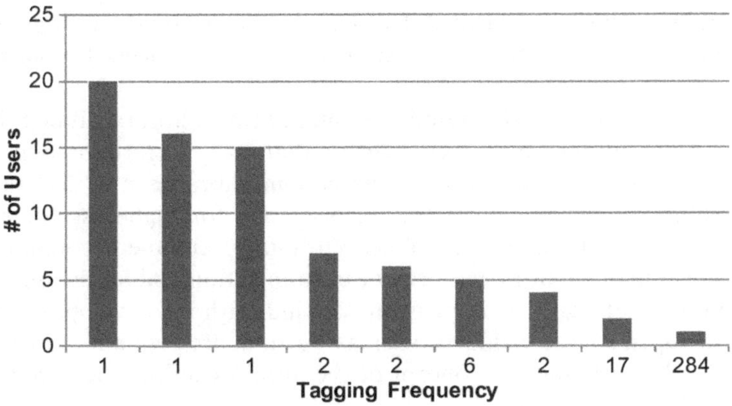

Chart 8.2: Tag Usage at UR (2012).

Some may argue if researchers are not making usage of tags or comment features then they are not needed or valued. However, a study done of tag usage at Wake Forest University demonstrated tags created by users were either of a process (i.e., research) focus or of a course focus (Mitchell, 2011). This study supports academic librarians' intuition that Web 2.0 tagging and comment features directly support researchers' information organization needs.

8.5. Conclusion

Libraries have struggled to improve their OPACs in order to maintain relevancy in the minds of information users. Users demand OPACs operate like search engines or stop using them. Libraries have limited options in improving their OPACs due either to constrained budgets that cannot accommodate high priced commercial products or to a lack of staff ability to implement open source products. VuFind has enabled a number of libraries to improve the searching results and features similar to how search engines operate. In addition to improved search functions, VuFind provides many of the Web 2.0 features web users come across in online article databases and shopping websites.

VuFind's ability to be completely customizable to suit the needs of a library's community is a major advantage of the product. Usability studies of VuFind demonstrate users' satisfaction with its search and Web 2.0 features. While many of the Web 2.0 features such as tagging and comments have not been heavily used as yet by library users, the potential for increased use is there. The sophisticated features within VuFind are appreciated by users, particularly suggested search phrases and facets for narrowing results.

VuFind is an inexpensive solution to an improved library catalog. It does require programming and server expertise that many libraries may not have in-house. Because of this learning curve, some libraries may feel the only viable solution for their communities is to pay for high-cost commercial products. However, there is a robust VuFind development community as well as a group of vendors that provide customization and hardware support for libraries that want to implement VuFind without developing internal expertise. Open source products, such as VuFind, are giving libraries a third way toward improving the concept of the library catalog, the core tool for accessing library holdings.

8.6. Term Definition

OPAC — An Online Public Access Catalog (often abbreviated as OPAC or simply Library Catalog) is an online database of materials held by a library or group of libraries. Users search a library catalog principally to locate books and other material physically located at a library.

Next-Generation Catalog: is referred as the New OPAC

Discovery systems — sometimes, is referred to Next-Generation Catalog. Such systems took things quite a bit further — in terms of interface design and content covered. The interfaces were built on more open technologies, and included design cues and features users have come to expect — like faceted browsing. In addition, these next generation catalogs often had the capacity to harvest other local collections into the same interface — like a library or institution's digital collections and institutional repository materials.

Web 2.0 — The term Web 2.0 is associated with web applications that facilitate participatory information sharing, interoperability, user-centered design, and collaboration on the World Wide Web. A Web 2.0 site allows users to interact and collaborate with each other in a social media dialog as creators (prosumers) of user-generated content in a virtual community, in contrast to websites where users (consumers) are limited to the passive viewing of content that was created for them. Examples of Web 2.0 include social networking sites, blogs, wikis, video sharing sites, hosted services, web applications, mashups, and folksonomies.

The term is closely associated with Tim O'Reilly because of the O'Reilly Media Web 2.0 conference in late 2004.

Web usability — Web usability is an approach to make websites easy to use for an end-user, without the requirement that any specialized training be undertaken. The user should be able to intuitively relate the actions he needs to perform on the web page, with other interactions he sees in the general domain of life, for example, press of a button leads to some action.

References

Antelman, K., Lynema, E., & Pace, A. K. (2006). Toward a twenty-first century library catalog. *Information Technology and Libraries*, *25*, 128–139.

Bauer, K. (2008). *Yale University VuFind Usability Test – Undergraduates*. Retrieved from https://collaborate.library.yale.edu/usability/reports/YuFind/summary_under graduate.doc. Accessed on September 17, 2012.

Breeding, M. (2007). Introduction to 'Next Generation' library catalogs. *Library Technology Reports*, *43*, 5–14.

Breeding, M. (2010). The state of the art in library discovery. *Computers in Libraries*, *30*, 31–34.

Columbia College Chicago Library. (2009). *VuFind Usability Report*. Retrieved from http://www.lib.colum.edu/CCCLibrary_VuFindReport.pdf. Accessed on September 17, 2012.

Desai, S., Piacentine, J., Rothman, J., Fulmer, D., Hill, R., Koparkar, S., Moussa, N., & Wang, M. (2011). *Mirlyn Search Satisfaction Survey*. Retrieved from http://www.lib.umich.edu/sites/default/files/usability_reports/MirlynSearchSurvey_Feb 2011.pdf. Accessed on September 17, 2012.

Emanuel, J. (2011). Usability of the VuFind next-generation online catalog. *Information Technology and Libraries*, *30*(1), 44–52.

Ex Libris (n.d.). *Primo. ExLibris Primo*. Retrieved from http://www.exlibrisgroup.com/category/PrimoOverview. Accessed on September 17, 2012. (last modified 2010).

ExLibris. (2009). *Unified resource management: The Ex Libris framework for next-generation library services*. Jerusalem: Ex Libris. Retrieved from http://www.exlibrisgroup.com/files/Solutions/TheExLibris-FrameworkforNextGeneration LibraryServices.pdf. Accessed on September 17, 2012.

Fagan, J. C. (2010). Usability studies of faceted browsing: A literature review. *Information Technology and Libraries*, *29*, 58–66.

Head, A. J., & Eisenberg, M. B. (2009). *Lessons learned: How college students seek information in the digital age*. Seattle, WA: Project Information Literacy, University of Washington Information School. Retrieved from http://projectinfolit.org/publications/. Accessed on January 5, 2011.

Hearst, M. A. (2008). UIs for faceted navigation: Recent advances and remaining open problems. *HCIR 2008: Proceedings of the second workshop on human–computer interaction and information retrieval*. Microsoft Research, Redmond (pp. 13–17). Retrieved from http://research.microsoft.com/en-us/um/people/ryenw/hcir2008/doc/HCIR08-Proceedings.pdf. Accessed on September 17, 2012.

Ho, B. (2012). Does VuFind meet the needs of Web 2.0 users? A year after. In J. Tramullas & P. Garrido (Eds.), *Library automation and OPAC 2.0: Information access and services in the 2.0 Landscape* (pp. 100–120). Hershey, PA: Information Science Reference.

Ho, B., & Bair, S. (2008). Inventing a Web 2.0 Catalog: VuFind at Western Michigan University. Presented at the annual meeting of the Michigan Library Association, Kalamazoo, MI, October. Retrieved from http://www.mla.lib.mi.us/files/Annual2008-1-4-1%201.pdf. Accessed on September 17, 2012.

Ho, B., Kelley, K. J., & Garrison, S. (2009). Implementing VuFind as an alternative to Voyager's Web-Voyáge interface: One library's experience. *Library Hi Tech*, *27*, 82–92.

Houser, J. (2008). The VuFind implementation at Villanova University. *Library Hi Tech*, *27*, 93–105.

Innovative Interfaces, Inc. (n.d.). Encore. *Innovative.* Retrieved from http://www.iii.com/products/encore.shtml. Accessed on September 17, 2012 (last modified 2008).

Katz, D., & Nagy, A. (2012). VuFind: Solr power in the library. In J. Tramullas & P. Garrido (Eds.), *Library automation and OPAC 2.0: Information access and services in the 2.0 Landscape* (pp. 73–99). Hershey, PA: Information Science Reference.

Mitchell, E. (2011). Social media web service VuFind, data from service user. *LITA, ALA annual conference*, Chicago, IL. Retrieved from http://connect.ala.org/files/Ala2011vufindzsr%201.pdf. Accessed on September 17, 2012.

Nagy, A., & Garrison, S. (2009). The Next-Gen catalog is only part of the solution. Presented at the LITA National Forum, October 3, Salt Lake City, UT. Retrieved from http://connect.ala.org/node/84816. Last Accessed on September 17, 2012.

OCLC, Inc. (n.d.). WorldCat® Local. *OCLC.org*. Retrieved from http://www.oclc.org/worldcatlocal/default.htm. Accessed on September 17, 2012 (last modified 2011).

Rochkind, J. (2007). (Meta)Search like Google. *Library Journal*, *132*(3), 28–30.

Seaman, G. (2012, March). *Adapting VuFind as a front-end to a commercial discovery system.* Retrieved from http://www.ariadne.ac.uk/issue68/seaman. Accessed on September 17, 2012.

Serial Solutions. (n.d.). *AquaBrowser®* Discovery Layer. *SerialSolutions.com.* Retrieved from http://www.serialssolutions.com/aquabrowser/Serial. Accessed on September 17, 2012 (last modified 2010).

Serial Solutions. (n.d.). The Summon Service. *SerialSolutions.com.* Retrieved from http://www.serialssolutions.com/Summon/. Accessed on September 17, 2012 (last modified 2010).

Villanova University. (n.d.). VuFind the library OPAC meets Web 2.0. *VuFind.org.* Retrieved from http://vufind.org. Accessed on September 17, 2012.

Xuemei, G. (2010). Information-seeking behavior in the digital age: A multidisciplinary study of academic researchers. *College & Research Libraries*, *71*(5), 435–455.

Yang, S. Q., & Hofmann, M. A. (2010). The next generation library catalog: A comparative study of the OPACs of Koha, Evergreen, and Voyager. *Information Technology in Libraries*, *29*, 141–150.

Yang, S. Q., & Wagner, K. (2010). Evaluating and comparing discovery tools: How close are we towards next generation catalog? *Library Hi Tech*, *28*, 690–709.

Yu, H., & Young, M. (2004). The impact of web search engines on subject searching in OPAC. *Information Technology & Libraries*, *23*(4), 168–180.

Chapter 9

Faceted Search in Library Catalogs

Xi Niu

Abstract

Purpose — In recent years, aceted search has been a well-accepted approach for many academic libraries across the United States. This chapter is based on the author's dissertation and work of many years on faceted library catalogs. Not to hope to be exhaustive, the author's aim is to provide sufficient depth and breadth to offer a useful resource to researchers, librarians, and practitioners about faceted search used in library catalogs.

Method — The chapter reviews different aspects of faceted search used in academic libraries, from the theory, the history, to the implementation. It starts with the history of online public access catalogs (OPACs) and how people search with OPACs. Then it introduces the classic facet theory and its relationship with faceted search. At last, various academic research projects on faceted search, especially faceted library catalogs, are briefly reviewed. These projects include both implementation studies and the evaluation studies.

Findings — The results indicate that most searchers were able to understand the concept of facets naturally and easily. Compared to text searches, however, faceted searches were complementary and supplemental, and used only by a small group of searchers.

Practical implications — The author hopes that the facet feature has not only been cosmetic but the answer to the call for the next generation catalog for academic libraries. The results of this research are intended

New Directions in Information Organization
Library and Information Science, Volume 7, 173–208

ISSN: 1876-0562/doi:10.1108/S1876-0562(2013)0000007013

to inform librarians and library information technology (IT) staff to improve the effectiveness of the catalogs to help people find information they need more efficiently.

9.1. Background

Mankind by nature is an information consumer. As information becomes more and more ubiquitously available, various search technologies are in demand to facilitate the access to information and to learn about the world. A current search system must go beyond the traditional query-response and ranked list paradigm to incorporate the increase in human searching behavior, such as filtering, browsing, and exploring, in addition to simple look-up. Modern search engine technology already does a reasonable job of tackling the problem of what library scientists call *known-item search*, in which the user knows which documents to search for, or at least knows about certain aspects of the documents. In contrast, comparably mature tools for exploratory search, where the information needs and target documents may not even be well established, are not well developed (Tunkelang, 2009). In addition, in order to organize search results, traditional search systems usually display results in a single list ranked by relevance. Information seekers, however, often require a user interface that organizes search results into meaningful groups in order to better understand and utilize the results (Hearst, 2006).

Faceted search, which categorizes and summarizes search results, is a way to extend ranked lists. It also helps mitigate difficulties in query formulation and incorporates browsing into the search process. Faceted search is widely used in both commercial web search engines and library catalogs. Faceted classification, a classic theory in library science of knowledge representation developed in the 1930s by Ranganathan, overcomes the rigidity of traditional bibliographic classifications by offering a flexible, multidimensional view of knowledge. Since 2006, facet theory has been actively used in information retrieval (IR) and employed to create numerous faceted search systems. Faceted search systems map the multidimensional classification of knowledge presentation level into multiple access points of knowledge access level. The central concept derived from early facet theory is that the facets are "clearly defined, mutually exclusive, and collectively exhaustive aspects" of knowledge (Taylor, 1992). In many current faceted search systems, however, the overlap of facets may occur, and the facets may not be exhaustive.

This chapter aims to survey the existing research on information-seeking behavior in an online public access catalog (OPAC) environment, facet theory and faceted search, and previous academic research into the topic of faceted search.

Section 9.1 starts with a review of information-seeking behavior in the setting of OPACs. Section 9.2 moves to the foundation of faceted search, that is, facet theory and faceted classification. Then, Section 9.3 surveys some well-known research projects on faceted search systems, which include faceted library catalogs, and also reviews the empirical research into ways that people search through a faceted system. Finally, Section 9.4 discusses some practical concerns and future directions for faceted search in library catalogs.

9.2. Context: Information-Seeking Behavior in Online Library Catalog Environments

The body of literature that concerns information-seeking behavior is quite large, and some of it focuses on a particular kind of information system. The focus of this study is OPACs because this research focuses on ways that people search through faceted library catalogs.

9.2.1. Brief History of Online Public Access Catalogs (OPACs)

A library catalog is an organized set of bibliographic records that represents the holdings of a particular collection and/or resources accessible in a particular location (Taylor, 2006). The two major reasons to use catalogs are for retrieval and inventory purposes. Library catalogs can assume different forms: book catalogs, card catalogs, microform catalogs, CD-ROM catalogs, and online catalogs (OPACs). The latter form is currently prevalent in libraries in the United States, and is the focus of this review.

Early online catalog systems appeared in the late 1970s and early 1980s and are considered to be the first generation of OPACs. These early systems tended to replicate card catalogs but in a digital environment, and contained the same bibliographic information as library cards and provided some access points. Using a dedicated terminal or telnet client, users could search a handful of pre-coordinate indices and browse the resulting display in much the same way they had previously navigated the card catalog. Most of these early catalogs required an exact match between the user's input and the bibliographic record, thereby reducing the recall rate. Users seemed inclined to conduct known-item searches on an OPAC.

The second-generation OPACs are catalogs with more user-friendly systems than the first-generation ones and are still found in many libraries.

Such OPACs include more sophisticated features, such as keyword searching on titles and other fields within the bibliographic record, Boolean matching, browsing functions, and ancillary functions. About the same time that these second-generation catalogs began to emerge, libraries began to develop applications to automate purchasing, cataloging, and circulation of books and other library materials. These applications, known as an integrated library system (ILS) or library management system, treated the OPAC as one module of the whole system.

Since the 1990s, rapid advances of computer and communication technologies and the fast growth of bibliographic utilities and networks have led to the development of OPACs. The Internet and, more specifically, the web undoubtedly have made OPACs remotely accessible and widely available, and web-based OPACs began to emerge in the late 1990s. In addition to web technology, these OPACs incorporated other new features, such as online resources, book covers, hyperlinks, and other features aimed at improving the interface. Despite the migration from catalogs to web interfaces, the underlying indices and exact-match Boolean search found in most library catalog systems, however, did not advance much beyond the second-generation catalogs. Web OPACs are considered to be advanced second-generation OPACs, which serve as a gateway to resources held not only by a particular library but also by other linked libraries, and further to regional, national and international resources (Babu & O'Brien, 2000).

Since the emergence of web OPACs, the major developments in OPAC technology are stabilized. Meanwhile, the industry outside of libraries has developed different types of web-based IR systems. Web search engines, such as Google, and popular e-commerce websites, such as Amazon.com, provide simple yet powerful search systems. As the Internet has become more and more accessible to people, OPAC users have grown more and more accustomed to these websites and search engines. As such, they began to express increasing dissatisfaction with library catalog systems. This dissatisfaction has led in recent years to the development of newer, often termed *next-generation*, catalogs that have brought back wide attention to OPAC research.

These next-generation catalogs use more advanced search technologies than their previous counterparts, including in particular, faceted search and features aimed at greater user interaction and participation with the system, including some Web 2.0 technology, such as tagging, reviewing, and RSS feeds. The collaboration of TLC, a library automation vendor, and Endeca, a software company that provides search applications, has served as a catalyst for the emergence of faceted library catalogs. One example is the NC State University library, which acquired Endeca's Information Access Platform (IAP) software in 2005 and started implementation of the new catalogs in early 2006.

9.2.2. Search Behavior

In order to investigate information-seeking behaviors in an OPAC environment, the situational nature of information behaviors and search activities needs to be understood. Järvelin and Ingwersen (2004) produced a model for searching context (Figure 9.1), which suggests that searching behavior is composed of multiple layered contexts wherein *information retrieval* is the most narrowly focused, *information seeking* is a larger context, and both are set within an even larger purview of *work task*. Information retrieval, as the smallest context in the model, represents the actions, usually keyword searches, by which users find relevant documents to match their query. Searchers may perform a series of information retrieval actions as part of broader information-seeking tasks. One or more information-seeking tasks are situated within the work task (or personally motivated goal), and are associated with the *socio-organizational and cultural* context, as described by the model.

This study situates searching activities in the context of Järvelin and Ingwersen's *Information Seeking* (Figure 9.1) because this focus is the primary lens for faceted search systems.

At the information-seeking (IS) level, search systems usually function beyond the query–result–evaluation cycle typically seen in IR systems. The IS search systems have more features that support IS tasks, such as search

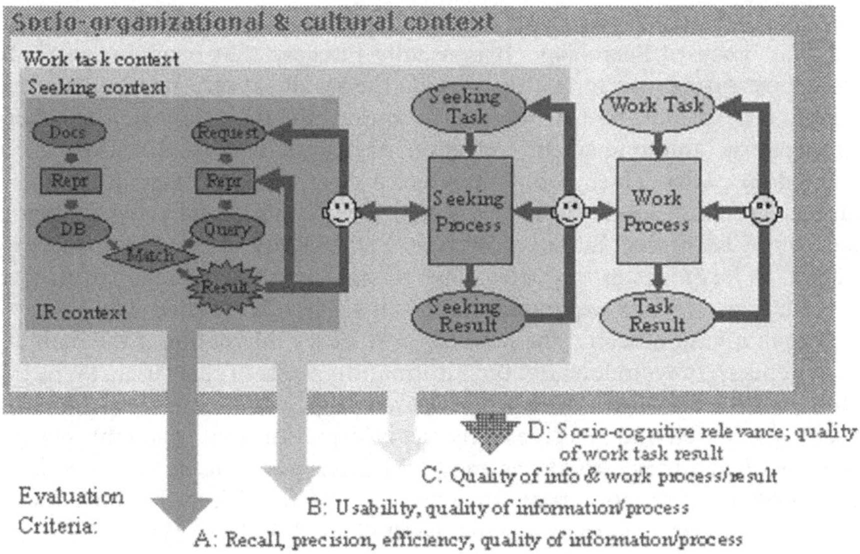

Figure 9.1: Model of search in context (Järvelin & Ingwersen, 2004).

history mechanisms for multiple-session searches, tagging mechanisms for grouping a set of documents to address a larger information need, overviews of collections, and browsing structures. Evaluations of systems that support IS tasks typically focus on assessing the quality of information acquired by users relative to the information need, rather than some system-oriented metrics, such as precision and recall, in the context of IR.

The information in the following sections provides types of information activities within the context of IS.

9.2.2.1. Searching and Browsing Searching and browsing represent two basic activities in IS. Searching is the most common and the most identified information activity of users. In searching, users express their information need in query terms that are understandable by the system, and then the users examine the results returned by the system until the target is found. In browsing, people are scanning information items, omitting irrelevant ones and occasionally picking up relevant ones. When browsing, each new information scent that is gathered can provide new ideas, suggest new directions, and change the nature of the information need (Bates, 1989). Browsing is an increasingly subtle searching activity in IS research (e.g., Ingwersen & Wormell, 1989; Noerr & Noerr, 1985). Ellis (1989) suggests that browsing features, for example, contents pages, lists of cited works, and subject terms, should be made available in automated catalog systems to accommodate searchers' browsing behaviors that usually occur physically in the library.

9.2.2.2. Focused Searching It is usually the case that people need to do some post-query searching after viewing the result set returned by an initial query. These post-query searches require system support for query specification and refinement, selection of search results, and post-query navigation paths. Thus, people may get a clear sense of their information targets and the trails to follow. Faceted navigation is one way to support post-query refinement in that it offers users the ability to extend the query by slicing a large result set down to a smaller size through controlled vocabularies, or even expanding the result set in a structured way.

The motivation behind the need for post-query interaction is the inability of systems to fully understand the information needs of their users (White & Roth, 2009). However, even if the search engine is able to understand a user's query well and return exactly the information that is sought, given a well-specified query, situations may still arise where users are unable to express their information need. In reality, people are observed to have a style of interaction referred to as *orienteering* (O'Day & Jeffries, 1993). The initial query and initial result set might be only partially relevant to the searcher. Through post-query interaction, people are taken to multiple result sets where they may be able to attain the complete set of information they need. Post-query navigation trails extracted from search logs exhibit traits of orienteering behavior (White & Drucker, 2007).

Another need for supporting post-query interaction lies in the inversely proportional relationship between precision and recall. An over-specified query may gain a high precision rate for the result set, but may hurt the recall, and many related but non-core documents might be excluded. On the other hand, an under-specified query may have good recall, but at the price of precision. To strike a balance between precision and recall, it is likely that users will find information from multiple result sets rather than from a single one, necessitating post-query interaction as a way of navigating the result sets.

9.2.2.3. Exploratory Search With more and more online information accessible to searchers, they are no longer satisfied with simply conducting a quick, look-up search. In addition to known-item, fact-finding searches, exploratory searching is another common type of search conducted by current library users. In addition, exploratory searching is an important use case for faceted search.

Exploratory searchers utilize a combination of searching and browsing behaviors to navigate through and to information that helps them to develop powerful cognitive capabilities and leverage their newly acquired skills to address open-ended, persistent, and multifaceted problems (White & Roth, 2009). According to White and Roth, exploratory searches comprise broader searching activities than traditional look-up searches, and include exploratory browsing, berry-picking, information foraging, comparing results, etc.

People who conduct exploratory searches generally (1) have vague information needs, (2) are unsure about the ways to satisfy their information needs, and (3) are unfamiliar with the information space. Exploratory searching usually involves complex situations. The problem context and the definition of the search task often are ill-structured, which requires searchers to clarify their search during the search process. Multiple information resources, including some partially relevant and irrelevant ones, are needed to satisfy the search task. In addition, information needs are always fluid and developing. Marchionini (2006) identifies two key components of the exploratory search: learning and investigation. In his proposed model (Figure 9.2), he depicts three search activities — look-up, learn, and investigate — and highlights exploratory search as related especially to the learning and investigating activities. The overlapping "clouds" of the three search activities suggest that some activities may be embedded in others, and that no clear boundary exists between them.

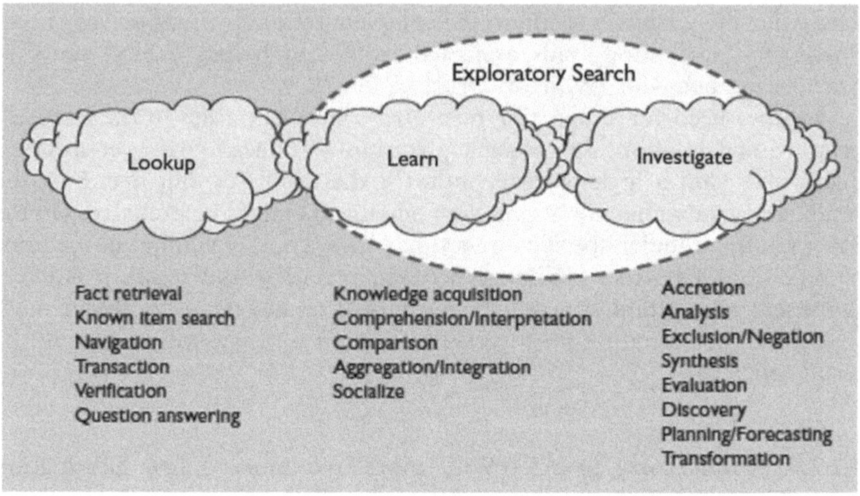

Figure 9.2: Exploratory search components (Marchionini, 2006).

9.2.3. Ways People Search Using OPACs

Basically, people conduct two types of searches when they use OPACs. One is the known-item search where the user wants to locate information about a specific item (e.g., author, title, and publication year). The other type of search is a subject search for a topic under a Library of Congress subject headings (LCSH) or other subject headings. Many researchers have examined the distribution of OPAC searches between the two types, and the results vary considerably. Sometimes, no clear boundary is found between the two search types.

Researchers are in general agreement that the known-item search type is less problematic than a subject search (Large & Beheshti, 1997). Research has shown that author and title searches are the most common search fields for known-item searches (Cochrane & Markey, 1983; Lewis, 1987). Compared to a known-item search, a subject search is much more open-ended, which may be popular, but is also problematic. Tolle and Hah (1985) found that subject searching is the most frequently used and the least successful of the search types. Hunter (1991) reports that 52% of all searches were subject searches, and 63% of those had zero hits. For a subject search, users need to know how to express their information need as subject "aboutness," how to map the subject "aboutness" to the controlled vocabulary of a LCSH, and how to re-conduct a search if no records, too many records, or irrelevant records are retrieved after the first attempt. These requirements may account for the fact that subject searching is being replaced by keyword searching. Knutson (1991) suggests that inadequate subject access is one of the reasons that many items in large academic libraries are rarely, if ever, checked out, and that libraries need to modify current subject cataloguing practices to make more items accessible to users.

Online catalogs have been criticized as being hard to use because their designs do not incorporate sufficient understanding of searching behaviors (Borgman, 1996). The ability of OPAC systems to analyze query terms and correctly interpret a user's information needs is still far from being perfect. For example, Large and Beheshti (1997) report that users encounter many problems in choosing suitable search terms to represent their subject interests. Some people enter very broad terms and then feel overwhelmed by the amount of results returned (Hunter, 1991). Some subjects enter very specified queries by pasting long phrases or sentences directly into the search box. Sit (1998) states that users' difficulties include finding subject terms to enter, using nondistinctive words, over-specification (e.g., a query that is too long), reducing results, and increasing results. Additional user difficulties include complex command syntax (e.g., Janosky, Smith, & Hildreth, 1986), scrolling through large retrieval sets and selecting appropriate database fields and keywords (e.g., Ensor, 1992; Yee, 1991), predicting the results of various search algorithms (e.g., Chen & Dhar, 1991), using multiple databases (e.g., Yee, 1991), error-recovery processes (Peters, 1989; Yee, 1991), and information comprehension and location in displays (Janosky et al. 1986; Yee, 1991). Therefore, a serious need exists to establish a closer working relationship between systems designers and users to develop useful IR systems. According to Warren (2000), the general design of the Urica OPAC system, for example, actually hindered rather than helped users in their search process. From the library organization perspective, difficulties might come from the restriction of the bibliographic records that are the basis for the catalog. O'Brien (1990) states that users do not necessarily understand the subject headings and classification numbers due to their artificial nature.

Borgman (1996) developed a three-layer framework of knowledge needed for successful OPAC searching: (1) conceptual knowledge for translating an information need into a searchable query, (2) semantic knowledge for how and when to use system features to implement a query, and (3) technical and basic computing skills. Borgman (1986b) concludes that people might have problems with each of the three layers. However, conceptual problems are more similar across types of systems than semantic and technical problems. Conceptual problems are essential because "only when the conceptual aspects of searching were understood could the user exploit the system fully and effectively." On the other hand, technical problems seem to be more common among novice catalog users.

People tend to use short queries when they search through OPACs. The most common length is one or two terms (Jones, Cunningham, & McNab,

2000; Lau & Goh, 2006; Mahoui & Cunningham, 2001; Wallace, 1993). People rarely use operators such as *AND*, *OR*, or *NOT*, and tend to use simple queries, although it is assumed by the system designer that the correct use of search operators would increase the effectiveness of the searches (Eastman & Jansen, 2003; Jansen & Pooch, 2001; Lau & Goh, 2006). The overall field of information-searching through OPACs has grown large enough to support investigations into demographic-based groups, for example, children (Borgman, Hirsh, Walter, & Gallagher, 1995; Hutchinson, Bederson, & Druin, 2007; Solomon, 1993), older adults (Sit, 1998), and university staff and students (Connaway, Budd, & Kochtanek, 1995).

Many research studies on OPACs include failure analysis in which a *failed search* is typically defined as a search that matches no documents in the collection (Jones et al., 2000). Generalizing from several studies, approximately 30% of all searches result in zero results. The failure rate is even higher, at 40%, for subject searches, as reported by Peters (1993). However, there is disagreement on the definition of *failed search* among researchers. Large and Beheshti (1997) state that not all zero hits represent failures, and not all hits represent successes. Some researchers also define an upper number of results for a successful search (e.g., Cochrane & Markey, 1983). Like the definition of *search failure*, the reasons for search failures also vary considerably in the literature. Large and Beheshti (1997) suggest that some of the failed searches are in fact helpful ones that could lead users to relevant information if users had more perseverance to look beyond the first results page rather than terminating the search.

Another stream of research reports feelings and reactions to OPAC searches through questionnaires and/or interviews. Satisfaction with search results often serves as a metric of utility (Hildreth, 2001). Measures, such as the wording "easy to use" and "confusing to use" (Dalrymple & Zweizig, 1992), or a high-to-low scale has been employed (Nahl, 1997) to assess user satisfaction. Many researchers have challenged the validity of using satisfaction and perception as evaluation measures for search systems. For example, Hildreth (2001) found no association between users' satisfaction and their search performance. He found that users often express satisfaction with poor search results and further investigated the phenomenon of false positives, which inflated assessments of the systems.

The availability of web technology and the appearance of web search engines in the 1990s had had a significant effect on OPACs. Jansen and Pooch (2001) report that 71% of web users use search engines. Many OPAC users in the library, especially in academic libraries, are also likely to be web search engine users, and bring their mental models and web search engine experience to OPACs (Young & Yu, 2004). Luther (2003) states in her study, "Google has radically changed users' expectations and redefined that experience of those seeking information." Furthermore, users tend to prefer a single search box type interface that conceptually allows them to perform a metasearch over all the library resources rather than performing separate searches (Hemminger, Lu, Vaughan, & Adams, 2007). "Users appear to be using the catalog as a single hammer rather than taking advantage of the array of tools a library presents to the user" (Young & Yu, 2004). Despite the popularity of web search engines, Muramatsu and Pratt (2001) report that users commonly do not understand the ways search engines process their queries, which leads to poor decisions and dissatisfaction with some search engines. Young and Yu (2004) believe that the same lack of understanding applies to OPACs. Features of web search engines and/or some online commercial websites could raise the bar for library catalogs; however, OPACs typically do not offer some of the features of web search engines and online commercial book stores (e.g., Amazon, Barnes, and Noble). Such features include: free-text (natural language) entry, automated mapping to controlled vocabulary, spell checking, relevance feedback, relevance-ranked output, popularity tracking and browsing functions (Young & Yu, 2004). "Search inside the book," that is, full text searching, as implemented by Amazon, Google Books, and some web search engines, is another feature that OPACs have not incorporated.

9.3. Facet Theory and Faceted Search

In order to understand the details of faceted search, the foundations of facet theory and faceted classification must be discussed. Then, the application of facet theory in the online digital environment, that is, faceted search, is examined.

9.3.1. Facet Theory and Faceted Classification

The notion of a *facet* is the central concept to the facet theory that was initiated by Ranganathan, an Indian mathematician and librarian. In facet theory, each characteristic (parameter) represents a *facet*. After Ranganathan, other researchers have contributed their summaries and understanding of *facets*. According to Taylor (1992), *facets* are "clearly defined, mutually exclusive, and collectively exhaustive aspects, properties, or characteristics of a class or specific subject." Hearst (2006) defines *facets* as categories that are a set of meaningful labels organized in such a way as to reflect the concepts relevant to a domain. In many current online faceted search systems, overlap of *facets* may occur, and the *facets* may not be exhaustive.

Vickery (1960) describes a faceted classification as "a schedule of standard terms to be used in document subject description" and in the assignment of notation. Vickery and Artandi (1966) notes that faceted classification, although "partly" analogous to the traditional rules of logical division on which classification has always been based, differs in three important ways:

1. Every facet is independent and clearly formulated.
2. Facets are left free to combine with each other so that every type of relation between terms and between subjects may be expressed.
3. Extend the hierarchical, genus–species relations of the traditional classification by combining terms in compound subjects. It introduces new logical relations between them, thus better reflecting the complexity of knowledge.

Since 1950s, researchers in library and information science (LIS) have devoted work to the application of the facet theory in special classifications, thesauri, and recently web applications. In the following sections is a brief summary of the work, not intended to be comprehensive, but to provide an idea of trends and strands for future research. This chapter groups the development into two phases — before the web and on the web.

9.3.1.2. Before the Web: Early Application (1950–1999) Application of facet theory has developed over years through intensive effort by three groups, the Library Research Circle (LRC), the Classification Research Group (CRG), and the Classification Research Study Group (CRSG) (La Barre, 2010). The early work has been around building and testing faceted classification schemes or using facet analysis to create indexing systems.

Early application of facet analysis to thesaurus construction was in the mid-1960s. Aitchison was a representative researcher back then. Her work on thesaurofacet, a faceted classification and controlled vocabulary for engineering and related subjects (Aitchison, 1970), was among the first to employ facet analysis explicitly and proved equally adaptable for use in computerized indexing in information retrieval systems and traditional library. Another of Aitchison's works was the development of UNESCO Thesaurus, a faceted system for use in indexing and information retrieval (Aitchison, 1977). Some important faceted bibliographic classification products in this time include Bliss Bibliographic Classification (BC2), a fully faceted system.

In 1980s, attention turned from creation of facet scheme or thesauri to integrating them to serve as meta-searching tools across databases (Aitchison, 1981; Anderson, 1979). Additionally, discussions of a faceted approach to hypertext on the web began during this period. In the meantime, the Bliss Classification (BC2) gained renewed attention at this time as a "rich source of structure and terminology for thesauri covering different subject fields," in spite of its limitations (Aitchison, 1986).

Since 1990, intensive effort of facet-directed research had been on the database construction, the design of information retrieval systems and interfaces, and testing the efficacy of facets in online environments.

9.3.1.3. On the Web: Faceted Information Retrieval (2000–present) Over the years, the potential for the application of facet theory to digital environments, especially on the web, has been discussed. Ellis and Vasconcelos (1999) referred to "the portability of Ranganatha's ideas across time, technology, and cultures, simply because they addressed the very foundations of the business of effective information storage and retrieval." They called attention of the contemporary web developers to Ranganathan's facet theory, which have been ignored by them in favor of algorithmic approaches. Foskett (2004) commented on the timeless influence of Ranganathan in the creation of special classification schemes. He favored the technique of facet analysis because it allows the uncovering of previously hidden or uncoordinated concepts in such a way that possible areas of future research are brought to light.

Fundamentally, faceted classification enables items to be classified in multiple ways. One can locate items by identifying the intersection of multiple characteristics. Therefore, there are multiple paths (access points) to the same target items. A faceted structure relieves a classification from a rigid hierarchical arrangement and from having to create fixed tons of "pigeonholes" for subjects that already existed or were foreseen. Such systems often left no room for future expansions and made no provision for the expression of complex relationships.

Since a faceted class notation is not necessarily meant to serve as a shelving device or call number, for which only a single order can be assigned, the individual facets can be accessed and retrieved either alone or in any desired combination. This feature is especially important for online retrieval.

9.3.2. Faceted Search

Faceted search is the application of classic facet theory in the online digital environment. It is the combination of free, unstructured text search, with faceted navigation. White and Roth (2009) describe faceted search interfaces as interfaces that seamlessly combine keyword searches and browsing, allowing people to find information quickly and flexibly based on what they remember about the information they seek. Faceted interfaces can help people avoid feelings of "being lost" in the collection and make it easier for users to explore the system. According to Ben-Yitzhak et al. (2008), a typical user's interaction with a faceted search interface involves multiple steps in which the user may (1) type or refine a search query, or (2) navigate through multiple, independent facet hierarchies that describe the data by drill-down (refinement) or roll-up (generalization) operations. Bast and Weber (2006) loosely define a faceted search interface as one that, in addition to showing ranked results for keyword queries as usual, organizes query results by categories. Figure 9.3 illustrates a website with a dynamic presentation of facets when searching for a laptop. The facets for a laptop are price range, manufacturers, screen size, memory size, and so on.

Faceted search enables users to explore a subject in terms of its different dimensions. Although keyword searches usually bring about a ranked result list, in faceted searches, users may filter the result set by specifying one or more desired attributes of the dimensions. The faceted interface gives users the opportunity to evaluate and manipulate the result set, typically to narrow its scope (White & Roth, 2009). It is important to recognize that primary attributes of "faceted search," as referred to in this work, are the interactive filtering along these multiple dimensions of information. And these dimensions do not formally adhere to facet theory definitions (for instance facets like date and time period are overlapping and not mutually exclusive). Yet, in the mainstream literature, and in this work, these interfaces will be referred to as "faceted interfaces" supporting "faceted search." Faceted search also gives users flexible ways to access the contents. Navigating within the hierarchy builds up a complex query over sub-hierarchies. As White and Roth (2009) describe, the approach reduces mental work by promoting recognition over recall and suggesting logical but perhaps unexpected alternatives, while avoiding empty result sets. Meaningful categories support learning, reflection, discovery, and information finding (Kwasnik, 1992; Soergel, 1999). The counts next to facet labels give users a quantitative overview of the variety of data available, thereby hinting at the specific refinement operations that seem most promising for targeting the information need(s) (Sharit, Hernández, Czaja, & Pirolli, 2008).

9.4. Academic Research on Faceted Search

This section introduces some important academic projects on faceted search and faceted library catalogs, and then enumerates some empirical studies on this subject.

9.4.1. Well-Known Faceted Search Projects

The query previews developed by Shneiderman and his colleagues (Doan, Plaisant, Shneiderman, & Bruns, 1997) probably serve as the catalyst for the current interest in faceted search. According to Shneiderman, query

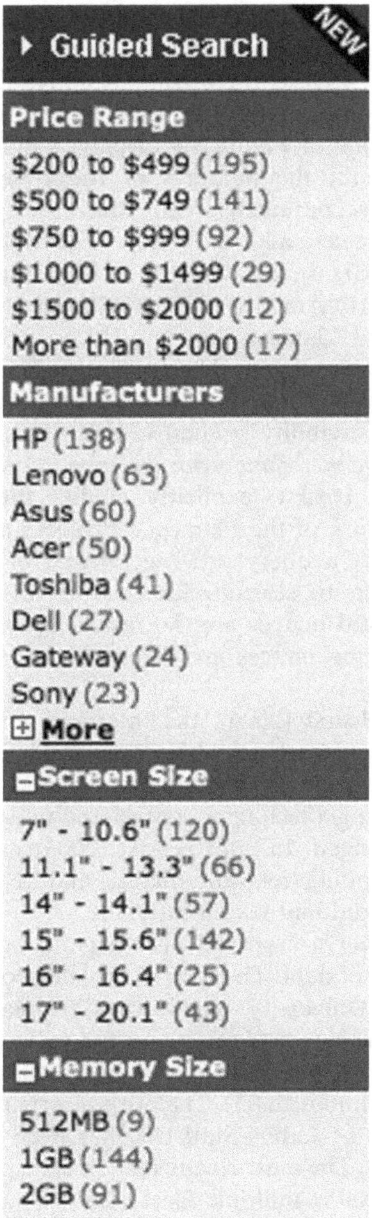

Figure 9.3: Facets for a laptop search.

previews allow users to specify the parameters that generate visually displayed results. Figure 9.4 shows the changes before and after selection of a geographic attribute, in this case, North America. The preview bar at the bottom of the map as well as the attributes above it update responsively. Users are able to obtain a sense of the overall collection and alleviate zero-hit queries. The left side of Figure 9.4 displays summary data on preview bars. Users learn about the holdings of the collection and can make selections over a few parameters (in this case geographic locations, environmental parameters, and the year). The right side of Figure 9.4 displays the updated bars (in less than 100 ms) when users select an attribute value (in this case, North America). The results bar at the bottom shows the total number of selected datasets.

The Flamenco Project led by Hearst at the University of California, Berkeley, represents work of almost a decade on developing faceted search tools and performing usability studies. (*Flamenco* is derived from ***fl**exible information **a**ccess using **me**tadata in **n**ovel **co**mbinations*.) The lead researcher of Flamenco, Marti Hearst, explicitly credits the query previews by Shneiderman in the work of the Flamenco Project and situates Flamenco's interface as a form of a query preview (Hearst et al., 2002). Flamenco allows users to navigate by selecting facet values. In the example shown in Figure 9.5, the retrieved images are the results of specifying a value from *Locations*. The matching images are displayed and grouped by the facet values from *People*.

As described by Hearst (2006), the interface aims to support flexible navigation, seamless integration with directed (keyword) searches, fluid alternation between refining and expanding, avoidance of empty results sets, and at all times retaining a feeling of control and understanding. A usability study by Yee, Swearingen, Li, and Hearst (2003) indicates that users are more successful at finding relevant images and report higher subjective measures than the traditional search interface.

The so-called *relation browser* (RB) is a generic search interface that can be applied to a variety of data. The RB is a tool developed by the Interaction Design Lab at the University of North Carolina at Chapel Hill for understanding relationships between items in a collection and for exploring an information space (Capra & Marchionini, 2008; Marchionini & Brunk, 2003; Zhang & Marchionini, 2005). The project, originally developed for the United States Bureau of Labor Statistics, has been through a number of major design revisions. The most recent version is displayed in Figure 9.6. In the figure 1 and 2 support multiple facet views; 3 supports multiple result views; 4 indicates the current query display and control; and 5 and 6 show the full-text search and search within results.

The RB combines simple text search and facet navigation as a way to refine the search. It provides searchers with a small number of facets (topic,

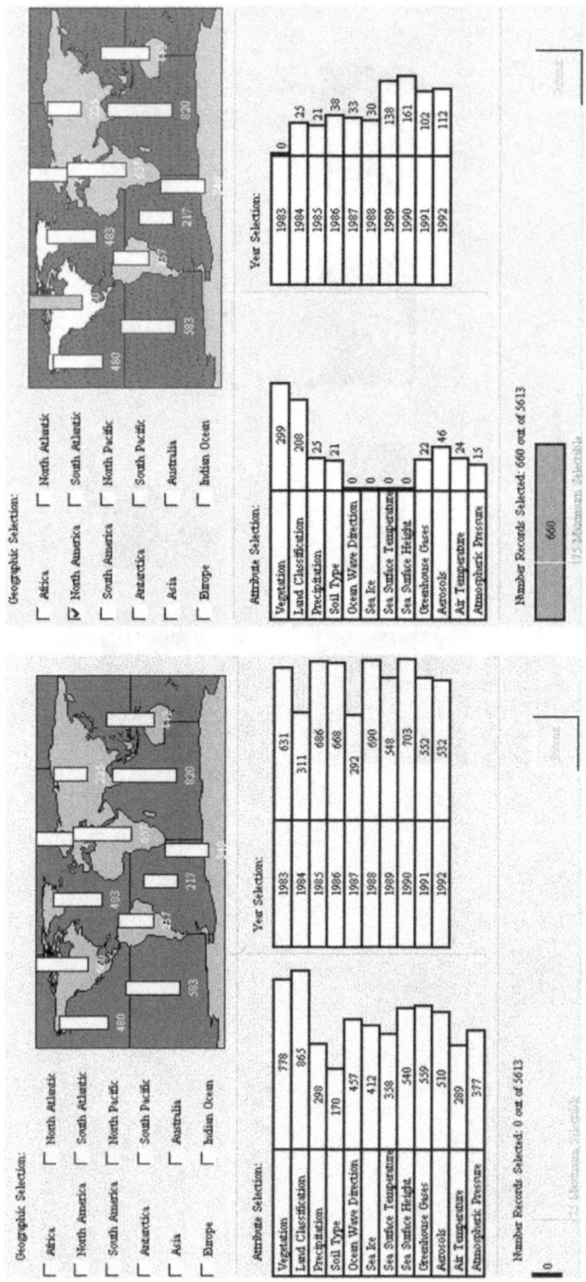

Figure 9.4: Collection of environmental data from the National Aeronautics and Space Administration (NASA).

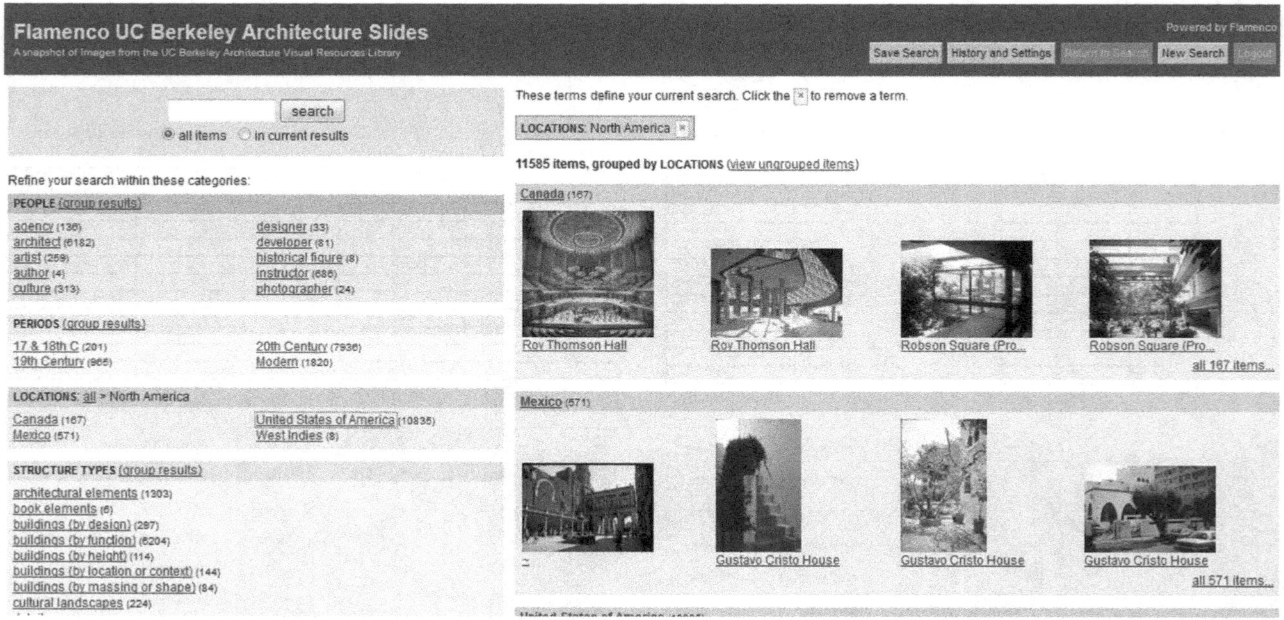

Figure 9.5: Hierarchical facet navigation in Flamenco.

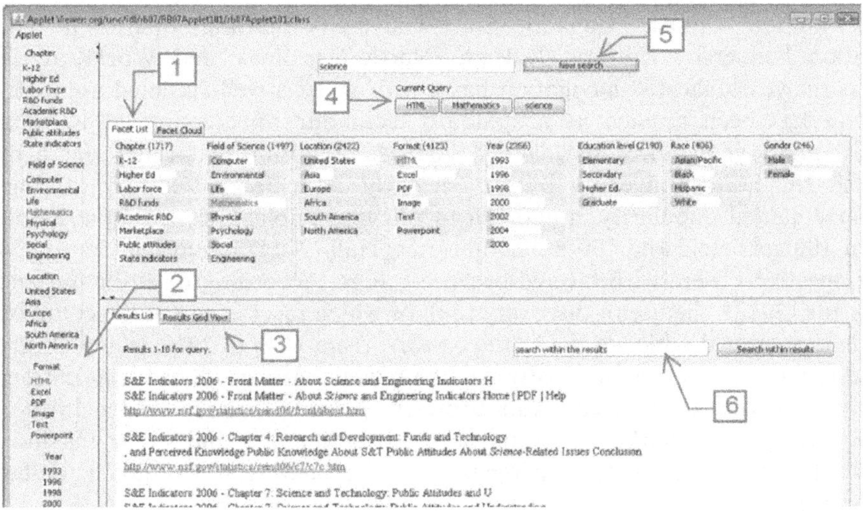

Figure 9.6: Relation browser.

time, data format) with a manageable size of values in each facet. Users can easily move between searching and browsing strategies. The current text query is displayed at the top of interface, and the current incorporated facet values are highlighted in red and shown below the current text query. Mouse-over capabilities allow users to explore relationships among the facets and attributes, and dynamically generate results as the mouse slides over them. One of the issues of RB lies in its dependence on dynamic client-side graphics to update the interface in real time. Scalability would be a problem for client applications if billions of records must be processed instantly.

Faceted search concepts can also be applied to the field of personal information management, where people acquire, organize, maintain, retrieve, and use information items (Jones, 2007). Information overload makes re-finding and re-using personal "stuff" similar to information discovery. Using facets in generic IR systems allows for pre-filtering personal information. A series of research studies has been conducted by Microsoft Research on applying facets to personal information management. *Phlat* (Cutrell, Robbins, Dumais, & Sarin, 2006) and *Stuff I've Seen* (Dumais et al., 2003) are two examples found in this series.

9.4.2. Faceted Search Used in Library Catalogs

Since 2006, some academic libraries have implemented faceted navigation on their online catalogs. Among them are McMaster University Library

(Hamilton, Ontario, Canada), State University Libraries of Florida, NC State University Library (Raleigh, North Carolina), and WorldCat. In recent years, faceted navigation has grown to be a well-accepted approach and has been applied as a standard technique on commercial websites for many years (Breeding, 2007). Since the adoption of faceted search by the NC State University Library in early 2006, faceted library catalogs have gained popularity in many academic and public libraries. In a sample of 100 academic and 100 public libraries, Hall (2011) found that 78 and 54 respectively were with faceted-based catalogs. According to Hofmann and Yang (2012), the use of discovery tool, of which facet is one of the common features, has doubled in the last two years, from 16% to 29%. Many library automation vendors and software companies have produced applications for facets (e.g., Endeca, AquaBrowser, Encore, Primo, Smart Library System, OPAC GiB, etc.), and some programmers and librarians have worked together to develop open source faceted ILS (Evergreen, Koha, VuFind, etc.).

Endeca, a well-known company for providing facet search applications to e-commerce sites, started the implementation of facet browsing in their catalog. Figure 9.7 presents the interface of NC State's library catalog, which acquired the Endeca applications in 2005. This new generation of library catalog gives its users both relevance-ranked keyword search results and rich facet metadata previously trapped in MARC records to enhance collection browsing and search refinement. The faceted metadata are grouped into subject, genre, format, location, author, etc. A user may enter the text query in the query box as a starting point and then click one attribute of facets from the left-hand box to filter the result set. An empty query in the query box will generate the results for the whole collection held by the library, organized by a set of facets. In addition to simple text search mode combined with facet browsing, users also can select other search modes, for example to browse through new titles that have been recently cataloged by the system, and to scan through the Library of Congress Subject Headings (LCSH).

AquaBrowser is another world leader application in visual faceted search that connects to heterogeneous data sources. It can be found in public, academic and special libraries around the United States and the world. It motivates users to explore the library's content by incorporating various common search behaviors. Its unique "search, discover, refine" methodology provides features that help users quickly and easily uncover relevant results. Figure 9.8 captures a screenshot from Edinburgh University Library, which implements AquaBrowser as its search solution. This OPAC's facet implementation is similar to that of the NC State University catalog, except that the facet panel is placed on the right side. Another major difference is the word cloud on the left side that explores associations between the current

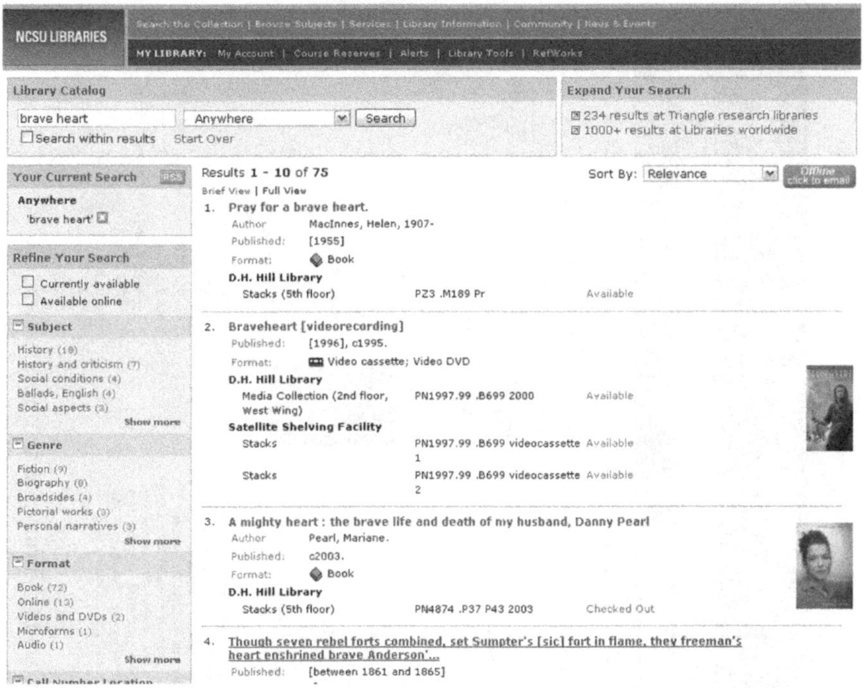

Figure 9.7: Interface of North Carolina State Universityapos;s faceted library catalog.

query and other vocabularies as a query recommendation tool. Another development is the separation of collections according to item type, that is, books, music, movies, etc.

Encore is another popular commercial application for faceted library catalogs. In addition to faceted navigation and relevance ranking, it also presents tag clouds, popular choices, and recently added suggestions. Encore even makes use of user contributions as a tool for discovery by incorporating community participation features, such as tagging.

Primo is an Ex Libris offering that aims to revitalize the library environment by creating next-generation interfaces. According to Ex Libris, Primo provides services for searching as well as delivering access to all of the library's resources, whether those resources are maintained and hosted locally or need to be accessed remotely. In addition to relevance ranking and faceted browsing, Primo indexes data from sources such as Syndetic Solutions, Blackwell, Amazon, and others to provide additional access points when searching. It also includes features that are popular in e-commerce websites, such as user-supplied reviews, recommendations

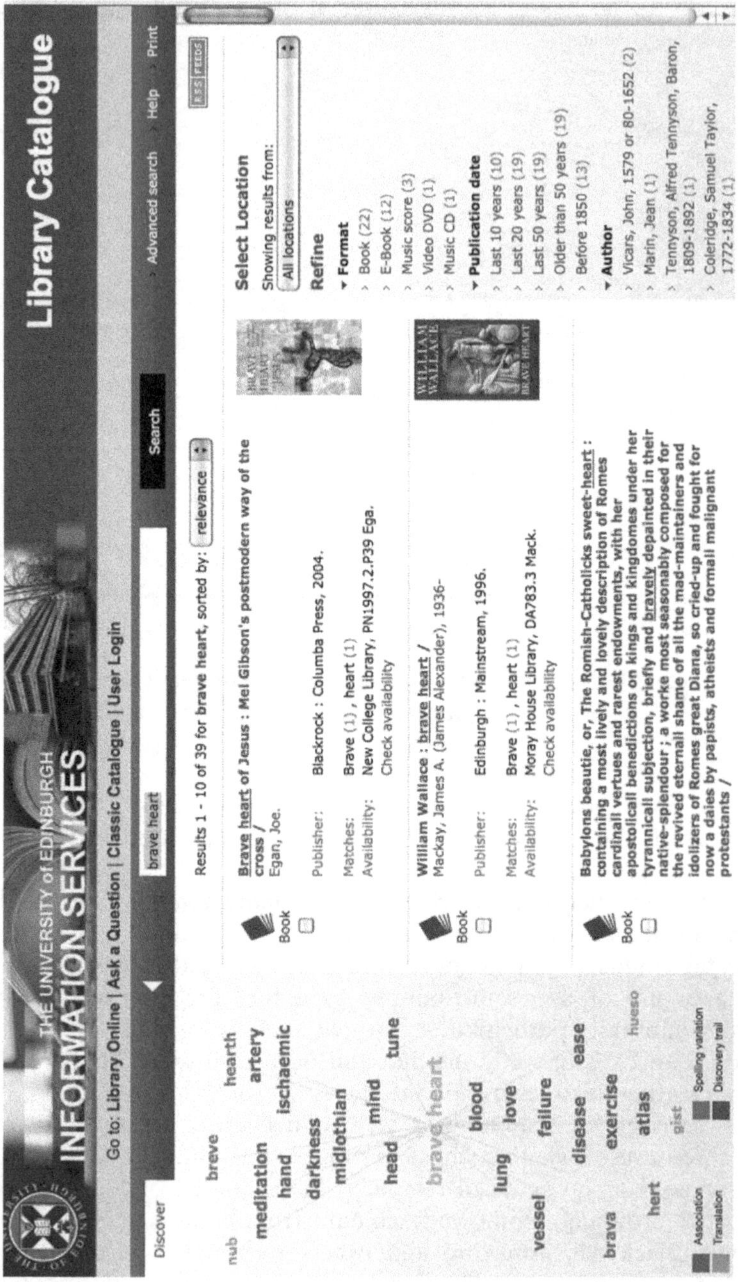

Figure 9.8: Interface of Edinburgh University Library faceted library catalog.

based on what others who viewed the same item selected, and grouping similar results. Primo also includes dictionaries and thesauri to provide search suggestions and structured lists as part of the search process.

In addition to commercial search solutions for faceted OPACs, some open source catalogs have been developed by programmers and librarians. These catalogs aim to be next-generation catalogs and regard facet searching as one of their major features. Also, open source OPACs are more cost-effective than proprietary ones, so many libraries choose to use open source solutions mainly for their affordability. Although users of open source OPACs may experience difficulties with installation and incomplete documentation, they are modestly more satisfied than users of proprietary OPACs (Riewe, 2008). Some common open source OPACs are Evergreen, Koha, VuFind, etc. For some libraries, the transition from commercial software to open source applications seems to be a recent trend. For example, Queens Library and Philadelphia Free Library have abandoned AquaBrower and been moving to VuFind; Florida State University Library has changed from Endeca to a Solr-based catalog. Some other universities adopted open source applications from the beginning as a discovery layer of their traditional systems, such as the University of Illinois at Urbana-Champaign Libraries, York University Libraries (in Toronto, Canada) (Figure 9.9). Both of the Universities overlaid VuFind on top of their traditional OPACs in the purpose of enhancing the catalogs' discovery ability.

VuFind is an open source catalog interface that gleans data from OPACs and other sources, such as digital repositories, creating a single searchable index (Sadeh, 2008). This decoupled architecture "provides the capability to create a better user experience for a given collection but also unifies the discovery processes across heterogeneous collections" (Sadeh, 2008, p. 11). Fagan (2010) explains that discovery layers like VuFind "seek to provide an improved experience for library patrons by offering a more modern look and feel, new features, and the potential to retrieve results from other major library systems such as article databases" (p. 58). VuFind is written in PHP and uses the search engine Solr to index MARC records. It was created by Andrew Nagy at Villanova University in 2007 to work with their Voyager system, and has since grown into a world-wide software project that can be placed in front of many different ILS. VuFind offers a single-box search, like Google, and decouples the Library of Congress Subject Headings to make each element of a subject heading searchable. Its relevancy rankings are adjustable so that each institution can customize the ordering of search results (Figure 9.9).

Blacklight is an open source OPAC being developed at the University of Virginia. It is a faceted discovery tool. Its special feature, other than those in other discovery tools, is that it searches both catalog records and digital

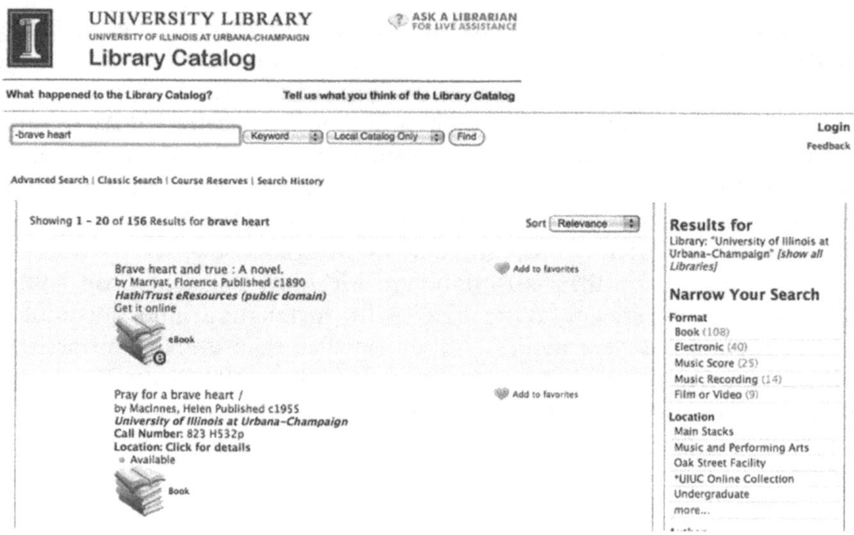

Figure 9.9: Interface of the University of Illinois at Urbana–Champaign Libraries faceted library catalog.

repository objects, making the latter more discoverable. It also has persistent URLs for each search result so that users could e-mail successful searches to others. An example of using Blacklight is the special collections at NCSU.

This section provides a comprehensive, but not necessarily exhaustive, overview of some well-known faceted search projects, for either general purposes, personal information management, or library catalogs. Despite the differences among the implementations, most faceted search systems offer users two-level faceted metadata for refining the text search or browsing the whole collection. Most systems allow a single choice of facet value under the same facet and multiple choices of facets. Overall, the facet feature has provided more powerful search assistance for users than was available prior to the introduction of facet searches.

9.4.3. Empirical Studies on Faceted OPAC Interfaces

Especially in North America, most research into faceted systems has been commercial, and proprietary reports generally are not published (La Barre, 2007). However, a small stream of research is available that has been conducted by either system implementers or interactive IR researchers and examines the effectiveness of various faceted interfaces.

OPAC studies suggest that users take advantage of facets or categories if these options are presented during the search process (Antelman, Lynema, & Pace, 2006; Lown, 2008). Antelman et al.'s log analysis (2006) of the NC State University faceted library catalog suggests that approximately 30% of searches involve post-search refinements from the facets on the results page. Lown's follow-up analysis (2008) indicates that faceted searches account for 15–18% of all requests. Users employ facets to help refine the search (Hearst, 2000), sharpen a vague query or formulate a new query (White & Roth, 2009), and browse the whole information collection (Shneiderman, 1994). For the dimension (facet) usage, according to Antelman et al. (2006), dimension use does not exactly parallel dimension placement in the interface. *LC Classification* is the most heavily used facet, followed closely by *Subject: Topic*, and then *Library*, *Format*, *Author*, and *Subject: Genre*. Query test results indicate that 68% of the top results in Endeca were judged to be relevant, whereas 40% of the top results in traditional catalogs were judged to be relevant. This finding suggests a 70% better performance for the Endeca catalog than the traditional catalogs.

Empirical research into faceted OPAC interfaces often uses two common methods to study the effectiveness of faceted search interfaces: large-scale log analysis and comparative user studies (Kules, Capra, Banta, & Sierra, 2009). Some studies use a combination of the two methods (e.g., Antelman et al., 2006). Log analysis employs server logs to examine users' interaction with the system and constitutes the most common research method in this field. Comparative user studies complement transaction log analysis in that they capture the context information for users' interaction with the system by directly observing the users' behaviors and actions. Most empirical research into faceted catalogs incorporates user studies as one of the data collecting methods. Beyond the two common research methods mentioned, Kules et al. (2009) adopt eye tracking, stimulated recall, and interviews to investigate important aspects of gaze behavior in a faceted catalog interface. The top 10 gaze transitions derive from the eye-tracking data that indicate what the searchers look at in the interface and suggest the specific part or component of the interface that plays an important role. Olson (2007) conducted qualitative research on 12 humanities Ph.D. students at the dissertation level. He found that nine of the participants reported finding materials that they had not found in their previous use of the traditional catalog interface.

User studies, also called *usability testing*, generally involve measuring how well test subjects respond in four areas: performance, accuracy, recall, and emotional response. Performance and emotional response are the two frequently examined measures for testing a faceted search system. Performance is often operationalized as the amount of time required for people to complete basic tasks. Emotional response is usually collected through post-search questionnaires to measure the participants' perception of the system. For example, Kules et al. (2009) confirm the users' perception that they are slightly more familiar with and more confident about the known-item tasks.

Time as a measurement is a point of discussion, as initiated by Capra et al. They suggest that time might not be a suitable measure for exploratory tasks. Completing an exploratory task quickly may suggest that a search system does not provide support for investigating and exploring. This finding is backed up by the Kammerer, Narin, Pirolli, and Chi' study (2009) results that suggest that the participants who used the MrTagyy interface spent more time and produced better reports than participants who used other interfaces. Time, in this case, is a positive measure for the system.

Recent years, there have been several usability studies on academic faceted library catalogs. Most of the studies used traditional usability testing methods, like assigning task-oriented questions, questionnaires, and interview. Examples are Denton and Coysh's research (2011) on a customized VuFind interface on York University Libraries, Emmanuel's work (2011) on a user study on the University of Illinois Champaign Library's new interface, and Synder's study (2010) on finding music materials with a AquaBrowser finder. All of the three studies have identified the dominant preference of the "next generation" interfaces over the traditional interfaces.

9.5. Overview of the Author's Dissertation

The dissertation (Niu, 2012) seeks to understand whether faceted search improves the interactions between searchers and library catalogs and to understand ways that facets are used in different library environments. Interactions under investigation include possible search actions, search performance, and user satisfaction. Faceted catalogs from two libraries, the University of North Carolina at Chapel Hill (UNC-CH) Library and the Phoenix Public Library, are chosen as examples of two different facet implementations.

To observe searchers in natural situations, two log datasets with over 3 million useful records were collected from the two libraries' servers. Logs were parsed, statistically analyzed, and visualized to gain a general understanding of the usage of these faceted catalogs. Two user experiments were conducted to further understand contextual information, such as the searchers' underlying motivations and their perceptions. Forty subjects were recruited to search different tasks using two different catalogs.

The results indicate that most searchers were able to understand the concept of facets naturally and easily. Compared to text searches, however, faceted searches were complementary and supplemental, and used only by a small group of searchers. When browsing facets were incorporated into the search, facet uptake greatly increased. The faceted catalog was not able to shorten the search time but was able to improve the search accuracy. Facets were used more for open-ended tasks and difficult tasks that require more effort to learn, investigate, and explore. Based on observation, facets support searches primarily in five ways. Compared to the UNC-CH Library facets, the Phoenix Library facets are not as helpful for narrowing the search due to its both essential and lightweight facet design. Searchers preferred the Book Industry Standards and Communications (BISAC) subject headings for browsing the collection and specifying genre, and the LCSH for narrowing topics. Overall, the results weave a detailed "story" about the ways people use facets and ways that facets help people employ library catalogs.

The results of this research can be used to propose or refine a set of practical design guidelines for designing faceted library catalogs. The guidelines are intended to inform librarians and library information technology (IT) staff to improve the effectiveness of the catalogs to help people find information they need more efficiently.

9.6. Conclusions and Future Directions

This chapter aims to survey existing research on faceted search used in an OPAC environment, facet theory and faceted search, and empirical research into faceted OPACs. An overview of the author's dissertation is also included.

Section 9.1 starts with a review of information-seeking behavior in the setting of OPACs. Section 9.2 moves to the foundation of faceted search, that is, facet theory and faceted classification. Then, Section 9.3 surveys some well-known research projects on faceted search systems, which includes faceted library catalogs, and also reviews the empirical research into ways that people search through a faceted system. Section 9.4 offers an overview of the author's dissertation on how people use facets in an academic OPAC setting and a public OPAC setting. The final section concludes the chapter, proposes a set of practical design guidelines, and provides some thoughts for future directions.

The information barriers in traditional library catalogs observed by Borgman (1996) are the "gap between the way a question is asked and ways it might be answered." Therefore, matching or entry vocabularies address the general problem of reconciling a user's query with the vocabulary presented in the catalog. Although faceted search reveals some authority data to searchers and addresses some information asymmetry between the information collection and the information need (as shown in Figure 9.10), its exposure of the index vocabulary to the user in the subject facet is limited

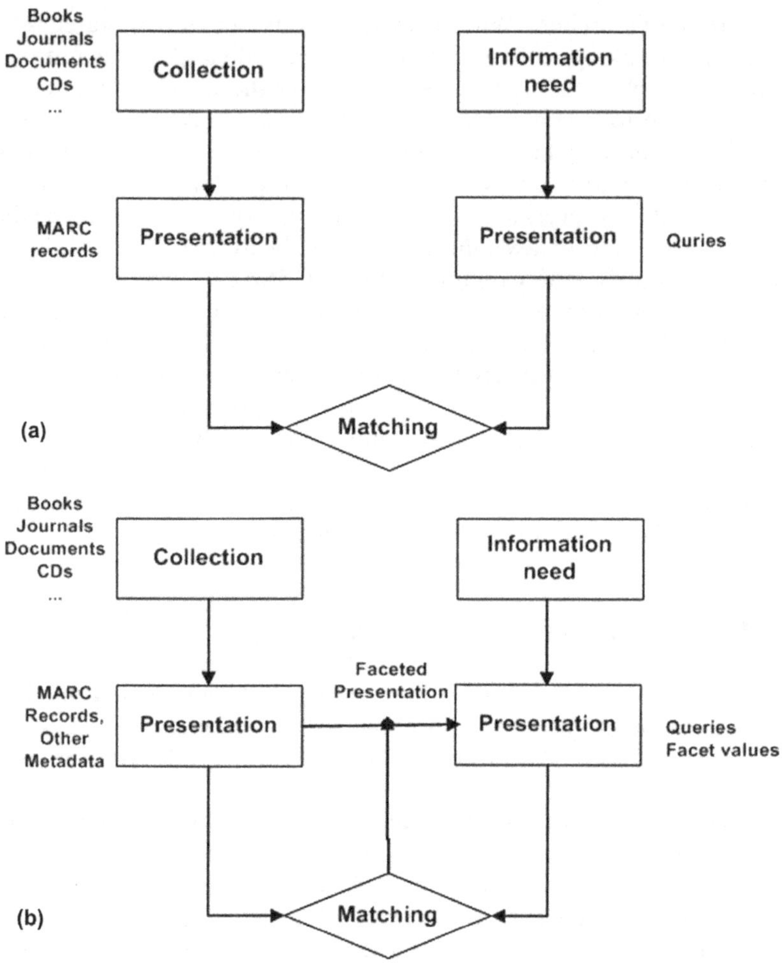

Figure 9.10: Before (a) and after (b) adding facets to library catalogs.

to controlled vocabulary derived from the bibliographic records. Relevant records may not be retrieved because of a mismatch between the vocabulary of the users and that of the bibliographic records, or because bibliographic record vocabulary is missing from the facets.

Research (Antelman et al., 2006) shows that users' vocabulary is large and diverse — that is, users rarely choose the same term to describe the same concept — and that users' vocabulary also is inflexible — that is, users are unable to repair searches using synonyms. Without the ability to stem or handle synonyms, users are not able to employ faceted search sufficiently to overcome such information barriers.

Another essential reason for the existence of information barriers lies in the presentation of the collection. Library catalogs, unlike web search engines, do not allow a search of the entire collection, but rather a search for the surrogates of the collection (MARC records). Any catalog with a slick appearance and fantastic facet design, but that misses the underlying artificial and inflexible surrogates that usually contain many typos, will not see a drastic improvement in user–catalog interaction.

Based on the author's dissertation research, we propose or refine a set of design guidelines for faceted library catalogs. Such guidelines are intended to inform librarians and library IT staff about ways to make the catalogs effective in helping people find the information they need. User interface design guidelines take into consideration constraints, capabilities, features, trade-offs, domain knowledge, and human factors. Through best practices, they provide practical advice to OPAC designers. The proposed principles are suggested to create guidelines that:

- Incorporate browsing facets
- Add/remove facets selectively
- Support including and excluding by facets
- Provide a flat vs. hierarchical structure
- Provide popular vs. long-tail data
- Consolidate the same types of facet values
- Support "AND," "OR," and "NOT" selections
- Incorporate predictable schema

9.6.1. Incorporate Browsing Facets

We find that people are able to take advantage of browsing facets, and that browsing facets boost the facet uptake. Future faceted OPACs could incorporate faceted browsing structures to accommodate searchers' browsing behavior. The depth and breadth of the hierarchy should be considered carefully to avoid any confusion or burden to searchers. Structures that are either too deep or too wide will cause usability issues. Arranging facet values into a meaningful hierarchy is also important because sometimes searchers require more effort to make sense of a browsing structure than to find value from it.

9.6.2. Add/Remove Facets Selectively

Due to space limitations and computational costs, facets must be chosen selectively for placement on the search interface. More importantly, a large number of facets can confuse searchers. From the log analysis conducted as part of this research, some participants rarely used some facets, such as the author facet or the MeSH facet. So, some facets should simply be removed if they are found not to be useful. On the other hand, some facets, such as the genre facet, should be added for their added value and usefulness.

9.6.3. *Provide a Flat vs. Hierarchical Structure*

Determining possible ways to present facets that have a large number of values is a matter of ongoing debate. A flat structure and a hierarchical structure are the two primary choices. In a flat structure, facet values are presented one by one, according to some ranking criterion. Due to the screen limit, the top ranked values are displayed by default, with the remaining ones in a "see more" option. Flat data are criticized for lacking a well-organized structure to lead users to the information they need. Presented with a long list, the participants in this study had to scan through the list one entry at a time in order to choose one. Presenting the users with only the top posted labels might also risk hiding the long-tail information that could be valuable.

An alternative to a flat structure is a hierarchical structure. A hierarchical structure offers a good way to organize the subject values. However, the depth and the width of the hierarchy must be considered carefully to avoid any confusion or burden to users. Facets are to help users, not to distract them with an impenetrable hierarchy (Tunkelang, 2009). The findings of this study suggest that, unless the hierarchy makes perfect sense to searchers, a flat structure should be used to present the facet values.

9.6.4. *Provide Popular vs. Long-Tail Data*

Many library catalogs display facets with a large number of values by "cutting off" a long list and showing only the top values. The underlying assumption is that the top posted values are more helpful to searchers than deeply buried ones. This assumption is somewhat problematic, however, because sometimes the long-tail data are actually valuable to searchers. Therefore, future catalogs should not only consider the popular values, but also provide a way for searchers to access the deeply buried long-tail data.

9.6.5. *Consolidate the Same Types of Facet Values*

Although the definition of *facet* is not as rigorous as the classic faceted classification that organizes a domain into mutually exclusive and collectively exhaustive dimensions, during the user experiments in this study, participants experienced confusion when *topical* and *name* subjects were separated, and *fiction* and *juvenile fiction* were split. Therefore, facets of the same type of value should be analyzed to determine whether they should be restructured and consolidated into one facet.

9.6.6. Support "AND," "OR," and "NOT" Selections

This study demonstrates that the user selects one value per facet, but people actually need multiple selections. When multiple selections were made available in this study, most participants were able to take advantage of them. So far, the logical relationships of queries supported by most faceted search systems are quite simple: an "or" relationship among facet values and an "and" relationship among facets. However, what if the user wants an "and" among facet values as well as an "or" among facets? The "not" relationship supported by the UNC catalog proved helpful to users as well. Ideally, future faceted catalogs should be able to support complex logical relationships among facets as much as SQL can.

9.6.7. Incorporate Predictable Schema

The study participants were found to incorporate facets at an early stage of their searches. Therefore, showing facets before searchers have seen any search results has the potential to quicken their search, but it can also lead them down the incorrect path because the searchers are not able to predict the effect of choosing these facets. This phenomenon is similar to the idea that Beaulieu and Jones (1998) refer to as "functional visibility" in the context of query expansion. They suggest that searchers must be aware of the options that are available at any stage, and also must be aware of the effect of these options. For example, the numbers next to facet labels are one type of predictable scheme. In addition, a preview of facet values, perhaps appearing by mouse over the facet value, could be potentially helpful for searchers to assess the facet values.

References

Aitchison, J. (1970). The thesaurofacet: A multipurpose retrieval language tool. *Journal of Documentation*, *26*(3), 187–203.

Aitchison, J. (1977). *Unesco thesaurus*. Paris: UNESCO.

Aitchison, J. (1981). Integration of thesauri in the social sciences. *International Classification*, *8*(2), 75–85.

Aitchison, J. (1986). A classification as a source for a thesaurus: The bibliographic classification of HE bliss as a source of thesaurus terms and structure. *Journal of Documentation*, *42*(3), 160–181.

Anderson, J. D. (1979). Prototype designs for subject access to the Modern Language Association's bibliographic database. *Proceedings of the IFIP working conference* (pp. 23–24).

Antelman, K., Lynema, E., & Pace, A. K. (2006). Toward a twenty-first century library catalog. *Information Technology and Libraries*, *25*(3), 128–138.

Babu, B. R., & O'Brien, A. (2000). Web OPAC interfaces: An overview. *The Electronic Library*, *18*(5), 316–330.

Bast, H., & Weber, I. (2006). When you're lost for words: Faceted search with auto completion. *Proceedings of ACM Special Interest Group on Information Retrieval* (*SIGIR 2006*) (pp. 31–35). Seattle, Washington, USA.

Bates, M. J. (1989). The design of browsing and berrypicking techniques for the online search interface. *Online Review*, *13*(5), 407–424.

Beaulieu, M., & Jones, S. (1998). Interactive searching and interface issues in the Okapi best match probabilistic retrieval system. *Interacting with computers*, *10*(3), 237–248.

Ben-Yitzhak, O., Golbandi, N., Har'El, N., Lempel, R., Neumann, A., Ofek-Koifman, S.,…, Yogev, S. (2008). Beyond basic faceted search. *The ACM international conference on web search and data mining (proceedings from WSDM 2008)*, Stanford, CA.

Borgman, C. L. (1986b). Why are online catalogs hard to use? Lessons learned from information-retrieval studies. *Journal of the American Society for Information Science*, *37*(6), 387–400.

Borgman, C. L. (1996). Why are online catalogs still hard to use? *Journal of the American Society for Information Science*, *47*(7), 493–503.

Borgman, C. L., Hirsh, S. G., Walter, V. A., & Gallagher, A. L. (1995). Children's searching behavior on browsing and keyword online catalogs: The science library catalog project. *Journal of the American Society for Information Science*, *46*(9), 663–684.

Breeding, M. (2007). Introduction to next-generation catalogs. *Library Technology Reports*, *43*(4), 5–14.

Capra, R. G., & Marchionini, G. (2008). The relation browser tool for faceted exploratory search. *Proceedings from JCDL '08: The 8th ACM/IEEE-CS joint conference on digital libraries*, Pittsburgh, PA.

Chen, H., & Dhar, V. (1991). Cognitive process as a basis for intelligent retrieval systems design. *Information Processing and Management*, *27*(5), 405–432.

Cochrane, P. A., & Markey, K. (1983). Catalog use studies – since the introduction of online interactive catalogs: Impact on design for subject access. *Library and Information Science Research*, *5*(4), 337–363.

Connaway, L., Budd, J., & Kochtanek, T. (1995). An investigation of the use of an online catalog: User characteristics and transaction log analysis. *Library Resources & Technical Services*, *39*(2), 142–152.

Cutrell, E., Robbins, D. C., Dumais, S. T., & Sarin, R. (2006). Fast, flexible filtering with Phlat-Personal search and organization made easy. *Conference on human factors in computing systems (proceedings from CHI 2006)*, Montreal, Canada.

Dalrymple, P. W., & Zweizig, D. L. (1992). Users' experience of information retrieval systems: An exploration of the relationship between search experience and affective measures. *Library and Information Science Research*, *14*, 167–181.

Denton, W., & Coysh, S. J. (2011). Usability testing of VuFind at an academic library. *Library Hi Tech*, *29*(2), 301–319.

Doan, K., Plaisant, C., Shneiderman, B., & Bruns, T. (1997). Query previews for networked information systems: A case study with NASA environmental data. *SIGMOD Record*, *26*, 75–81.

Eastman, C. M., & Jansen, B. J. (2003). Coverage, relevance, and ranking: The impact of query operators on web search engine results. *ACM Transactions on Information Systems (TOIS)*, *21*(4), 383–411.

Ellis, D. (1989). A behavioural approach to information retrieval design. *Journal of Documentation*, *45*(3), 171–212.

Ellis, D., & Vasconcelos, A. (1999). Ranganathan and the Net: Using facet analysis to search and organize the World Wide Web. *Aslib Proceedings*, *51*(1), 3–10.

Emmanuel, J. (2011). Usability of the VuFind next generation online catalog. *Information Technologies & Libraries* (March 2011), 44–52.

Ensor, P. (1992). User characteristics of keyword searching in an OPAC. *College and Research Libraries*, *53*(1), 72–80.

Fagan, J. C. (2010). Usability studies of faceted browsing: A literature review. *Information Technology and Libraries*, *29*(2), 58–66.

Foskett, D. J. (2004). *From librarianship to information science: Pioneers of information science*. Retrieved from http://www.libsci.sc.edu/bob/isp/foskett2.htm. Accessed on March 1, 2010.

Hall, C. E. (2011). Facet-based library catalogs: A survey of the landscape. *Proceedings of the 74th annual meeting of ASIS&T*. New Orleans, Louisiana.

Hearst, M., Elliott, A., English, J., Sinha, R., Swearingen, K., & Yee, P. (2002). Finding the flow in web site search. *Communications of the ACM*, *45*(9), 42–49.

Hearst, M. A. (2000). Next generation web search: Setting our sites. *Bulletin of the Technical Committee on Data Engineering*, *23*(3), 38–48.

Hearst, M. A. (2006). Clustering versus faceted categories for information exploration. *Communications of the ACM*, *49*(4), 59–61.

Hemminger, B. M., Lu, D., Vaughan, K., & Adams, S. J. (2007). Information seeking behavior of academic scientists. *Journal of the American Society for Information Science and Technology*, *58*(14), 2205–2225.

Hildreth, C. R. (2001). Accounting for users' inflated assessments of on-line catalog search performance and usefulness: An experimental study. *Information Research*, *6*(2). Retrieved from http://InformationR.net/ir/6-2/paper101.html

Hofmann, M. A., & Yang, S. Q. (2012). "Discovering" what's changed: A revist of the OPACs of 260 academic libraries. *Library Hi Tech*, *30*(2), 253–274.

Hunter, R. N. (1991). Successes and failures of patrons searching the online catalog at a large academic library: A transaction log analysis. *RQ*, *30*(3), 395–402.

Hutchinson, H., Bederson, B. B., & Druin, A. (2007). Supporting elementary-age children's searching and browsing: Design and evaluation using the international children's digital library. *Journal of the American Society for Information Science and Technology*, *58*(11), 1618–1630.

Ingwersen, P., & Wormell, I. (1989). Modern indexing and retrieval techniques matching different types of information needs. In S. Koskiala & R. Launo (Eds.), *Information, knowledge, evolution* (pp. 79–90). London: North-Holland.
Janosky, B., Smith, P., & Hildreth, C. (1986). Online library catalog systems: An analysis of user errors. *International Journal of Man-Machine Studies*, *25*(5), 573–592.
Jansen, B. J., & Pooch, U. (2001). A review of web searching studies and a framework for future research. *Journal of the American Society for Information Science and Technology*, *52*(3), 235–246.
Järvelin, K., & Ingwersen, P. (2004). Information seeking research needs extension towards tasks and technology. *Information Research*, *10*(1), 212. Retrieved from http://InformationR.net/ir/10-1/paper212.html
Jones, S., Cunningham, S. J., McNab, R., & Boddie, S. (2000). A transaction log analysis of a digital library. *International Journal on Digital Libraries*, *3*(2), 152–169.
Jones, W. P. (2007). *Keeping found things found: The study and practice of personal information management*. San Francisco, CA: Morgan Kaufmann.
Kammerer, Y., Narin, R., Pirolli, P., & Chi, E. (2009). Signpost from the masses: Learning effects in an exploratory social tag search browser. *The 27th international conference on human factors in computing systems (proceedings from CHI 2009)*, Boston, MA (pp. 625–634).
Knutson, G. (1991). Subject enhancement: Report on an experiment. *College and Research Libraries*, *52*(1), 65–79.
Kules, B., Capra, R., Banta, M., & Sierra, T. (2009). What do exploratory searchers look at in a faceted search interface? *The joint international conference on digital libraries (proceedings from JCDL 2009)*, Austin, TX (pp. 313–322).
Kwasnik, B. H. (1992). A descriptive study of the functional components of browsing. *Engineering for human-computer interaction: The IFIP TC2/WG2.7 working conference on engineering for human-computer interaction*, Ellivuori, Finland (pp. 191–203).
La Barre, K. (2007). The heritage of early FC in document reference retrieval systems. *Library History*, *23*(2), 129–149.
La Barre, K. (2010). Facet analysis. *Annual Review of Information Science and Technology*, *44*, 243–284.
Large, A., & Beheshti, J. (1997). OPACs: A research review. *Library and Information Science Research*, *19*(2), 111–133.
Lau, E. P., & Goh, D. H. L. (2006). In search of query patterns: A case study of a university OPA. *Information Processing and Management*, *42*(5), 1316–1329.
Lewis, D. W. (1987). Research on the use of online catalogs and its implications for library practice. *Journal of Academic Librarianship*, *13*(3), 152–157.
Lown, C. (2008). *A transaction log analysis of NCSU's faceted navigation OPAC*. Master's Paper. University of North Carolina, Chapel Hill, NC.
Luther, J. (2003). Trumping google? Metasearching's promise. *Library Journal*, *128*(16), 36–40.
Mahoui, M., & Cunningham, S. J. (2001). Search behavior in a research-oriented digital library. *Lecture Notes in Computer Science*, *2163*, 13–24.

Marchionini, G. (2006). Exploratory search: From finding to understanding. *Communications of the ACM*, *49*(4), 41–46.

Marchionini, G., & Brunk, B. (2003). Towards a general relation browser: A GUI for information architects. *Journal of Digital Information*, *4*, 1.

Muramatsu, J., & Pratt, W. (2001). Transparent queries: Investigation users' mental models of search engines. *The 24th annual international ACM SIGIR conference on research and development in information retrieval (proceedings from SIGIR 2001)*, New Orleans, LA (pp. 217–224).

Nahl, D. (1997). Information counseling inventory of affective and cognitive reactions while learning the internet. *Internet Reference Services Quarterly*, *2*(2–3), 11–33.

Niu, X. (2012). *Beyond text queries and ranked lists: Faceted search in library catalogs*. Doctoral Dissertation. University of North Carolina, Chapel Hill, NC.

Noerr, P. L., & Noerr, K. T. B. (1985). Browse and navigate: An advance in database access methods. *Information Processing and Management*, *21*(3), 205–213.

Olson, T. A. (2007). Utility of a faceted catalog for scholarly research. *Library Hi Tech*, *25*(4), 550–561.

O'Brien, A. (1990). Relevance as an aid to evaluation in OPACs. *Journal of Information Science*, *16*, 265–271.

O'Day, V., & Jeffries, R. (1993). Orienteering in an information landscape: How information seekers get from here to there. *The ACM SIGCHI conference on human factors in computing systems (proceedings from CHI 1993)*, Amsterdam, The Netherlands (pp. 438–445).

Peters, T. A. (1989). When smart people fail: An analysis of the transaction log of an online public access catalog. *Journal of Academic Librarianship*, *15*(5), 267–273.

Peters, T. A. (1993). The history and development of transaction log analysis. *Library Hi Tech*, *11*, 41–66.

Riewe. (2008). *Survey of open source integrated library systems*. Master's Paper. San Jose State University.

Sadeh, T. (2008). User experience in the library: a case study. *New Library World*, *109*(1/2), 7–24.

Sharit, J., Hernández, M. A., Czaja, S. J., & Pirolli, P. (2008). Investigating the roles of knowledge and cognitive abilities in older adult information seeking on the web. *ACM Transactions on Computer-Human Interaction (TOCHI)*, *15*(1), Article 3.

Shneiderman, B. (1994). Dynamic queries for visual information seeking. *IEEE Software*, *11*(6), 70–77.

Sit, R. A. (1998). Online library catalog search performance by older adult users. *Library and Information Science Research*, *20*(2), 115–131.

Soergel, D. (1999). The rise of ontologies or the reinvention of classification. *Journal of the American Society for Information Science*, *50*(12), 1119–1120.

Solomon, P. (1993). Children's information retrieval behavior: A case analysis of an OPAC. *Journal of American Society for Information Science and Technology*, *44*(5), 245–264.

Synder, T. (2010). Music materials in a faceted catalog: Interviews with faculty and graduate students. *Music Reference Services Quarterly*, *13*(3/4), 66–95.

Taylor, A. G. (1992). *Introduction to cataloging and classification*. Englewood, CO: Libraries Unlimited.

Taylor, A. G. (2006). *Introduction to cataloging and classification*. Westport, CT: Libraries Unlimited.

Tolle, J. E., & Hah, S. (1985). Online search patterns: NLM CATLINE database. *Journal of the American Society for Information Science and Technology*, *36*(2), 82–93.

Tunkelang, D. (2009). *Faceted search*. San Rafael, CA: Morgan & Claypool Publishers.

Vickery, B. C. (1960). *Faceted classification: A guide to construction and use of special schemes*. London: Aslib.

Vickery, B. C., & Artandi, S. (1966). *Faceted classification schemes*. New Brunswick, NJ: Rutgers University.

Wallace, P. M. (1993). How do patrons search the online catalog when no one. *RQ*, *33*(2), 239–252.

Warren, P. (2000). Why they still cannot use their library catalogues. *Proceedings of informing science conference* (pp. 19–22).

White, R. W., & Drucker, S. M. (2007). Investigating behavioral variability in web search. *The 16th annual World Wide Web conference (proceedings from WWW 2007)*, Banff, Alberta, Canada (pp. 21–30).

White, R. W., & Roth, R. A. (2009). *Exploratory search: Beyond the query-response paradigm*. San Rafael, CA: Morgan & Claypool Publishers.

Yee, K. P., Swearingen, K., Li, K., & Hearst, M. (2003). Faceted metadata for image search and browsing. *The 21st conference on human factors in computing systems (proceedings from CHI 2003)*, Fort Lauderdale, FL (pp. 401–408).

Yee, M. M. (1991). *System design and cataloging meet the user: User interfaces to online public access catalogs*. Retrieved from http://www.Escholarship.org/uc/item/2rp099x6. Accessed on March 21, 2010.

Young, M., & Yu, H. (2004). The impact of web search engines on subject searching in OPAC. *Information Technology and Libraries*, *23*(4), 168–180.

Zhang, J., & Marchionini, G. (2005). Evaluation and evolution of a browse and search interface: Relation browser. *Proceedings of the national conference on digital government research* (pp. 179–188). Atlanta, GA, USA.

Chapter 10

Doing More With Less: Increasing the Value of the Consortial Catalog

Elizabeth J. Cox, Stephanie Graves, Andrea Imre and Cassie Wagner

Abstract

Purpose — This case study describes how one library leveraged shared resources by defaulting to a consortial catalog search.

Design/methodology/approach — The authors use a case study approach to describe steps involved in changing the catalog interface, then assess the project with a usability study and an analysis of borrowing statistics.

Findings — The authors determined the benefit to library patrons was significant and resulted in increased borrowing. The usability study revealed elements of the catalog interface needing improvement.

Practical implications — Taking advantage of an existing resource increased the visibility of consortial materials to better serve library patrons. The library provided these resources without significant additional investment.

Originality/value — While the authors were able to identify other libraries using their consortial catalog as the default search, no substantive published research on its benefits exists in the literature. This chapter will be valuable to libraries with limited budgets that would like to increase patron access to materials.

New Directions in Information Organization
Library and Information Science, Volume 7, 209–228

ISSN: 1876-0562/doi:10.1108/S1876-0562(2013)0000007014

10.1. Introduction

Contemporary library patrons are savvy consumers who expect easy and efficient access to an abundance of content and services. Providers like Netflix, GameFly, Amazon, and Redbox promise speedy delivery of immense collections of content. Local libraries lack the purchasing power to compete with these commercial entities. Yet libraries remain an important resource for many patrons who do not wish to purchase content outright. Libraries struggle to do more with less as collection budgets shrink. Increased use of interlibrary loan services is one important way to meet patrons' needs for more content. Many academic libraries, however, still promote their local catalog as the starting point for resource discovery, despite robust consortial borrowing arrangements. Is there an advantage to library patrons seeing all the resources they have available to them? Could libraries actually do more with less by leveraging discovery tools to take advantage of consortial resources?

In January 2011, the Dean of Library Affairs at Southern Illinois University Carbondale (SIUC) Morris Library brought a proposal to the Information Services department. Over the past decade, the library's monograph budget has been in decline due to journal inflation costs and flat library funding. We needed a way to provide access to more materials without significant additional investment. SIUC's Morris Library has been a member of a consortial borrowing system, now called I-Share, since 1983. Seventy-six of the 152 members of the Consortium of Academic and Research Libraries in Illinois (CARLI) participate in I-Share, the consortial catalog, which boasts approximately 32 million items. In order to expose our patrons to a broader collection of materials available at other consortial libraries in the state of Illinois, the library's Dean proposed changing our default catalog search on the library homepage from the local catalog to the consortial catalog. Patrons are able to borrow materials through our consortium's universal borrowing system. Requested materials are sent to the borrower's library for check-out. Most consortial libraries offer links within their local catalog to I-Share, provide direct links to I-Share from their websites, and provide a link to re-execute a search in I-Share when the search in the local catalog fails. Despite I-Share's massive holdings, most participating libraries, including Morris Library, offer their local catalogs as the default search for their patrons.

The Information Services librarians were intrigued by the proposal but raised a number of concerns. If we made this change, we would be the first library in I-Share to default to the consortial catalog. Would we continue to have a local catalog? How would we deal with proprietary electronic resources that appeared in the I-Share catalog but were inaccessible to our local patrons due to licensing issues? Would we be able to customize the appearance of the catalog? Would our local edits of bibliographic records appear in the consortial catalog? Several librarians volunteered to investigate these and other yet-to-be-discovered issues. What initially appeared to be a simple idea proved to be a large project with significant implications.

10.2. Project Background

After the Dean's proposal in January 2011, two librarians teleconferenced with CARLI staff members to discuss the implications of using the consortial catalog as the local default search. After that initial phone call, the reference librarians originally tasked with investigation of the proposal recognized that additional expertise was necessary. In February 2011 the project was brought to the library's Virtual Library Group (VLG) for discussion and technical assistance. Later that month Information Services librarians also met to further discuss impacts on public access and services. While they thought the proposal had considerable merit, they unanimously agreed to ask the Dean to delay implementation until the completion of the Spring academic semester. The librarians were concerned that an immediate change would adversely affect instructional efforts, handouts, preexisting library assignments, and reference interactions. The Dean agreed to wait until summer semester and a meeting was convened in March 2011 with a working group comprised of: the Head of Circulation, the Electronic Resources Librarian, the Head of Reference, the Virtual Reference Coordinator, the Web Development Librarian, the Associate Dean for Information Services, the Special Formats Cataloger, and a graphic specialist. Each member of the working group was assigned to investigate a specific concern relative to their expertise (e.g., the Head of Circulation was tasked with investigating universal borrowing issues, the e-Resources librarian was tasked with investigating the inclusion of e-resource records into the consortial catalog, etc.). Once the group had developed solutions, a forum for all library staff was held at the end of the spring semester to inform and train staff.

10.2.1. Catalog System and Organization

Switching the default search from the local catalog to the consortial catalog was not technically difficult to implement, although a few issues required work from library and consortial staff. The consortial catalog runs on Voyager 7.2.5 from Ex Libris. Voyager's configuration in the I-Share environment allows each participating library to have their own instance that includes each library's holdings. In addition, a consortial catalog is generated with the holdings of all member libraries.

Voyager has been in place since 2002 and has become a well-established and reliable consortial borrowing system. In the late 2000s, CARLI began investigating open source products to overcome the limitations of commercial products. VuFind, a library resource discovery layer, was developed as an open source product by Villanova University. Starting in 2008, CARLI began offering VuFind as an alternative interface to Voyager. Each library could choose to run their local catalog with either the WebVoyage Classic or the VuFind search interface. SIUC offered the VuFind interface as an alternative to the local catalog starting in the Fall of 2008 under the name SIUCat Beta. In the summer of 2010, shortly after CARLI made VuFind the only catalog interface for I-Share, SIUC made VuFind the primary interface for the local catalog.

Consortial staff at the CARLI office maintain the servers, implement system upgrades, provide technical support to member libraries, provide remote backup in case of disasters, and implement new features for both the integrated library system (Voyager) and the I-Share consortial catalog. This consortial support of Voyager and VuFind relieves libraries of a large portion of system maintenance tasks. The arrangement also results in certain limitations when local customization is needed. CARLI staff welcome suggestions for improvements to the catalog, but each proposed change goes through a thorough vetting process and not all local customizations are implemented.

10.2.2. Interface Customization

Since the VuFind interface is maintained by CARLI office staff, individual libraries have limited customization choices. Customization options include the choice of colors for links on the page, feedback contact information, local catalog name, choice about inclusion or exclusion of links to WebVoyage and course reserves, header image, initial search page text, footer, text for the top portion of the login page, and text for account creation.

Prior to the project, the local catalog and the consortial catalog had different customized headers at the top of their respective interfaces. Because of technical issues, a switch to the consortial catalog as the default would only allow for a single header image. This raised issues related to customization, branding, and functionality.

At the time, the header was the primary section of the catalog interfaces that could be customized by local libraries. Morris Library had provided a number of links unique to SIUC in the local catalog header such as storage retrieval forms, Ask A Librarian reference services, e-journal finder, and a link to the library homepage. Local links would need to be retained in the new merged header to maintain functionality for local patrons. In addition, at the insistence of the reference librarians, a link was included to the WebVoyage interface, relabeled as "Classic Search." It was also important to re-brand the header for both I-Share and Morris Library so that both organizations could be recognized from the same header image.

For public services librarians, the primary issue of header customization was the disappearance of the local catalog, called SIUCat, as a distinct named entity. Librarians had been teaching with and referring to our local catalog as SIUCat for almost a decade. However, it would be misleading to brand the header with SIUCat, since this name historically referred only to the local catalog. In the new shared environment, patrons would see holdings from all I-Share libraries. The header image would remain the same regardless of whether the patron was looking at the consortial catalog or local catalog. After numerous discussions, Morris Library staff decided to phase out the use of the "SIUCat" name for the local catalog in favor of "I-Share @ Morris Library" as a descriptor for both catalogs (see Figures 10.1–10.3 for former and current headers). The phrase captured

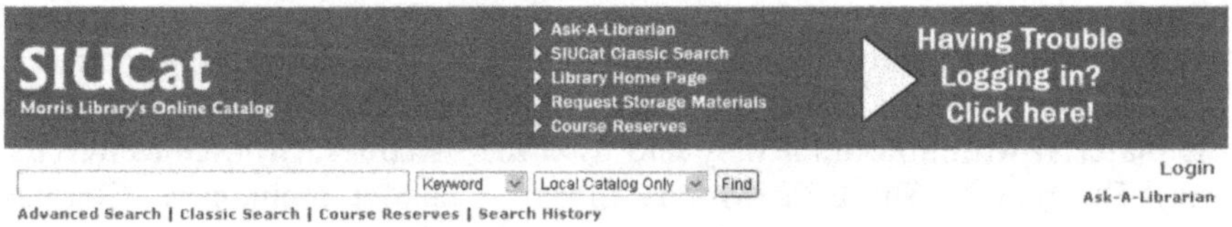

Figure 10.1: Former SIUCat header.

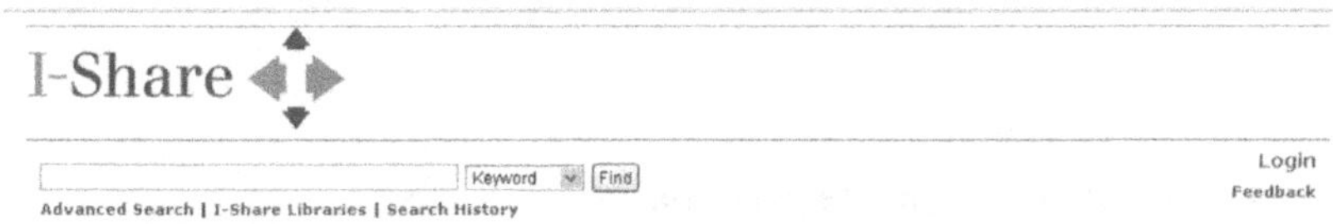

Figure 10.2: Former I-Share header.

Figure 10.3: Current "I-Share @ Morris Library" header.

the local connection to the library while honoring the partnership with I-Share. A librarian worked with a graphic specialist to develop a merged header that included the new name, as well as links important to local library patrons.

10.2.3. Universal Borrowing

As stated earlier, I-Share libraries allow patrons at other I-Share institutions to borrow materials from their collections. A "Request 1st Available" tab in the consortial catalog facilitates this function. Morris Library's recent renovation, however, presented a unique issue related to the request option. During the renovation, the majority of the collection was moved to a remote storage facility. The library retrieves items from this facility twice daily for patrons who initiate a storage retrieval request via a web form on the library's website. Despite our best efforts to place the storage retrieval link prominently on the website, the Head of Circulation reported that most of our local patrons used the request function in the catalog instead of using the "Request Storage Materials" link in the catalog header. Nothing prevents patrons from using the request function in the catalog, but the library only runs a report of these items daily, thus items are not retrieved from the storage facility on the regular schedule. This can cause a request to be delayed until the following day, when the patron could have had the material within hours if they had used the "Request Storage Materials" link. The new "I-Share @ Morris Library" header includes a "Request Storage Materials" link to avoid confusion, but the problem persists. Because the library has limited control over I-Share customizations, we must rely on educating our patrons on the difference between the two retrieval options.

10.2.4. Universal Borrowing Implications

Individual CARLI libraries can choose to allow an item to circulate to local patrons only, a practice most often implemented with items that can be checked out for short loan periods. Libraries commonly restrict formats like DVDs, journals, multimedia, and special collections materials. However, the records for such items still appear in the consortial catalog. If a patron attempts to borrow an item that is "unrequestable," they receive a standard error message provided by the consortium that directs them to contact their local library. Librarians and staff at Morris Library anticipated that the change to the consortial catalog as the default would likely increase the number of reference questions related to borrowing items that were "unrequestable."

In preparation for those questions, the Head of Circulation and the Virtual Reference Coordinator created a help document on Morris Library's website (http://libguides.lib.siu.edu/aecontent.php?pid=184214&sid=1570072) for patrons. This site provides patrons with a chart describing which item types typically circulate and which do not. It also provides a direct link to the local interlibrary loan website and the library's virtual reference services.

The help guide was initially linked in the new header image in the catalog. Beginning in 2011, CARLI allowed individual libraries to customize the error message so that libraries could embed direct links to their local interlibrary loan units. We immediately took advantage of this customization. Any patron that tries to request an "unrequestable" item is directed to our help guide.

Librarians were also concerned that the switch to the consortial catalog would result in unnecessary borrowing of items that are held locally. The catalog uses a relevance ranking algorithm to determine the order in which results appear. The ranking algorithm does not take into consideration whether the local library holds an item or not. Patrons cannot see which libraries own an item from the results list. They must view the item level record to see which libraries in the consortium own the item. If our library owns the item, our holdings information will appear first in the individual item record, followed by other libraries in the consortium.

CARLI has made considerable efforts to reduce duplicate records in the consortial catalog. However, when a patron is looking for something as ubiquitous as "Hamlet," they are presented with several hundred items from multiple libraries. The number of results found in the consortial catalog is overwhelming. CARLI has implemented two location facets to expedite discovery of local items. The first allows patrons to limit to local library holdings only (e.g., SIUC only). The second allows collection of specific facets as designated by the local library (e.g., Special Collections, Government Documents, Morris Library, storage). The latter, however, display in the local catalog only. Patrons need to be familiar with facets and know how to limit their searches to be able to filter out unwanted items from the large result sets I-Share offers.

10.2.5. Account Creation

The consortial catalog requires patrons to create an account with a unique username and password to access many functions, including universal borrowing and renewals. With 76 participating libraries, CARLI must assure unique usernames across the consortium and login information cannot be preloaded into the system. This prevents our library from using students' preexisting campus network IDs. Each patron must create his or her own personalized account before they can make requests or access their accounts. This approach unfortunately creates many difficulties and misunderstandings among patrons and extra work for public services staff.

Several librarians and staff were concerned that patrons would not understand that their campus Network ID was not synonymous with their I-Share account. To address this concern, a team of public services librarians and staff developed a program called "Set Up For Success." During the first two weeks of the Fall 2010 semester, the staff at the Information Desk, Circulation Desk, and Help Desk provided assistance in creating all of the accounts needed at SIUC. In addition to setting up their I-Share username and password, staff also assisted students with their interlibrary loan accounts, campus Network IDs, and campus email accounts. The program was advertised with flyers and targeted email messages to select campus courses, such as University 101.

The first year of "Set Up For Success" was very popular. Reference questions for the areas of Network ID creation, interlibrary loan, reference, and policy doubled from the previous year, from 1449 in the first two weeks of 2009 to 3089 in 2010. In 2011, the "Set Up For Success" team decided to incentivize the program, in part to address concerns about the switch to the consortial catalog. They deployed volunteer library student workers to talk to their fellow students and pass out "Set Up For Success" tickets throughout campus. Every student who came to the library, created their library accounts, and handed in a completed ticket which was entered into a drawing for a $100 gift certificate for textbooks at the University Bookstore. The library student workers who had the most tickets redeemed also won a $100 gift certificate. As a result of these efforts, the number of recorded questions for the period rose to 3314, a 7% increase from 2010. This number represents accounts created during a two-week period drawn from a total student population of over 20,000. However, it does mean that these students are now aware of their universal borrowing privileges. The total number of current I-Share accounts, 34,901, is more indicative of local usage. However, we are unable to determine if this number includes duplicate and inactive accounts. We continue to be concerned that I-Share account creation is an inconvenience for patrons to utilize universal borrowing in the consortial catalog. However, if a patron has forgotten their I-Share account information, they can simply create a new one. Despite our concern, patrons are making use of the system, as universal borrowing has increased.

10.2.6. Concerns Related to Local Cataloging Practices

The consortial catalog includes de-duplicated bibliographic records of member libraries with member library holdings attached to the appropriate bibliographic record. CARLI staff make use of the field weights of various indexes in the duplicate detection process and use a quality hierarchy in identifying the record to be retained in the consortial catalog. CARLI extracts data from each library's local database on an hourly basis and then loads the extracted data into the consortial catalog at the end of each day. The duplicate detection and the quality hierarchy settings in the consortial catalog mean local changes made to the catalog record may not be available in the consortial catalog. This is a concern for special collections material where catalogers include unique information about a locally held item and for formats such as maps where catalogers enhance records. In addition, contents notes in the 505 field are added locally to newly acquired books to enhance discovery, but many of these contents notes do not appear in the consortial catalog due to the de-duplication and quality hierarchy process. Technical Services staff must continue to be vigilant in following the consortial guidelines for replacement and updating of bibliographic records to ensure that the most current and up-to-date version of the record is available in the consortial catalog. This also ensures that Morris Library's holdings are accurately reflected in the consortial catalog.

Switching to the consortial catalog as a default search therefore may have negative effects on the discovery of several of our collections and limits the usefulness and availability of locally added cataloging information. Some staff expressed concern early on that this information would be lost if the library switched from the local catalog to the consortial catalog. The library addressed this shortcoming by including the option to limit searches to SIUC holdings only, as well as providing links to WebVoyage, the "classic" interface of the local catalog. Despite these concerns, it was determined that the benefits of accessing the consortial holdings would outweigh any loss of local catalog information.

The vast majority of Morris Library's holdings are available in the consortial catalog. A small number of nonelectronic titles currently have brief, local records that are suppressed from I-Share, but local catalogers are in the midst of a project to replace these with full bibliographic records. Other records that do not appear in the consortial catalog are order records for monographs and a small portion of the Instructional Materials Center's posters.

However, the largest collection of items absent from the consortial catalog were electronic resources. Since 2004, Morris Library has added over 250,000 vendor-provided MARC records for large literary collections, other e-books, e-journals, and reference works. Many of these records were excluded from the consortial catalog either because the vendor imposed restrictions on sharing or because these records lacked appropriate control numbers to be used in the consortial catalog's de-duplication process. In addition, since the consortial catalog was used for universal borrowing and lending of electronic books was not allowed in most of our licenses, MARC records for electronic books were also excluded from the consortial catalog. MARC records for electronic journals were loaded and updated on a monthly basis with thousands of deletions, changes, and updates made each time. In order to avoid complications with this update process, a local decision was made to exclude electronic journal records from the consortial catalog as well. When the decision was made to switch to the consortial catalog as the default, library staff reexamined this practice. Library staff wanted to ensure that the consortial catalog represented as many locally held items as possible, including electronic resources. At this point, the only electronic resources excluded from the I-Share catalog are those with licensing restrictions. This is limited to one specific vendor and applies to about 75,000 records. As we move forward on the implementation of a discovery service, we have developed a solution to this problem.

Staff decided that MARC records without vendor restrictions on sharing would be loaded into the consortial catalog. Before this could happen, the library needed to update the MARC records of electronic resources by removing the 049 field in a batch process using a script. This field was used to suppress records from the consortial catalog. Through trial and error we also found that many of the electronic resource MARC records had another field that caused serious problems in the consortial catalog's de-duplication process. The 010 field holds the Library of Congress Control Number specific to the print version and was often left in the electronic resource records by vendors who derived their MARC records for the electronic resource from the existing MARC records for the print version. When SIUC originally loaded these records into the local catalog, the 010 did not cause any problems because locally created bulk import rules ignored this field. In the consortial de-duplication process, however, the 010 is weighted very strongly. When the 010 field is included in the electronic record, it is likely that an existing MARC record for the print version of an item already included in the consortial catalog with other institution's holdings attached will be overwritten by the MARC record for the electronic version from SIUC. This goes against the consortial recommendation of using separate bibliographic records for electronic resources and print resources. When the problem with the 010 field was discovered, SIUC librarians worked with CARLI staff to resolve the issue by identifying the incorrectly overlaid records in the consortial catalog and removing them. SIUC staff then had to edit the electronic resource records to remove the 010 field and then reloaded those records into I-Share.

10.2.7. Website Changes

The changes to branding and search options necessitated changes to Morris Library's web page. References to SIUCat were removed and replaced with the I-Share name and URLs were corrected. In the quick search box on the homepage the default option was the consortial catalog; patrons had the option to use a pull-down menu to search SIUC only (see Figure 10.4). We needed the assistance of a local, skilled programmer to create the script that enabled this choice.

It was important to prepare our patrons for this significant change. In the spring of 2011, a website was created (http://libguides.lib.siu.edu/I-Share-atMorris) containing information about the switch to the consortial catalog as the default. A link to this page was added in a prominent location on the library's homepage in May 2011, two weeks before the consortial catalog was activated as the default. The link read: "Changes to the catalog coming soon! Click here for more info." The website included an FAQ, a list of what can be borrowed, and instructions on how to set up an I-Share account.

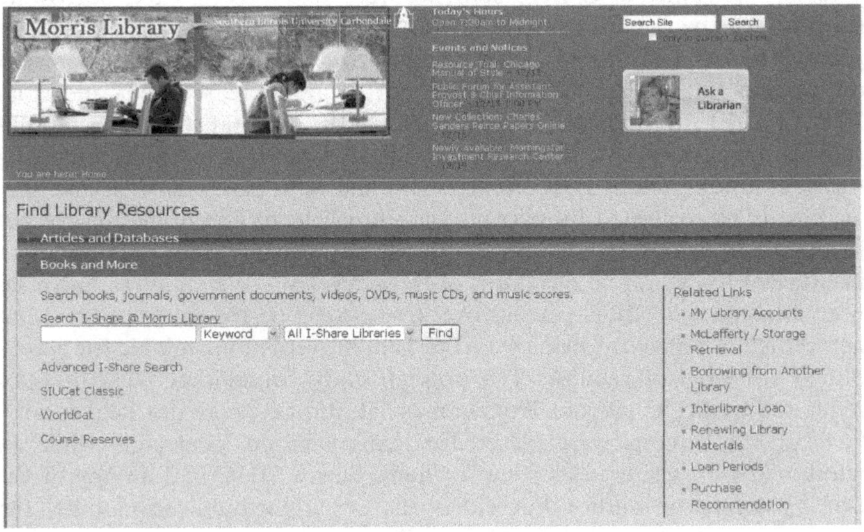

Figure 10.4: Screen shot of Morris Library's home page, showing the contents of the "Books and More" tab.

The librarians also had to remove references to the old local catalog name, SIUCat, from handouts and web pages. This was not easily done with a "find and replace" function. In many cases, subject librarians needed to decide if they wanted patrons to be defaulted into a search for local holdings only or if they wanted to default patrons into the consortial catalog. The librarians administer their own subject LibGuides and were able to make decisions based on the needs of their particular fields and students. The Web Development Librarian provided code for librarians to embed a simple search of the consortial or local catalog in their LibGuides.

10.3. Evaluation and Assessment

After implementation in Summer 2011, librarians were anxious to determine the impact of the change to I-Share as the default catalog. However, it was necessary to wait until sufficient time had passed and data was available. The decision was made to evaluate the program using consortial borrowing statistics and usability testing in the latter half of the semester.

10.3.1. Consortial Borrowing Statistics

With the assistance of CARLI staff, we were able to review our borrowing statistics for the same time period (June 1–October 31) for four consecutive years, 2008–2011. Consortial borrowing by SIUC patrons steadily increased during that time. From 2008 to 2009, borrowing increased 12% and from 2009 to 2010, the increase was 7%. However, the statistics show a substantial increase of 24% from 2010 to 2011. A study analyzing borrowing statistics among OhioLINK libraries (Prabha & O'Neill, 2001) found that 76% of titles requested by patrons were not held by the home library but further analysis of the remaining 24% was not possible since their data was insufficient to determine the status of those requests. We analyzed universal borrowing data of SIUC patrons over a one-week period to determine what percentage of borrowed items were not held or were not available for checkout at the time of request. The present study found that 80% of titles requested by SIUC patrons from consortial libraries were not held locally: 66% of the requests were placed for items with no local copy while an additional 14% of requests were for items where SIUC had a copy of the title by the same author but either the copyright/publication date, the publisher, or the format differed from the one borrowed via the consortial catalog. In the latter group the item borrowed from another library was attached to a different bibliographic record in the consortial catalog than the one to which the SIUC holding was attached. Based on data available to us it is impossible to determine with certainty whether patrons were looking for a specific edition requested via the consortial catalog or if they just overlooked the SIUC holdings. Because the item borrowed from another library was not an exact copy of the locally held item, requests in this group were categorized as valid requests. Unlike the OhioLINK study, our study focused on the borrowing data of a single institution and determining item availability for the remaining 20% of the requests was possible using catalog information, circulation data, and in many cases by checking the availability of the items on the shelves. Our study found that 18% of these requests were for items where the local copy was not available (e.g., checked out, on reserve, noncirculating, missing, at preservation). Only 2% of the items were held and were available for check-out at the time of request. In these cases patrons likely overlooked the SIUC copy in the I-Share catalog and used the "Request this item" link displayed under each I-Share library's holding. This data indicate that switching to the I-Share consortial catalog resulted in a small percentage of unnecessary or invalid requests for items SIUC owned but that much of the increase was due to valid requests made for items SIUC doesn't have a copy of. These statistics validate our hope that using I-Share as the default catalog would encourage patrons to use the wider consortial collection more frequently. However, the increase does affect daily workflow and staffing, as our staff and the lending libraries' staff must cope with increased requests.

10.3.2. Usability Testing

For this publication, as well as for our own local use and information, the authors created a brief usability test to determine how students use the default consortial catalog configuration. The test subjects included six undergraduates ranging from sophomore to senior, three graduate students, and one PhD candidate. Such a small number of subjects is normal for usability tests. Research has shown that five users will uncover about 80% of usability problems on a website. Each tester beyond that provides a diminishing number of usability insights (Nielsen, 2012). Some of the students were more advanced library users than others. During the testing, we discovered that one of the graduate students also worked at the library's main reference desk. Although we considered excluding her from the testing, we determined that she had limited experience using I-Share and would be acceptable. One of the primary goals of this assessment was to test known problems, such as account creation.

Despite the apparent popularity of the VuFind interface, there are few studies assessing its use by patrons in libraries. The studies related to VuFind are divided into those that focus on the implementation and customization of the system by various libraries (Digby & Elfstrand, 2011; Featherstone & Wang, 2009; Ho, Kelley, & Garrison, 2009; Houser, 2009) and those that address aspects of the usability of VuFind implementations (Denton & Coysh, 2011; Emanuel, 2011; Fagan, 2010). In addition, Yale University published a summary of a usability test of VuFind librarians conducted in 2008 on their website (Bauer, 2011). Ho's team at Western Michigan University also ran usability tests but have not published a summary. Unlike the current examination, none of these libraries use a consortial catalog as the default search. While a cursory web search provides examples of other libraries that are using a consortial catalog as their default search, no substantive published research on the benefits of doing so is found in the literature.

The study conducted at the University of Illinois at Urbana-Champaign (UIUC) by Emanuel examines a version of VuFind that, like SIUC's instance, is maintained by CARLI. Subjects included undergraduates, graduate students, and faculty members. Unfortunately, the questions included in the article show that subjects were directed to examine certain features of the interface, in addition to tasks to complete using the interface. Such direction masks problems patrons have coming to the interface without instruction. Even so, issues similar to those uncovered by the authors in the current study were reported. Patrons were unclear on how to switch between results limited to their campus library and the full consortium's holdings and encountered problems with terminology commonly used by librarians.

The testing of undergraduates at Yale (2008) is most informative and similar to the current study. Testing undergraduates, subjects were asked to complete a number of nondirective tasks. Subjects quickly executed known item and subject searches, determined availability status, and located the request function. They, however, were unable to effectively use the facets even though three out of the five subjects located and attempted to narrow searches with them (Bauer, 2011).

10.3.3. Usability Test Results

For the current usability test, eight questions were created to test a variety of functions within I-Share. These questions are included in the appendix at the end of the chapter.

The first question asked students to access their accounts and look at items checked out. If the student did not have an active account, he or she was asked to create one. Since I-Share requires an account separate from other university accounts, we wanted to examine whether this process created problems. Most students knew they needed to login to *an* account, but some were not sure if they had one. Four of the students already had an account set up. For those that did not have an account, success in creating one was mixed. Most followed the instructions but were stumped by a field asking for their library barcode number, despite an explanation at the top of the screen. One did read the instructions and was able to follow them without trouble (see Figure 10.5).

Another test question asked students to find a specific book that was checked in and not housed in storage. This task provided students the opportunity to make a choice between searching all I-Share libraries and SIUC holdings only using a pull-down menu located between the search box and search button. It also tested their ability to use the facets in the results page to limit by two different levels of location: between SIUC only and all I-Share libraries and by location in the Morris Library building. Most students realized that they would need to find a book in Morris Library, not in storage. Few of the subjects used the pull-down menu to limit the search to SIUC only. None of the students found or used the facets which are

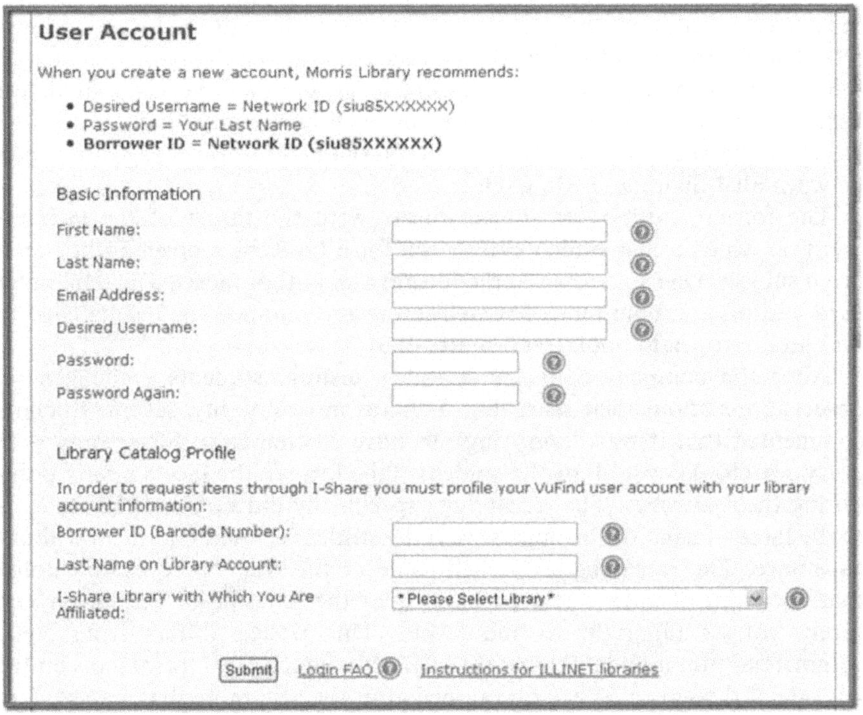

Figure 10.5: Partial screen shot showing account creation page.

located on the right side of the results page. When searching the consortial catalog, students generally opened multiple holdings' item records and looked at the "Location & Availability" tab in search of SIUC.

A question was developed to examine whether the student could find a known book and its availability. Because the question asked if Morris Library owned the title, most students searched SIUC holdings only. Many students entered multiple variations of the title, expecting to get different results. Almost all found the item by re-executing the search in I-Share by selecting that option from the pull-down menu near the search box. None used the location facet on the results page to broaden their search to all I-Share libraries.

Students were also told that a copy of a known title was checked out from Morris Library and to obtain a copy. This question provided the largest variety of responses. Search strategies varied between keyword and title searches and both the local and consortial catalog. Of those that searched SIUC only, one said she would have given up and gone to interlibrary loan, one was confused by the word "biography" in the test question and searched for an article on the library databases page, one noticed that the first title was checked out and said she would request the second title (which was not the correct item), and one said that she would wait until the local copy was returned. Of those that searched all I-Share libraries initially or switched to this option when they discovered that the local copy was checked out, all test subjects were able to navigate to the universal borrowing function quickly. None of the students used the library facet on the results page to switch between all I-Share and SIUC Only.

The format, author, or subject facets were the target of the last test question which asked students to search for a book by a given author on a given subject. One student used the format and author facets. The remainder used various combinations of search terms and scanned the results page to find an appropriate book (see Figure 10.6).

After the completion of the usability testing, students made general observations about their searching. Perhaps most notably, several students commented that it was "annoying" to have to change to SIUC only with every search. Almost all of the students failed to see the facets at any point during their searches. The researchers specifically did not lead the students to the facets during the testing to see if the students would find them without assistance. The researchers watched some of the students' eyes and noted that they almost always started looking at the left side of the screen and rarely got as far right as the facets. This design differs from some commercial sites and databases (e.g., EBSCO) which have their facets on the left side of the screen. When questioned after the test, more than one student mentioned that they either did not notice the facets or did not think they would be helpful. While librarians thought that facets were one of the major

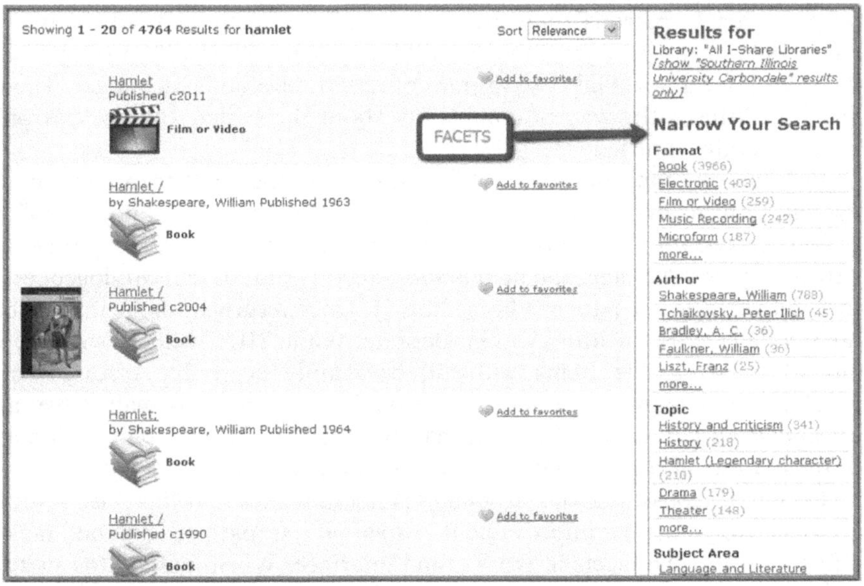

Figure 10.6: Partial screen shot of search results showing facets.

benefits of the VuFind interface, our usability testing illustrates that facets are not being utilized effectively. Only 1 of 10 test subjects actually found and used the facets in the catalog.

A feedback link was embedded in the merged header of the consortial and local catalog. A survey with three questions and an open comment box, developed in Survey Monkey, provided a mechanism to assess patron satisfaction with "I-Share @ Morris Library." Only 31 responses were collected: 11 undergraduate, 14 graduate, 5 faculty, and 1 staff. Respondents tended to be regular library users with 65% using the catalog for research on a daily or weekly basis. When asked the question, "Which do you prefer as the default search: SIUC Library only or all I-Share libraries?," 57% chose SIUC only. Open comments generally related to collection development issues, remote storage retrieval, or account creation. The response pool was too small to derive any statistically significant data, and further investigation is warranted. Therefore, it was decided to leave the survey open in the hopes of collecting additional responses.

10.4. Conclusions and Next Steps

The first six months after implementation have been an adventure. We believe that defaulting to the consortial catalog is serving its intended purpose. SIUC patrons' universal borrowing has increased substantially, rising 19% in the past year. Our local library patrons are discovering more items without additional cost to our collection development budget. There has been little in the way of complaints about the switch and our patrons seem generally satisfied.

In addition, the consortium has announced the implementation of a Patron Driven Acquisitions program. The consortium will load bibliographic records for a number of titles into the consortial catalog. When a patron requests the item, the item is subsequently purchased, cataloged, and then delivered to the patron's home library. Once returned, the items will be housed in a central location within the state. While SIUC will not own these individual items, the items will still be readily accessible through this purchase-on-demand program. Additionally our patrons will have an advantage in requesting these purchasable titles, since the records display in the consortial catalog only, now our default search.

Despite the positives, our usability testing indicates that there are several areas needing further improvement. Most of our patrons did not make effective use of the facets in the VuFind interface. When making the switch to the consortial catalog, we anticipated that the facets would help patrons considerably reduce the number of irrelevant sources. We hypothesize that the location of the facets on the right side of the page makes them all but invisible for the students we tested. Repeated eye-tracking studies of users' focus show that they heavily favor the left side of a webpage to the near total exclusion of the right (Nielsen, 2010). Commercial websites address this behavior by placing important links and facets on the left and advertising on the right. As a next step, we will recommend to CARLI that the location of the facets be moved to the left side. Usability testing following that change could corroborate our hypothesis.

Our library is also investigating a webscale discovery tool, such as EBSCO Discovery Service, WorldCat Local, Summon, or PRIMO. The addition of a discovery tool would dramatically change the way our patrons find library resources. If we are successful in purchasing and implementing a discovery tool, we will need to make decisions whether to include item records from the local or the consortial catalog.

The licensing cost of a discovery tool is a primary concern as our library attempts to provide patrons with easy access to content from various providers. Currently no library is using an open source discovery tool that would offer the ability to integrate a universal borrowing feature, similar to the one in I-Share. However, if our budget continues to decrease, an open source application may be our only option. The consortial borrowing model currently in use between I-Share libraries provides easy access and quick delivery of millions of items at no additional cost. There may be options in the future for an open source solution, such as the eXtensible

Catalog from the University of Rochester. CARLI is currently a development partner in this project. Regardless of the choice of discovery service, libraries should pursue integration of consortial holdings in their discovery service offerings.

The change to the consortial catalog as the default search for our local patrons was an experiment that has proven successful based on universal borrowing statistics. We will continue to monitor universal borrowing and lending statistics as the project moves forward. In the past decade libraries have been focused on leveraging the accessibility of online resources. In today's economic climate, libraries must take advantage of every opportunity to expose patrons to more content, regardless of the format. This study provides one low- to no-cost example of how libraries may take advantage of expanded resources already at hand. Based on this test case, other consortial libraries may want to take note. This project describes one attempt to allow our local patrons to discover more resources and our library is able to do more with less.

10.A.1. Appendix. Usability Test Questions

1. You think your book is overdue. Check.
2. Your professor has recommended the book *The United States during the Civil War* and you want to check it out. Find the call number and where it is located.
3. You know that your professor has placed a book about Congress on reserve. Find the reserves list for History 392.
4. Your professor has asked you to bring a copy of Shakespeare's Hamlet to class. Class starts in 45 minutes. Can you get a copy from the library and get to class in time? What steps do you need to take to get it?
5. Find a CD of Mozart's *Requiem.*
6. A friend has recommended a book to you, *Queen Victoria: Demon Hunter*. Does Morris Library own this book?
7. You would like to read a biography of Jennifer Jones, *Portrait of Jennifer*, but it is checked out. What can you do?
8. Do a search for jazz music. Does Morris Library own any books by Gary Giddins?

References

Bauer, K. (2011). *Yale University Library VuFind Test — Undergraduates.* Retrieved from http://collaborate.library.yale.edu/usability/reports/YuFind/summary_undergraduate.doc.

Denton, W., & Coysh, S. J. (2011). Usability testing of VuFind at an academic library. *Library Hi Tech*, *29*(2), 301–319.

Digby, T., & Elfstrand, S. (2011). Discovering open source discovery: Using VuFind to create MnPALS Plus. *Computers in Libraries*, *31*(2), 6–10.

Emanuel, J. (2011). Usability of VuFind Next-Generation online catalog. *Information Technology and Libraries*, *30*(1), 44–52.

Fagan, J. C. (2010). VuFind. *The Charleston Advisor*, *11*(3), 53–56.

Featherstone, R., & Wang, L. (2009). Enhancing subject access to electronic collections with VuFind. *Journal of Electronic Resources in Medical Libraries*, *6*(4), 294–306.

Ho, B., Kelley, K., & Garrison, S. (2009). Implementing VuFind as an alternative to Voyager's WebVoyage interface: One library's experience. *Library Hi Tech*, *27*(1), 82–92.

Houser, J. (2009). The VuFind Implementation at Villanova University. *Library Hi Tech*, *27*(1), 93–105.

Nielsen, J. (2010, April 6). *Horizontal attention leans left*. Retrieved from http://www.useit.com/alertbox/horizontal-attention.html

Nielsen, J. (2012, June 4). *How many test users in a usability study?* Retrieved from http://www.useit.com/alertbox/number-of-test-users.html

Prabha, C., & O'Neill, E. (2001). Interlibrary borrowing initiated by patrons: Some characteristics of books requested via OhioLINK. *Journal of Library Administration*, *34*(3/4), 329–338.

Chapter 11

All Metadata Politics Is Local: Developing Meaningful Quality Standards

Sarah H. Theimer

Abstract

Purpose — Quality, an abstract concept, requires concrete definition in order to be actionable. This chapter moves the quality discussion from the theoretical to the workplace, building steps needed to manage quality issues.

Methodology — The chapter reviews general data studies, web quality studies, and metadata quality studies to identify and define dimensions of data quality and quantitative measures for each concept. The chapter reviews preferred communication methods which make findings meaningful to administrators.

Practical implications — The chapter describes how quality dimensions are practically applied. It suggests criteria necessary to identify high priority populations, and resources in core subject areas or formats, as quality does not have to be completely uniform. The author emphasizes examining the information environment, documenting practice, and developing measurement standards. The author stresses that quality procedures must rapidly evolve to reflect local expectations, the local information environment, technology capabilities, and national standards.

Originality/value — This chapter combines theory with practical application. It stresses the importance of metadata and recognizes

New Directions in Information Organization
Library and Information Science, Volume 7, 229–250

ISSN: 1876-0562/doi:10.1108/S1876-0562(2013)0000007015

quality as a cyclical process which balances the necessity of national standards, the needs of the user, and the work realities of the metadata staff. This chapter identifies decision points, outlines future action, and explains communication options.

11.1. Introduction

The former U.S. Speaker of the House Tip O'Neill is credited with the phrase "All politics is local," meaning a politician's success is directly tied to his ability to understand those issues important to his constituents. Politicians must recognize people's day to day concerns. The same can be said of metadata. Metadata issues are discussed nationally, but first and foremost, it serves the local community. Just as electorates in different regions have specific local concerns, libraries, archives, and museums have local strengths which local metadata must reflect and support. Metadata should adapt to changes in staff, programs, economics, and local demographics. Customers used to walk through the door, but globalized access to networked information has vastly expanded potential users and uses of metadata.

Metadata, data about data, comprises a formal resource description. Data quality research has been conducted in fields such as business, library science, and information technology because of its ubiquitous importance. Business has traditionally customized data for a consumer base. Internet metadata supports many customer bases. Heery and Patel (2000), when describing metadata application profiles, explicitly state that implementers manipulate metadata schemes for their own purposes. Libraries have traditionally edited metadata for local use. While arguing against perfectionism, Osborn observed "the school library, the special library, the popular public library, the reference library, the college library, and the university library — all these have different requirements, and to standardize their cataloging would result in much harm" (1941, p. 9). Shared cataloging requires adherence to detailed national standards. Producing low-quality records leads to large scale embarrassment as an individual library's work is assessed nationally and sometimes globally. A 2009 report for the Library of Congress found that 80 percent of libraries locally edit records for the English-language monographs. Most of this editing is performed to meet local needs. Only 50 percent of those that make changes upload those local edits to their national bibliographic utility. Half of those that do not share their edits report the edits are only appropriate to the local catalog (Fischer & Lugg, 2009). A study on MARC tag usage reported that use can vary from the specific local catalog to the aggregated database

(Smith-Yoshimura et al., 2010). Though local edits are common, Simpson (2007) argues it is an unnecessary, dated practice, identifying an over-emphasis on the needs of highly specialized user groups as a failing of research libraries. Catalogers must relinquish excessive localization of catalog records to be more productive and relevant. Calhoun (2006) lists unwillingness or inability to dispense with highly customized cataloging operations, the "not created here" mindset preventing ready acceptance of other people's records, and resistance to simplified cataloging as obstacles to innovation and cost reduction.

11.2. The Importance of Quality

Metadata quality standards vary. Different settings require different levels of metadata quality because the organizations have very distinct standards and purposes. The museum and archives communities have different ideas of what constitutes high-quality metadata. The metadata created for the same resource would look different for all setting, but neither is better. Quality is user dependent (Robertson, 2005).

Quality standards may differ, but there is no doubt that metadata quality is important. Poor quality data has significant social and economic impacts. The Data Warehouse Institute estimated that poor data quality cost US companies more than 600 billion annually and half of the companies surveyed had no plan for managing data quality. The business costs of low-quality data, including irrecoverable costs, workarounds, and lost or missing revenue may be as high as 10–25 percent of revenue or total budget of an organization (Eckerson, 2002).

Even Google is not exempt from metadata quality issues. Google Books metadata has been labeled a "train wreck" and "a mess." Itunes also has faced criticism of its metadata. Data important to jazz music, such as liner text, photographs, and sidemen is not included, thus significantly diminishing the context needed to develop a full understanding of the genre Misleading date information can also cause confusion. "Coleman Hawkins Encounters Ben Webster" listed a 1997 date, when actually it is a rerelease of 1957 recording (Bremser, 2004).

Napoleon Bonaparte said war is 90 percent information. Poor data quality hampers decision making, lessens organizational trust, and erodes customer satisfaction. Quality is especially important because negative events have a greater impact than positive ones. It's easy for the user to acquire feelings of learned helplessness from a few failures, but hard to undo those feelings, even with multiple successes (Hanson, 2009). With the exponential increase in the size of the databases and proliferation of information systems, the magnitude of the data quality problems is continuously growing, "making data quality management one of the most important IT challenges in this early part of the 21st century" (Maydanchik, 2007).

In libraries the most obvious result of poor metadata quality is low or inaccurate search results. Barton, Currier, and Hey (2003) found poor quality metadata leads to invisible resources within digital repositories. Lagoze et al. (2006) argue that even if all other aspects of a digital library work perfectly, poorly created metadata will disrupt the library services. According to Guy, Powell, and Day (2004) "there is an increasing realization that the metadata creation process is key to the establishment of a successful archive." Zeng and Qin (2008) report poorly created metadata records result in poor retrieval and limit access to collections, resulting in a detrimental impact on the continuing adoption and use of a digital library. Robertson (2005) went so far as to say that "supporting the development of quality metadata is perhaps one of the most roles of LIS professional."

11.3. Defining Quality

Considering how important quality is, it is interesting that there are different definitions of quality, with no single definition accepted by researchers. Even the American Society for Quality admits it is subjective term for which each person or sector has its own definition (American Society for Quality, n.d.). Bade (2007) suggests that quality may be understood as a social judgment which reflects the goals of a larger institution. Recent studies within Information systems indicate that culture plays a significant role in the construction of quality practice with policies "representing the values and norms of that culture" (Shanks & Corbitt, 1999).

Business generally defines quality as meeting or exceeding the customers' expectations (Evans & Lindsay, 2005). Understanding consumers have a much broader quality conceptualization than information system professionals realize, Wang and Strong (1996) and many other general data literature studies use the definition "data that is fit for use by information consumers." It is generally recognized that the user defines the level of quality required to make the data useful. Data by itself is not bad or good. It can only be judged in context and cannot be assessed independently from the user assigned tasks. Business academics and practitioners recognize however that merely satisfying a customer is not enough. Delighting customers is necessary to produce exceptional behavioral consequences such as loyalty or positive word-of-mouth (Füller & Matzler, 2008). Libraries should consider following this lead as customer loyalty leads to donations, fund raising, and positive publicity. In politics it leads to reelection.

Redman (2001) uses a slightly more internally focused definition: fit for their intended uses in operations, decision making, and planning, free of defects and possess desired features. Kahn, Strong, and Wang (2002) have dual requirements defining quality as conforming to specifications and meeting or exceeding customer expectations. This definition acknowledges that it is not enough for data simply to meet local specifications, it must meet customer needs.

The Library of Congress forum "Quality Cataloging Is ..." concluded that quality is "accurate bibliographic information that meets users' needs and provides appropriate access in a timely fashion, perhaps implying that appropriate access might not be needed by users." Justifying the time component, Thomas noted that the last 20 years have seen "an increasing awareness of cost in libraries and a shift from quality of records as an absolute toward a redefinition of quality service rather than strictly quality cataloging" (1996).

Data quality is perceived through multiple layers: hardware, applications, schemas, and data. Any of these factors, if faulty, can create a less than satisfactory user experience. To find the root cause of information quality problems, realize that high-quality data in a low-quality application or with inferior hardware will not meet customer expectations. Information consumers do not distinguish between the quality of the data and the quality of the hardware and software systems that deliver them (Kahn et al., 2002). Users also do not draw a distinction between the content of the information and technical problems, users commonly reporting technical problems such as poor response time and an inability to access information when asked about problems with completeness or timeliness of information found (Klein, 2002). OCLC found that a user's perception of quality involves more than the quality of the data itself. How the data is used and presented can be just as critical a factor in creating a positive experience for the user (Calhoun & Patton, 2011). Data quality should be evaluated in conjunction with system quality. Neither high-quality metadata in a low-quality system nor a high-quality discovery layer with low-quality metadata will meet user expectations or complete required tasks.

Quality data is a moving target. User expectations change as they become accustomed to new technology. Metadata quality requirements change as the state of the information resources change, the needs of the user communities evolve, and the tools used to access metadata and e-resources strive to keep up. Maintaining high-quality metadata isn't free. Costs of quality include: prevention costs and appraisal costs. The cost of improving quality must be met with an increase in value of the metadata. Not all lapses in quality are equivalent and not all quality expenditures are justifiable.

Costs of low quality may be difficult to measure, but include: inability of staff and public to find resources, public complaints, ill will, and clean-up projects. Quality decisions should balance metadata functionality against time and staffing constraints, the knowledge that can be expressed, and the effort and expense budgeted for metadata creation, organization, and review (Bruce & Hillman, 2004).

11.3.1. Quality and Priorities

All metadata is not created equal. According to the OMB's Data Quality Act federal agencies are advised to apply stricter quality control for important or "influential" information. Influential information is defined as information that will or does have a clear and substantial impact on important public policies or important private sector decisions. Agencies were encouraged to develop their own criteria for influential information which should be transparent and reproducible (Copeland & Simpson, 2004).

In business it is widely accepted that companies should set clear priorities among their customers and allocate resources that correspond to these priorities. The idea of customer prioritization implies that selected customers receive different and preferential treatment. Importance refers to the relative importance a firm assigns to a particular customer based on organizational specific values (Homburg, Droll, & Totzek, 2008).

A value-impact matrix is sometimes used in libraries. Data that impacts a large number of individuals will have high impact and data that has a high value placed on it by end users has a high value. The highest priority is given to a combination of high value and high impact data (Matthews, 2008).

11.4. What to Measure: Dimensions of Quality

It is not surprising with multiple definitions of quality that there are multiple approaches to measuring it. There is no general agreement on which set of dimensions defines the quality of data, or on the exact meaning of each dimension.

11.4.1. General Data Studies

Wang and Strong (1996) conducted the first large scale research designed to identify the dimensions of quality. The focus of the work was on understanding the dimensions of quality from the perspective of data users, not criteria theoretically or intuitively produced by researchers. Using methods developed in marketing research, they developed a framework of 15 dimensions of quality: believability, accuracy, objectivity, reputation, value added, relevancy, timeliness, completeness, appropriate amount of data, interpretability, ease of understanding, representational consistency, concise representation, accessibility, and access security. In a later study, Kahn et al. (2002) developed 16 dimensions, dropping accuracy and adding ease of manipulation and free of error.

Many later studies use Wang and Strong's dimensions of quality. Stvilia, Gasser, Twidale, and Smith (2007), while echoing accuracy, relevancy, and consistency, include the concept of naturalness. In a remarkably concise list the Department of Defense includes: accuracy, completeness, consistency, timeliness, uniqueness, and validity as its data quality criteria.

11.4.2. Web Quality Studies

In her study on World Wide Web quality, Klein (2002) noted that while the Wang and Strong framework, originally developed in the context of traditional information systems, has also been applied successfully to information published on the World Wide Web. The Semantic Web Quality page refers to both Wang and Strong (1996) and Kahn et al. (2002). SourceForge.net developed its quality criteria for linked data sources using studies of data quality and quality for web services. Their chosen criteria are data content, representation, and usage: consistency, timeliness, verifiability, uniformity, versatility, comprehensibility, validity of documents, amount of data, licensing, accessibility, and performance.

11.4.3. Metadata Quality Studies

Bruce and Hillman (2004) examined the seven most commonly recognized characteristics of quality metadata: completeness, accuracy, provenance, conformance to expectations, logical consistency and coherence, timeliness, and accessibility. As the Library of Congress added cost to the definition of quality, Moen, Stewart, and McClure (1998) included financial considerations of cost, ease of creation, and economy. Some additional customer expectations were added including fitness for use, usability, and informativeness.

All data, especially metadata, are a method of communication, so it is not surprising to see data quality concepts echoed in the cooperative principle of linguistics, which describes how effective communication in conversation is achieved in common social situations. The cooperative principle is divided into four maxims —the maxim of quality: do not say what you believe is false and lack adequate evidence; the maxim of quantity of information: make your contribution of information as required and do not contribute more than is required; the maxim of relevance: be relevant; and the maxim of manner: avoid obscurity of expression, avoid ambiguity, be brief, and be orderly (Grice, 1975).

11.4.4. User Satisfaction Studies

By definition quality requires satisfaction of internal and external users. Humans have an inborn drive to evaluate. Negative experiences are more noticeable and consequential (Hanson, 2009). Satisfaction has a three-factor structure. Basic factors are the minimum requirements that cause dissatisfaction if not fulfilled, but do not lead to customer satisfaction if met or exceeded. Dissatisfiers in self-service technologies may include technology failures and poor design. Usually less than 40 percent of dissatisfied people complain. Excitement factors surprise the customer and generate delight, increase customer satisfaction if delivered but do not cause dissatisfaction if not delivered. Performance factors lead to satisfaction if performance is high and dissatisfaction if performance is low. These factors are not concrete, as what one customer group might consider basic or exciting, could be irrelevant or expected by another (Füller & Matzler, 2008).

Customer satisfaction with technology has special mitigating factors. As most have experienced, personal technology use involves dual experiences of effectiveness and ineptitude. These experiences can happen within seconds of each other. It is not surprising that research has shown technological experiences of isolation and chaos can create anxiety, stress, and frustration (Johnson, Bardhi, & Dunn, 2008). Ambiguous emotions result from the conflict between expectations and reality. Consumers often feel ambivalent about their experiences with personal technology. Customers who have ambiguous experiences have lower rates of satisfaction than those who have unambiguous experiences. Traits of the user such as: technology readiness, motivation, ability, self-consciousness also impact adoption of technology (Johnson et al., 2008).

11.4.5. Dimension Discussion

Organizations may select whichever quality dimensions apply and define the terms as needed, seriously considering concepts common to both data quality studies and customer satisfaction research. Accuracy is the term most commonly associated with quality. It has been defined as the degree to which data correctly reflects the real world object or event being described or the degree to which the information correctly describes the phenomena it was designed to measure (McGilvray, 2008). Values need to be correct and factual. Some expand the scope of accuracy to include concepts such as objectivity. The Office of Management and Budget reverses that idea and includes accuracy as a part of objectivity (OMB, 2002). Traditionally accuracy is decomposed into systemic errors and random errors. Systemic errors may be due to problems such as inputters not changing a default value in a template. Common examples of random errors are typos and misspellings. Measuring accuracy can be complicated, time-intensive, and expensive. In some cases correctness may simply be a case of right and wrong, but the case of subjective information is far more complicated. Sampling is a common method to develop a sense of accuracy issues.

11.4.6. Timeliness

Timeliness is related to accuracy. Online resources may change while the metadata remains static. Controlled vocabularies also change and these changes should be included in the metadata. Bruce and Hillman (2004) separate timeliness into two concepts: currency and lag. Currency reflects instances when the resource changes, but the metadata does not. Lag occurs when the object is available but the metadata is not. Measuring lag, or what could be called a backlog, will help inform metadata management and maintenance decisions.

11.4.7. Consistency

Consistency is a facet of dimensions such as conformance to expectations, logical consistency, and coherence. Consistency is the degree to which the same data elements are used to convey similar concepts within and across systems (McGilvray, 2008). Like judgment, consistency is a natural drive. According to the cognitive consistency theory inconsistency creates a dissonance, and this dissonance drives us to restore consistency (Hanson, 2009). To minimize dissonance language and fields should be used consistently within and across collections. The ordinary user reasonably expects a search conducted across collections will generate similar responses. The MARC analysis report recommended "Strive for consistency in the choice and application of fields. Splitting content across multiple fields will negatively impact indexing, retrieval and mapping" (Smith-Yoshimura et al., 2010). Completeness standards should articulate the expectations of the community. Community expectations need to be managed realistically considering time and money constraints. If there is a large gap between user expectations and what can be managed financially, this fact needs to be communicated and a compromise must be reached. Like good politicians we must manage expectations. Consistency lapses may be caused when standards change over time or when records are created by separate groups with varying amounts of experience and judgment. Consistency suffers when different communities use different words to convey identical or similar concepts, or the same word is used to express different concepts. Consistency can be measured by comparing unexpected terms, data outside of accepted standards with all accepted terms. Consistency is enhanced by written instructions, web input forms, and templates.

11.4.8. Completeness

Completeness, the degree to which the metadata record contains all the information needed to have an ideal representation of the described object, varies according to the application and the community use. Completeness may be observed from a lack of desired information. Completeness may be hard to define, as even the Library of Congress task force said there was no persuasive body of evidence that indicates what parts of a record are key to user access success (Working group on the future of bibliographic control, 2007). Markey and Calhoun (1987) found that words in the contents and summary notes contributed an average of 15.5 unique terms, important for keyword searching. Dinkins and Kirkland (2006) noted the presence of access points in addition to title, author, and subject improves the odds of retrieving that record and increases the patron's chances at determining relevance. Tosaka and Weng (2011) concluded that the table of contents field was a major factor leading to higher material usage. Completeness should describe the object as completely as economically reasonable. Completeness is content dependent, thus a metadata element that is required for one collection may be not applicable or important in another collection. Complete does not mean overly excessive. There is a fine line between a complete record and metadata hoarding. Metadata should not be kept simply because it might be useful someday to someone. Some metadata fields may have been required for earlier technology, but now are obsolete. Consider use when determining completeness. At some point unnecessary and superfluous metadata is an error in itself. As with consistency, community participation is necessary to determine user needs. Measuring completeness starts with the determining the existence of documentation and the completeness of documentation. Documentation should reflect current technology and agreed upon community standards. All metadata should reflect the documentation. One way to determine completeness is to count fields with null value, or nonexistent fields which is a process often easily automated.

11.4.9. Trust

Metadata can be highly complete and consistent, but it won't be used if it isn't trusted. Trust is a measure of the perception of and confidence in the data quality from those who utilize it. Users need to trust the data and trust the technology. Trust in technology is an expectation of competent and reliable performance and is important in customer satisfaction (Luarn & Lin, 2003). Trust may be produced when we know who created the metadata, their experience, and level of expertise. Quality also depends on the changes that have been made to the metadata since its creation. There are significant limits to what can be assumed about quality and integrity of data that has been shared widely (Hillman & Phipps, 2007). Wang and Strong (1996) considered reputation to be an intrinsic data quality and data source tagging to be a good step in that direction. Measuring trust is difficult. Google uses an algorithm intending to lower the rank of "low-quality sites" and return higher quality sites near top of search results. They first developed a survey to determine what factors people took into consideration to develop trust in a website. Later they attempted to automate that process based on factors identified in the surveyed population (Rosenthal, 2011). Measuring a belief or feeling, must be done initially by surveys focus groups or some other customer-based method.

11.4.10. Relevance

Even if the metadata is trusted, accurate, timely, and complete, it has to represent something a user wants. Relevance reflects the degree to which metadata meets real needs of the user. Along with relevance metadata needs to be easy to use, concise, and understandable. To communicate well we must share understanding of the meaning of the codes. If ideas represented by symbols or abbreviations are not shared, communication breaks down. Metadata should be beneficial and provide advantages from its use. This may mean placing an item in context, providing user reviews or comments. Like trust, relevance is only discernible to the individual user and requires a consumer-based measurement. Metadata also should be accessible and secure. It might be unreadable for a variety of technical or intellectual reasons such as obsolete or proprietary file formats. Access to metadata may be restricted appropriately to maintain its security, but who can access what should be explained to the public. Metadata should be safe from hacking and users should be secure when using the site.

11.5. What Tasks Should Metadata Perform?

Before applying quality dimensions to local metadata populations it is necessary to understand both the tasks the data is expected to perform and the user expectations. The National Information Standards Organization website (NISO, 2004) clearly states metadata purposes: resource discovery, organizing e-resources, facilitating interoperability, digital identification, archiving, and preservation. OCLC found that MARC tasks include: user retrieval and identification, machine matching, linking, machine manipulations, harvesting, collection analysis, ranking, and systematic views of publications. Metadata may allow for discovery of all manifestations of a given work, interpret the potential value of an item for the public's needs, limit or facet results, deliver content, and facilitate machine processing or manipulation (Smith-Yoshimura et al., 2010).

11.6. User Expectations

11.6.1. User Needs

Metadata consumers judge quality within specific contexts of their personal, business, or recreational tasks and bring to searches their expectations. Data might have acceptable quality in one context, but be insufficient to another user. Redman (2001) recognized that customers have only a superficial understanding of their own requirements at best. Beyond the usual "timely accurate data," customers almost always want: data relevant to the task at hand, clear intuitive definitions of fields and values, the "right" level of detail, a comprehensive set of data in easy to understand format presentation, at low cost. User needs may conflict and certainly change constantly. Contemplating user needs quickly brings to mind the old truism you can't keep everyone happy all the time.

11.6.2. Online Expectations

User expectations of search tools and metadata are shaped by their other online experiences. Users have become accustomed to sites where resources relate to each other, and customers have an impact. Pandora is a popular internet radio station based on the Music Genome Project. Trained music analysts assign up to 400 distinct musical characteristics significant to understanding music preferences of users. When the user like or dislikes a song, their radio station automatically is fine tuned to these personal preferences. Itunes provides users with value additions such as cover art and celebrity playlists. Amazon remembers previous purchases and suggests items of future interest.

11.6.3. Online Reading

In 2008 Carr's article "Is Google making us stupid" noted people are losing their ability to read long articles. "It is clear that users are not reading online in the traditional sense; indeed new forms of 'reading' are emerging as users power browse horizontally through titles, contents pages, abstracts going for quick wins. It almost seems they go online to avoid reading in the traditional sense."

11.6.4. Online Searching

A study of web searches found 67 percent of people did not go beyond their first and only query. Query modification was not a typical occurrence (Jansen, Spink, & Saracevic, 2000). The Ethnographic Research in Illinois Academic Libraries Project found students tend to overuse Google and misuse databases. "Students generally treated all search boxes as the equivalent of a Google box and searched using the any word anywhere keyword as the default. Students don't want to try to understand how searches work" (Kolowich, 2011). Calhoun also found that preferences and expectations are increasingly driven by experiences with search engines like Google and online bookstores like Amazon (Calhoun, Cantrell, Gallagher, & Hawk, 2009).

Vendors have picked up on this. In a national library publication a Serials Solutions representative said company employees ask themselves "What would Google do?" In same article the author describes someone experiencing a "come to Google" moment. While giving Google God-like status may be excessive, it shows how much prestige and power it has in the world of information discovery (Blyberg, 2009).

11.6.5. Local Users and Needs

National tasks and expectations are important, but do not replace the need to determine local users' tasks and expectations. Transaction analysis logs reveals failure rates, usage patterns, what kind of searches are done, and what mistakes are made. The results of transaction log analysis often challenge management's mental models of how automated systems do or should work (Peters, 1993). Tools like Google Analytics will indicate how users get to our websites. Also take into consideration the internal staff transactions and local discovery tool requirements.

11.7. Assessing Local Quality

11.7.1. Define a Population

Quality assessment is done to create accountability and improve service. Once user tasks are determined, select a population of metadata. One possibility is to support a specific project of a narrow and focused scope, or to screen the most influential population. This can be done to meet a critical need, start the conversation, or proactively meet a need where high quality is critical. Supporting a specific smaller project will give experience in the process and make later, larger projects easier. A second option is to assess data in an entire database. This enables a broader look at the data, which can be more efficient and yield more results, and create potentially a bigger impact. The third option is to evaluate all data. Data across databases is often related and this would allow many related problems to be solved simultaneously (McGilvray, 2008).

To decide which approach is best, consider money, time, staffing, and impact. Data quality is not a project, it is a lifestyle, but evidence provided by a successful project might be required by administrators before a drastic lifestyle change. Start assessing the impact and make priorities correspondently. Consider metadata of the broadest value, the greatest benefit to the majority of users. Select a method where a high amount of data can be cleaned at the lowest cost. Consider your responsibilities to other users if you plan on sharing the data. Before starting a project, understand the need you are filling and why it is important to the organization. Will the time and money spent be justified? Are searches facets unreliable because data is incorrect or missing? Are dead links frustrating users? Are searches missing resources because of nonexistent subject headings or insufficient keywords? Do some resources lack metadata completely? Does offsite material have appropriate representation?

Without standards there is no logical basis for making a decision or taking action. It helps to start with a clearly articulated vision of data quality so everyone is on the same page and understands institutional priorities. Ideally this vision should primarily reflect the needs of the users, taking into account the beliefs of the organization's administrators. Be aware of the fact the organizations often believe their data quality is higher than it actually is and user expectations, though estimated, should be assessed directly (Eckerson, 2002).

11.7.2. Understand the Environment

Once a metadata population has been selected, determine the information environment. Understand the various ways metadata is created through purchase, import and internal creators, and how metadata is updated or edited. How is the metadata used, by whom, and through what discovery layers? What metadata fields are used to create displays and for searching.

You cannot tell if something is wrong unless you can define what right is. Examine national and local data requirements. Determine whether current quality expectations are the same for all metadata populations or do some areas of strength have higher standards. Do old or rare resources have different metadata quality expectations? Should they? Are high-quality expectations in place for a collection no longer an area of strength? Should other standards be raised? Have all standards been documented in writing? Are current practices realistic considering new technology, staffing levels, and workload? Sometimes pockets of metadata creators, intentionally or unintentionally have differences in their quality expectations. What are the lowest national standards? What is the minimal level of quality the institution is willing to produce? Based on this analysis identify the macro and micro functional requirements for metadata (Olson, 2003).

11.7.3. Measuring Quality

Quality dimensions should be chosen based on organizational values and the needs of the population under examination. Specific quality metrics and their range values can only be determined based on specific types of metadata and its local cost and value (Stvilla, Gasser, Twidale, Shreeves, & Cole, 2004). Prioritizing these criteria is far from uniform, and is dictated by the nature of the objects to be described and perhaps how the metadata is to be constructed and derived.

11.7.4. Criteria

There are criteria to keep in mind when selecting quality measurements. Measurements need to be meaningful and significant. Einstein reportedly had a sign on his wall that said "Not everything that counts can be counted and not everything that can be counted counts." Redman (2008) expressed the same thought saying data that is not important should be ignored. The most impactful and improvable data should be addressed first. Accuracy, objectivity, and bias may be very important but may require much staff time to assess. Completeness and timeliness may be less important, but easier to have an automated report generated. Subjective quality of dimensions like trust and relevancy are very important, but require a different kind of data collection and depending on the administration may have less of a decision-making impact. What gets measured gets done. Measures should be action oriented. Measure only what really matters. Solve existing problems that impacts users. It is easy to measure things not important to the organization's success. Spend only time testing when you expect the results will give you actionable information. Because of the fluid nature of quality, errors not currently considered "important" may become important later when user expectations or the capabilities of the search software change. Errors that exist but do not currently have a large impact should be measured, but are not included in the grading (Maydanchik, 2007).

Measures should be cost effective, simple to develop and understand. In a limitless world all quality parameters could be measured and considered, however programs usually are limited by cost and time. With these constraints selecting the parameters that have the most immediate impact and are the simplest measurements is smart. Sometimes the cost of assessing the data will be prohibitive. As in politics, quality requires that everyone agree how to compromise. Most agree that the appropriateness of any metadata elements need to be measured by balancing the specificity of the knowledge that can be represented in it and queried from it and the expense of creating the descriptions (Alemneh, 2009). Quality schemes inevitably represent a state of compromise among considerations of cost, efficiency, flexibility, completeness, and usability (Moen et al., 1998).

Which metric to use for a given IQ dimension will depend on the *availability*, *cost*, and *precision* of the metric and the *importance* of the dimension itself and the tools that exist to manipulate and measure data. There is no one universal invariant set of quality metrics, no universal number that measures information quality. An aggregate weighted function can be developed, but this is specific to one organization and reflect subjective weight assignments (Pipino, Lee, & Wang, 2002). The process should end with measurements that mirror the value structure and constraints of the organization. A data quality framework needs to have both objective and subjective attributes in order to reflect the contextual nature of data quality and the many potential users of the data (Kerr, 2003). Metrics should measure information quality along quantifiable, objective variables that are application independent. Other metrics should measure an individual's subjective assessment of information quality. Other metrics should measure quality along quantifiable, objective variables that are application dependent (Wang, Pierce, Madnick, & Fisher, 2005). Compare what measurements are needed to what measurements are possible. Take into consideration which measurements can be automated. How much money or staff time is available for this process? Manually comparing an item with a record requires much staff time. If in the course of a project objects and records are being compared, then accuracy analysis could take place as part of an ongoing project, but otherwise the process might not be cost effective. Automated data quality reports and sample scanning are methods to obtain a total quality picture. How these are used depends on staffing, collection size, size of problem, and institutional support. Localities will need to create a survey that will determine the basic factors, excitement factors, and performance factors of customer satisfaction.

11.7.5. Understand the Data

After measuring quality dimensions, get a report of the data. Compile data into an error catalog that will aggregate, filter, and sort errors, identify overlaps and correlations, identify records afflicted with a certain kind of error, and the errors in a single record. This will assist to determine trends and patterns. What deviated from expectations? What are the red flags? What are the business impacts? Explore the boundaries of the data and the variations within the data. Assign quality grades and analyze problems. Determine what it means for a record to be seriously flawed. Is there such a thing as flawed but acceptable? What is the impact on decisions making and user satisfaction? Grades can be assigned based on the percentage of good records to all records. Consider the average quality score, high score, and low score. Grades can be developed for each quality dimension measured.

Two keys to metadata quality are prevention and correction. Clean up can never be used alone. Error prevention is superior to correction because detection is costly and can never guarantee to be totally successful. Corrections mean that customers may have been unable to locate resources and damage has been done (Redman, 2001). Identify where procedural changes are necessary to reduce future errors. Sources of poor quality may include: changing user expectations, data created under older standards national, and/or local, system gaps, and human error. Some small group within the organization may have "special" procedures that do not mesh with larger organizational standards or metadata may have originated in a home grown system that did not follow national standards at that time.

11.8. Communication

11.8.1. Communicate Facts

In order to be effective a message has to be communicated well. Good communication should be complete, concise, clear, and correct and crystallize information for all decision makers. The measuring required to support effective decision making needs to be aggregated and presented in an actionable way. Always understand what should happen with the results. More than how many problems exist, describe the impact of the problem, and cost to fix and not to fix.

While data itself is normative, there will be a range of interpretations. Political differences, challenges to cultural practices, and different ways of socially constructing an interpretation of data introduce biases into the meaning of data assigned by different social groups (Shanks & Corbitt, 1999). An important aspect of all data interpretation is to have an awareness of bias. Biases such as anchoring and framing involve experience with previous events. The wording of a document can impact subsequent decisions.

11.8.2. Remember All Audience Members

The metadata environment will be healthier when everyone understands their metadata quality rights and responsibilities. Provide to all internal and external metadata creators the content expectations and why quality is important. Users of the metadata also have responsibility to provide feedback good and bad, report errors, and unclear metadata. Users should also be provided with the information needed to understand the strengths and limitations of the metadata being provided.

11.8.3. Design a Score Card

Many use scorecards as a means of communication. Well-designed scorecards are specific, goal driven, and allow for better decisions. The purpose of a scorecard is to encourage conformation to standards and ensure transparency of quality rankings. A scorecard should allow for the planning and prioritizing of data cleansing while conveying both the source of existing problems and ways of improving them. Remember to discuss new uses of metadata data and impact of quality on new services. The score card should explain the data set, its size, and the user group it supports. It describes clearly both the objective and subjective measurements.

The scorecard should contain specific sections for each quality dimension, so that strengths and weaknesses of the data are clear. Separated scores allow the reader the capacity to analyze and summarize data quality. Consider creating multiple levels of documentation. A summary level should be an easy to read, including targets, actual data quality and status, what needs to be improved and at what cost. A secondary, more detailed level of documentation might also be necessary. That level would include fuller descriptions and the error catalog.

11.9. Conclusion

While many of the reasons for quality appear to be universal psychological needs, almost every step in quality process requires local decisions. From selecting a definition, to choosing quality dimensions and measurements, decisions are based on local hardware, software, tools, metadata populations, and staffing capabilities. Quality is determined by the use and the user. National standards are created to satisfy a generic worldwide need, but local organizations have much more specific demands. Organizations have the enormous responsibility of negotiating a balanced approach to metadata quality and delighting the customer. Politicians who do not satisfy their constituents can be voted out of office. Unhappy people can express apathy by failing to vote. Few institutions outside of the government can afford to have an apathetic constituency. Through the effective understanding, assessment, and communication of metadata quality, all organizations have the opportunity, maybe an obligation, to create happier, even delighted, users.

References

Alemneh, D. G. (2009). *Metadata quality: A phased approach to ensuring long-term access to digital resources*. UNT Digital Library. Retrieved from http://digital.library.unt.edu/ark:/67531/metadc29318/

American Society for Quality. (n.d.). *Glossary online*. Retrieved from http://asq.org/glossary/q.html

Bade, D. (2007). Rapid cataloging: Three models for addressing timeliness as an issue of quality in library catalogs. *Cataloging and Classification Quarterly*, *45*(1), 87–121.

Barton, J., Currier, S., &,Hey, J. (2003). Building quality assurance into metadata creation: An analysis based on the learning objects and e-prints communities of practice. *Proceedings of DC-2003*, Seattle, Washington, DC. Retrieved from http://www.sideran.com/dc2003/201_paper60.pdf. Accessed on December 11, 2011.

Blyberg, J. (2009). A show of cautious cheer. *American Libraries*, *40*(3), 29.

Bremser, W. (2004, February 28). *Jazz in 2500: Itunes vs preservation*. Retrieved from http://www.harlem.org/itunes/index.html

Bruce, T., & Hillman, D. (2004). The continuum of metadata quality: Defining, expressing, exploiting. In D. Hillman & E. Westbrooks (Eds.), *Metadata in practice* (pp. 238–256). Chicago, IL: ALA Editions.

Calhoun, K. (2006, March 17). *The changing nature of the catalog and its integration with other discovery tools*. Retrieved from http://loc.gov/catdir/calhoun-report-final.pdf

Calhoun, K., Cantrell, J., Gallagher, P., & Hawk, J. (2009, March 3). *Online catalogs: What users and librarians want*. Retrieved from http://www.oclc.org/reports/onlinecatalogs/fullreport.pdf

Calhoun, K., & Patton, G. (2011). *WorldCat quality: An OCLC report*. Retrieved from http://www.oclc.org/reports/worldcatquality/default.htm

Carr, N. (2008, July). Is Google making us stupid? *Atlantic Monthly*. Retrieved from http://www.theatlantic.com/magazine/archive/2008/07/is-google-making-us-stupid/6868/

Copeland, C., & Simpson, M. (2004). *The information quality act: OMB's guidance and initial implementation*. Washington, DC: Congressional Research Service.

Dinkins, D., & Kirkland, L. (2006). It's what's inside that counts: Adding contents notes to bibliographic records and its impact on circulation. *College& Undergraduate Libraries*, *13*, 61.

Eckerson, W. (2002, February 1). *Data quality and the bottom line: Achieving business success through commitment to high quality data*. Retrieved from http://download.101com.com/pub/tdwi/Files/DQReport.pdf

Evans, J., & Lindsay, W. (2005). *The management and control of quality* (6th ed.). Mason, OH: South-Western.

Fischer, R., & Lugg, R. (2009). *Study of the North American MARC records marketplace*. Washington, DC: Library of Congress.

Füller, J., & Matzler, K. (2008). Customer delight and market segmentation: An application of the three factor theory of customer satisfaction on life style groups. *Tourism management*, *29*, 116–126.

Grice, P. (1975). Logic and conversation. In P. Cole & J. Morgan (Eds.), *Syntax and semantics, 3: Speech acts*. New York, NY: Academic Press. Reprinted in *Studies in the way of words* (H. P. Grice, ed., pp. 22–40). Cambridge, MA: Harvard University Press.

Guy, M., Powell, A., & Day, M. (2004). Improving the quality of metadata in eprint archives. *Ariadne*, 38.

Hanson, R. (2009). *Buddha's brain: The practical neuroscience of happiness, love and wisdom*. Oakland, CA: New Harbinger Publications.

Heery, R., & Patel, M. (2000). Application profiles mixing and matching metadata schemas. *Ariadne*, 25.

Hillman, D., & Phipps, J. (2007). *Application profiles: Exposing and enforcing metadata quality*. Retrieved from http://ecommons.cornell.edu/bitstream/1813/9371/1/AP_paper_final.pdf

Homburg, C., Droll, M., & Totzek, D. (2008). Customer prioritization does it pay off, and how should it? *The Journal of Marketing*, *72*, 110–130.

Jansen, B., Spink, A., & Saracevic, T. (2000). Real life, real users, and real needs: A study and analysis of user queries on the web. *Information Processing and Management*, *36*, 207–277.

Johnson, D., Bardhi, F., & Dunn, D. (2008). Understanding how technology paradoxes affect customer satisfaction with self service technology: The role of performance ambiguity and trust in technology. *Psychology and Marketing*, *25*(5), 416–443.

Kahn, B., Strong, D., & Wang, R. (2002). Information quality benchmarks: Product and service performance. *Communications of the ACM*, *45*(4), 184–192.

Kerr, K. (2003). *The development of a data quality framework and strategy for the New Zealand Ministry of Health.* Retrieved from http://mitiq.mit.edu/Documents/IQ_Projects/Nov%202003/HINZ%20DQ%20Strategy%20paper.pdf

Klein, B. (2002). When do users detect information quality problems on the world wide web? Retrieved from http://sighci.org/amcis02/RIP/Klein.pdf

Kolowich, S. (2011, August 22) What students don't know. *Inside Higher Ed.* Retrieved from http://www.insidehighered.com/news/2011/08/22/erial_study_of_student_research_habits_at_illinois_university_libraries_reveals_alarmingly_poor_information_literacy_and_skills

Lagoze, C., Krafft, D., Cornwell, T., Dushay, N., Eckstrom, D., & Saylor, J (2006). Metadata aggregation and "Automated Digital Libraries": A retrospective on the NSDL experience, JCDL-2006: Joint conference on digital libraries, Chapel Hill, NC.

Luarn, P., & Lin, H. (2003). A customer loyalty model for e-service context. *Journal of Electronic Commerce Research*, *4*(4), 156–167.

Markey, J., & Calhoun K. (1987). Unique words contributed by MARC records with summary and/or contents notes. Retrieved from http://works.bepress.com/Karen_calhoun/41

Matthews, J. (2008). *Scorecards for results: A guide for developing a library balanced scorecard.* Westport, CT: Libraries Unlimited.

Maydanchik, A. (2007). *Data quality assessment.* Bradley Beach, NJ: Technics Publications.

McGilvray, D. (2008). *Executing data quality projects: Ten steps to quality data and trusted information.* Boston, MA: Morgan Kaufmann/Elsevier.

Moen, W., Stewart, E., & McClure C. (1998) Assessing metadata quality: Findings and methodological considerations from an evaluation of the U.S. Government Information Locator Service (GILS). In *Proceedings of ADL'1998* (pp. 246–255). Washington, DC.

National Information Standards Organization. (2004). *Understanding metadata, a framework for guidance for building good digital collections.* Retrieved from http://www.niso.org/publications/press/UnderstandingMetadata.pdf

Office of Management of Budget Information Quality Guidelines. (2002 October 1). Retrieved from http://www.whitehouse.gov/omb/info_quality_iqg_oct2002/

Olson, J. (2003). *Data quality: The accuracy dimension.* San Francisco, CA: Morgan Kaufmann.

Osborn, A. (1941). *Crisis in cataloging: A paper read before the American Library Institute at the Harvard Faculty Club*. Chicago, IL: American Library Institute.
Peters, T. (1993). History and development of transaction log analysis. *Library Hi Tech*, *11*(2), 41–66.
Pipino, L., Lee, Y., & Wang, R. (2002). Data quality assessment. *Communications of the ACM*, *45*(4), 211–218.
Quality criteria for linked data sources. (2011). *General format*. Retrieved from http://www.sourceforge.net
Redman, T. (2001). *Data quality: The field guide*. Boston, MA: Digital Press.
Redman, T. (2008). *Data driven: Profiting from your most important business asset*. Boston, MA: Harvard Business Press.
Robertson, R. (2005). Metadata quality: Implications for library and information science professionals. *Library Review*, *54*(4), 295–300.
Rosenthal, M. (2011, March 28). *Why panda is the new Coke: Are Google's results higher in quality now?* Retrieved from http://www.webpronews.com/google-panda-algorithm-update-foner-books-2011-03. Accessed on December 14, 2011.
Shanks, G., & Corbitt, B. (1999). Understanding data quality: Social and cultural aspects. In *Proceedings of 10th Australasian conference on information systems*. Wellington, New Zealand.
Simpson, B. (2007). Collections define cataloging's future. *The Journal of Academic Librarianship*, *33*(4), 507–511.
Smith-Yoshimura, K., Argus, C., Dickey, T., Naun, C., Rowlison de Ortiz, L., & Taylor, H. (2010). *Implications of MARC tag usage on library metadata practices*. Dublin: OCLC.
Stvilia, B., Gasser, L., Twidale, M., Shreeves, S., & Cole, T. (2004). Metadata quality for federated collections. In *Proceedings of the international conference on information quality — ICIQ 2004*, Cambridge, MA (pp. 111–125).
Stvilia, B., Gasser, L., Twidale, M., & Smith, L. (2007). A framework for information quality assessment. *JASIST*, *58*(12), 1720–1733.
Thomas, S. (1996). Quality in bibliographic control. *Library Trends*, *44*(3), 491–505.
Tosaka, Y., & Weng, C. (2011). Reexamining content-enriched access: Its effect on usage and discovery. *College and Research Libraries*, *72*(5), 419.
Wang, R., Pierce, E., Madnick, S., & Fisher, C. (2005). Information quality. *Advances in Management Information Systems*, *1*, 37.
Wang, R., & Strong, D. (1996). Beyond accuracy: What data quality means to data consumers. *Journal of Management Information Systems*, *12*(4), 5–35.
Working group on the future of bibliographic control. (2007). *On the record: Report of the working group on the future of bibliographic control*. Retrieved from http://www.loc.gov/bibliographic-future/news/lcwg-ontherecord-jan08-final.pdf
Zeng, & Qin. (2008). *Metadata*. New York, NY: Neal-Schuman.

Conclusion: What New Directions in Information Organization Augurs for the Future

Introduction

In the introduction to this edited volume, we outlined topical areas which we considered characteristic of key trends and fresh perspectives in a rapidly evolving landscape of information organization in the digital environment. Broadly speaking, we chose to situate the 11 chapters within three sections, labeled as: (1) Semantic Web, Linked Data, and RDA; (2) Web 2.0 Technologies and Information Organization; and (3) Library Catalogs: Toward an Interactive Network of Communication. Following a brief summary of each chapter, we concluded with a hope that the volume would stimulate "new avenues of research and practice," and also contribute "to the development of a new paradigm in information organization." Lest anything be left to chance, we propose in this final chapter to highlight particular aspects addressed across the various chapters that evoke, in our opinion, opportunities for further reflection, a call to action, or a notable future shift in perspectives around information organization. We conclude with suggestions of what the chapters, collectively, might augur regarding the future direction of information organization.

Semantic Web, Linked Data, and RDA

This seems an auspicious time to be issuing a collection of chapters focused on *new directions* given the convergence of several significant developments that have been fomenting over the past dozen years. Barbara Tillett establishes the connection that has been developing during that time between the design of a significant rethinking of the *Anglo-American Cataloging Rules* and a parallel reconceptualization of the Internet — as

Yang and Lee note — from that of a Web of linked documents, to that of a Web of linked data. Tillett sees the Semantic Web as a logical home for the kinds of "well-formed, interconnected metadata for the digital environment" that will derive from the "alternative to past cataloging practices" that *RDA: Resource Description and Access* (released in July 2010) will yield. She also sees the Semantic Web as "offering a way to keep libraries relevant" at a time when they are "in danger of being marginalized by other information delivery services."

Yang and Lee similarly make the case for using RDA to "organize bibliographic metadata more effectively, and make it possible to be shared and reused in the digital world," RDA is based on the Functional Requirements for Bibliographic Data (FRBR), and Functional Requirements for Authority Data (FRAD) — conceptual models that make explicit entities, their attributes, and relationships. The Semantic Web is, as Yang and Lee note, "based on entity relationships or structured data." Consequently, they posit, "The significance of RDA lies in its alignment with Semantic Web requirements," and "Implementing RDA is the first step for libraries to adopt Semantic Web technologies and exchange data with the rest of the metadata communities." They conclude that, "Linking data will be the next logical move."

Just as the Semantic Web projects Tim Berners-Lee's original vision of networked information into a future of linked meaning, RDA propels organization of bibliographic data along a trajectory of structured metadata shared among a diversity of communities. As Yang and Lee illustrate, "Searching in the Semantic Web will retrieve all the relevant information on a subject through relationships even though the searched keywords are not contained in the content." Likewise, linking data around an author can yield a map of his or her birthplace, events occurring during the year of his or her birth, and similar information about a co-author, or illustrator, or translator, with whom the author has collaborated. Such enhanced content, made possible by machine-level inference, and relationships established through structured data, will, in Tillett's words, "display information users want." Exposing RDA bibliographic and authority data, as well as other library-derived controlled vocabularies and other structured data to registries, not only adds to the growing cloud of linked data, both open and closed, but also showcases the professional expertise and wealth of tools that have been instrumental to building catalogs of library collections, and repositories of digital objects over decades. Park and Kim emphasize the benefits — and *necessity* — of exposing "library bibliographic data created as linked data" broadly, highlighting a number of major library-related linked data implementations to illustrate the importance and future of sharing.

Focusing on the importance and future of sharing brings us back to two cautionary, even contrary notes. The first is our observation that, while the

Semantic Web may offer a second life to libraries, it may be because of libraries that the vision of the Semantic comes to fruition. The momentum toward creating a "critical mass" of linked data, evolving from the first undertakings of DBpedia continues to grow. Investments from large players, such as Google, Facebook, and Microsoft, are instrumental for the growth of infrastructure and expertise. Public sector contributors — essential to creating and maintaining open linked data resources — understand the potential benefits of sharing structured data, but usually lack the same kind of financial reserves for investing in large-scale implementations. Libraries are numerous and in possession of volumes of structured data. Pairing with other cultural heritage institutions, with publishers, vendors, and important stakeholders, such as OCLC, IFLA, and national libraries, will yield a larger presence, as a group, to the Semantic Web space. Libraries have much to contribute; our relationship with the Semantic Web seems a symbiotic one.

The second cautionary, even contrary note is raised by Alan Poulter. As he observes, RDA, as originally conceived and structured, "was intended to also provide subject access," with Chapters 12–16, 23, and 33–37 left open for establishing those guidelines. Chapter 16, "Identifying Places" is complete, while the others remain "blank." Poulter describes the highly problematic challenge of extending the entity-relationship modeling of FRBR (bibliographic data) and FRAD (authority data) to subjects (entities, attributes, relationships, AND the full range of subject access tools). He elaborates further on "the task of developing a conceptual model of FRBR Group 3 entities within the FRBR framework as they relate to the 'aboutness' of works." The resulting Functional Requirements for Subject Authority Data (FRSAD), a more abstract model than either FRBR or FRAD, and based on "thema" and "nomen," is well-suited to the Semantic Web environment, as Poulter explains, in that it "matches well with schemas such as SKOS (Simple Knowledge Organization System), OWL (Web Ontology Language), and the DCMI Abstract Model." He observes that, while "this paper found no fundamental criticisms of FRSAD ... it is almost as though FRSAD itself has never appeared" at least as far as its incorporation into the structural foundations of subject access (and chapters) in RDA is concerned. Poulter's chapter suggests that, "there seems to be a general denial of the FRSAD model," and offers a "mechanism, based on PRECIS, for putting into practice this [FRSAD] model."

In the spirit of everything old is new again, Poulter's exploration of Derek Austen's Preserved Context Indexing System (PRECIS) (1974) as a practical "procedure" for implementing an abstract model (FRSAD) underlines the theoretical and structural congruence or alignment of the old ("tried and tested") and new. Moreover, PRECIS's use of subject strings, each assigned its own Subject Indicator Number (SIN), and generated based on syntactic "roles," bears a striking resemblance to

Uniform Resource Identifiers (URIs) — the DNA of the Semantic Web. It is intriguing to contemplate a new direction based on an old solution; Poulter leaves us with delicious food for thought.

Web 2.0 Technologies and Information Organization

We are reminded of that same thread running from past to future in the opening sentence of Shawne Miksa's chapter. She invokes Jesse Shera's assessment that, "The librarian is at once historical, contemporary, and anticipatory" (Shera, 1970, p. 109) in framing her examination of the role of the cataloger in the era of social tagging. Miksa notes the increase in the amount of user-contributed content to library catalogs, suggesting that this type of engagement, "affords us the opportunity to see directly the users' perceptions of the usefulness and about-ness of information resources." She defines this "social cataloging" as, "the joint effort by users and catalogers to interweave individually- or socially-preferred access points in a library information system as a mode of discovery and access to the information resources held in the library's collection." Hence, both user and information professional offer perspective, "… interpreting the intentions of the creator of the resources, how the resource is related to other resources, and perhaps even how the resources can be, or have been, used." Since librarians have, traditionally, been the intermediaries between users and the catalog, sharing the role of record creator, even partially, has presented challenges to the professional identity of some catalogers. What happens to ones sense of having cultivated a certain level of professional expertise when ones voice is "simply one among the many?"

Miksa contends that Shera's concept of "social epistemology" offers a framework for making the shift from the historical to the anticipatory when it comes to sharing responsibilities for record creation. The "social cataloger" may feel a greater affinity to accommodating and engaging with user-generated content recognizing that social tagging represents, in Shera's terms, "the value system of a culture," as well as part of the means in which a society "communicates" and "utilizes" knowledge (Shera, 1970, p. 131). An enduring process of describing and providing access to resources may be changed, if not enhanced, by a new direction toward cocreation of bibliographic records through a more social cataloging. Again we see the intertwining of historical perspective and emerging reality to offer an innovative way forward. Whereas catalogers may have been viewed, historically, as the denizens of the backroom, the future suggests highly skilled individuals who work in partnership with individuals within a public domain to ensure effective sharing and use of a culture's or a society's vital knowledge resources — a new direction for an old professional identity, to be sure.

Miksa's article sets the stage nicely for Choi's subsequent assessment of how social indexing may be applied to addressing problems associated with traditional approaches to providing subject access to resources on the Web. She investigates "the quality and efficacy" of social indexing, pointing out the challenges of using controlled vocabularies, and emphasizing "the need for social tagging as natural language terms." Choi notes, further, that tagging may offer a more accurate description of resources, and reflect more current terminology than that provided by controlled vocabularies which are slow to be revised. From her doctoral research (2011) comparing "indexing similarity between two professional groups, i.e., BUBL and Intute, and also [comparing] tagging in Delicious and professional indexing in Intute," she concludes that, "As investment in professionally-developed subject gateways and web directories diminishes, it becomes even more critical to understand the characteristics of social tagging and to obtain benefit from it." She also notes the potential for assigning subjective or emotional tags as "crucial metadata describing important factors represented in the document."

Choi speaks to a future where a "decline in support for professional indexing" is occurring as "web resources continue to proliferate and the need for guidance in their discovery and selection remains." A remedy for that growing gap might appear to be social indexing; however, as the final section of this volume portends, a move toward the Semantic Web, and to a greater need for, and reliance on, linked data, may exert a counter pressure. To the extent that controlled vocabularies are crucial to the exchange of trusted data — now and in the future — the role of natural language tags supported through Web 2.0 technologies may be muted to some degree. Continuing with the theme of everything old is new again, the solutions proffered by a social Web, may be different from those required for a *Semantic* Web. While the ascendancy of user tagging and folksonomies may continue within the realm of socially mediated exchange on the Web, activities requiring structured data for sharing information will demand more formalized approaches within a framework of international standards. As with Miksa's social cataloging, the future of social indexing may involve a partnership of user and professional navigating a course somewhere between the social Web 2.0, and the structured data of the Semantic Web.

Choi's reference to subjective or emotional tags segues to Emma Stuart's past and future of organizing photographs. Nineteenth century analog photography, first introduced in 1839, limited the kinds of things that could be photographed because of expense and long exposure times. Digital photography introduced a playfulness and flexibility beyond the limitations of temporal and spatial affiliations, allowing for features, such as color, shape, and what Stuart refers to as, "cognitive facets." Web 2.0 photo management sites, such as Flickr, allow for social sharing of images, facilitated by the use of tags, alignment with groups, and other community-focused features. Research has suggested that social tagging of images is done for self-organization, for self-communication (e.g., memory), for social organization, or for self-communication (e.g., expressing emotion or opinion). The latter two motivations are most popular among Flickr users. Camera phones have further opened the world of photography, allowing for seamless uploading and sharing of images, often reflecting, "the emotional or communicative intent" with which the photograph had been taken. As Stuart concludes, "The ubiquity of the camera phone and its coupling with web 2.0 technology has led to a new form of everyday photography, one that is keen to capture the mundane and fleeting aspects of daily life." She suggests that the future organization of photos will depend on available technology. She speculates no further than that.

We might conjecture that, while current Web 2.0 applications support a greater sharing of images, and GPS will allow for tagging geographic coordinates which can then attach a photo with a place — thus realizing one vision for linked data and the Semantic Web — there are human factors that may suggest a more conservative future. The photograph, as Stuart suggests, functions, not only as public and/or private record of the "mundane everyday," but also as an image aesthetically pleasing in its own right. As Stuart notes, "… whilst we are moving forward into a new genre of photography on the one hand, we are also anchoring ourselves to the past on the other hand, reluctant to truly let go of older forms of photography." While digital technology may be changing the ways we take, organize, and store images, it cannot take away from the ways we see, interpret, and communicate the relationships we form with the people, places, and events represented in a photograph. Might it be that the future direction accommodates, equally and readily, an analog aesthetic in parallel with a digital functionalism. In that case, both the available technology, and those inclinations that make us human will determine the future organization of photos.

Library Catalogs: Toward an Interactive Network of Communication

Birong Ho's and Laura Horne-Popp's chapter, "VuFind — an OPAC 2.0?" offers an assessment of Web 2.0 features supported by open source library online public access catalog (OPAC) software, VuFind. In framing the evaluation Western Michigan University (WMU) undertook of a next generation open source discovery tool, Ho and Horne-Popp describe Web 2.0 applications as those that facilitate interaction and collaboration, and user-generated content. So-called OPAC 2.0 implementations support such features as user-tagging and reviews, faceted searching, a Google-like search box, relevancy rankings, and RSS feeds. While libraries assess what the authors characterize as a "new bevy of discovery tools," OPAC 2.0 users may not be responding, as anticipated, in optimizing enhanced social networking functionality. For example, the WMU Web team noticed that few users added tags despite the ready availability to do so.

This may sound a note of caution as libraries strive to maintain both the currency and relevancy of OPACs. In a social media and networking landscape that is constantly and quickly changing, is it possible for libraries — themselves constrained fiscally — to anticipate the next new development and stay ahead of the curve? Does the experience of WMU and other libraries suggest that, by the time open source software has been programmed to incorporate a trend in the social media sphere, it is already passé in the minds (and responses) of users who, themselves, are determining relevance in real time? Would libraries find it a better use of their resources and expertise to focus on enhancing what OPACs are intended to do — to provide access to digital and physical assets in their collections, and to facilitate the user experience in doing so? Ho and Horne-Popp describe open source products as "giving libraries a third way toward improving the concept of the library catalog." While this may be so, perhaps there is a third way that goes beyond open source solutions, to rethinking, carefully and thoughtfully, the role of the OPAC as the rhetoric of Web 3.0 suggests yet another development — a trend? — that must be anticipated and requiring response.

Might this "third way" resurface and build on incremental expertise regarding information-seeking behaviors and appropriate information search and retrieval strategies and functionalities to address them? There may be value to building on the knowledge accrued in designing, for example, second-generation OPACs with enhanced user interfaces, then WebPACs incorporating simple search box and advanced Boolean search features. Xi Niu's chapter, "Faceted Search in Library Catalogs," hints at the kind of third wave (re)thinking we might envision, exploring research on the long-standing concept of facets, and tracing their application and efficacy in more recent faceted search-enabled OPACs. Incorporating an understanding of how facets accommodate and enhance user browsing behaviors is one approach to improving on the design of next-generation discovery tools. Users may be more inclined to use an OPAC that facilitates ready access to needed information, than to engage in adding tags and reviews simply because one can.

As Elizabeth J. Cox, Sephanie Graves, Andrea Imre, and Cassie Wagner observe in their chapter, "Doing More with Less: Increasing the Value of the Consortial Catalog," commercial content providers, such as Amazon and Netflix (among others) are successful because they deliver on their promise to supply an enormous collection of content and services quickly and easily. The authors acknowledge the fiscal constraints that prevent libraries from competing head-on-head with private sector suppliers and then ask, "Could libraries actually do more with less by leveraging discovery tools to take advantage of consortial resources?" The Morris Library (Southern Illinois University, Carbondale) experiment with providing users with easy access to content from various providers within the consortium, proved successful, based on borrowing statistics. At the same time, usability testing found that searchers were not making effective use of facets located on the right side of the interface, rather than on the left side preferred by the human eye — a problem remedied by moving facets to the left side of the display. Nonetheless, there is a third way implied in exploiting the "public good" of the networked collections of consortial catalogs to supply an enormous amount of content to users who do not wish to purchase or own it outright. This seems a kind of "working smarter" that thinks strategically about how to make a voluminous quantity and quality of publicly funded resources available to larger numbers of the tax-paying public within a model of cost-containment. This approach clearly distinguishes libraries from commercial content-providers, using what is both mandated for, and characteristic of libraries to their own institutional benefit.

Conclusions

The path to the future of information organization may, ultimately, rely on that well-worn path of focusing on the user. We are reminded of the importance of local decisions by Sarah H. Theimer's chapter, "All Metadata Politics Is Local: Developing Meaningful Quality Standards." While libraries adhere to national (and international) standards in creating records for catalogs that live in the shared environment of bibliographic utilities, consortial networks, and the Web, Theimer notes that, "libraries have traditionally edited metadata for local use" — in essence recognizing and supporting the particular needs of the local user, serving the local community. Or, as the author observes further, "... libraries, archives and museums have local strengths which local metadata must reflect and support." Moreover, "Quality is determined by the use and the user. National standards are created to satisfy a generic worldwide need, but local organizations have much more specific demands."

The theme of understanding the user, his or her information needs and uses, and subsequent behaviors in engaging with information search tools and systems, is a recurring one throughout preceding chapters. New directions in information organization will necessarily involve international standards continuously under revision, enhanced software tools and applications, and strategic, collaborative approaches to enhancing public access to an increasing array of resources while also balancing fiscal and other constraints. What should remain a focus, and the guiding principle for responding to change, and determining future courses of action, is the information user and his or her need to locate the right information at the right time, easily and readily. A new direction may depend on little more than an old direction considered in light of present realities, and astute divination of emerging possibilities. Finally, new directions in information organization will also necessarily entail fostering greater partnership and dialog among those who create, organize, provide, and use information in a world where the distinction between and among each has become increasingly indistinguishable.

Lynne C. Howarth
Jung-ran Park

Reference

Shera, J. H. (1970). *Sociological foundations of librarianship*. Bombay: Asia Publishing House.

Index